ON THE

HISTORY OF THE DOCTRINE

OF THE

PROCESSION OF THE HOLY SPIRIT,

FROM THE APOSTOLIC AGE TO THE DEATH
OF CHARLEMAGNE.

ON THE HISTORY OF THE DOCTRINE OF THE PROCESSION OF THE HOLY SPIRIT,

FROM THE APOSTOLIC AGE TO THE DEATH OF CHARLEMAGNE.

BY

H. B. SWETE, B.D.,

FELLOW AND DIVINITY LECTURER OF GONVILLE AND CAIUS COLLEGE.

ἡμεῖς δὲ οὐ τὸ πνεῦμα τοῦ κόσμου ἐλάβομεν, ἀλλὰ τὸ Πνεῦμα τὸ ἐκ τοῦ Θεοῦ.

Wipf & Stock
PUBLISHERS
Eugene, Oregon

Per te sciamus da PATREM
Noscamus atque FILIUM:
Te UTRIUSQUE SPIRITUM
Credamus omni tempore.

Wipf and Stock Publishers
199 W 8th Ave, Suite 3
Eugene, OR 97401

On the History of the Doctrine of the Procession of the Holy Spirit
From the Apostolic Age to the Death of Charlemagne
By Swete, H. B.
ISBN: 1-59244-969-7
Publication date 10/28/2004
Previously published by Deighton, Bell, and Co., 1876

THE aim of this Essay is to collect and arrange materials for a history of the Procession-dogma which lie scattered in the ecclesiastical writers and councils of the first eight centuries.

Authorities have been quoted for the most part in the original Greek or Latin, under the belief that a majority of readers will prefer to interpret the evidence for themselves.

The *Patrologiae* and the *Concilia* have been my chief books of reference; but free use has also been made of the historical and controversial works which have fallen into my hands. I hope that particular obligations will be found to be duly acknowledged in the notes.

The revision of the proof-sheets has been kindly undertaken by the Rev. C. G. BROWNE, of Balliol College, Oxford. To the Rev. Professor JONES, of S. Beuno's College, S. Asaph, I am indebted for much valuable information upon the bibliography of the subject. My thanks are also due to R. L. BENSLY, Esq., of the Cambridge University Library, whose help I have never sought in vain.

H. B. S.

GONVILLE AND CAIUS COLLEGE,
Whitsuntide, 1876.

ἐξαποστελεῖς τὸ Πνεῦμά σου καὶ κτισθήσονται· καὶ ἀνακαιεῖς τὸ πρόσωπον τῆς γῆς.

CONTENTS.

CORRIGENDA.

Page 8, *line* 14, *for* Procopowitz *read* Procopowicz.
,, ,, 29, *for* 101 *read* 111.
,, 13, ,, 17, [The MS. recently discovered at Constantinople contains the entire Greek Ep. of Barnabas: cf. Bryennius, προλεγ. η′.]
,, 53, ,, 31, *for* processions *read* procession.
,, 57, ,, 18, *for* Patri *read* Patris.
,, 85, *last line*, *for* מֵעִם *read* מֵעִם.
,, 97, ,, 16, *for* συμπεριχώρησις *read* περιχώρησις.
,, ,, ,, 32, *for* ὃ *read* ὁ.
,, 107, ,, 32, *for* σαφηνεέας *read* σαφηνείας.
,, 108, ,, 18, *for* μεγάλω *read* μεγάλῳ.
,, 124, ,, 27, *for* obtineret *read* obtineant.
,, 131, *last line*, *after* ἁγιάζειν *dele* comma.
,, 133, *note* 2, *transfer to note* 1 *all that follows the reference.*
,, 135, *line* 34, *for* canonis *read* canones.
,, 139, ,, 23, *for* 11, 12 *read* 13—15.
,, 158, ,, 1, *for* will *read* shall.
,, 181, ,, 30, *for* ὁ *read* ὃ.
,, 183, *note* 3, *dele* Nullam nunc—sunt.

SI QUA DE MEO, ET TU IGNOSCE ET TUI.

ON THE

HISTORY OF THE DOCTRINE OF THE PROCESSION OF THE HOLY SPIRIT.

Ἓν Σῶμα καὶ ἓν Πνεῦμα.

S. Paul, *Ephes.* iv. 4.

THE whole Church believes and teaches that the Holy Spirit "proceedeth from the Father[1]." But to this article of the Catholic Faith the Eastern Churches for the most part annex the limitation which they conceive to be implied in the original words, "From the Father only[2]." The Churches of the West, on the contrary, extend the language of the Creed, adding, "And from the Son[3]." It is

[1] Πιστεύομεν ... εἰς τὸ Πνεῦμα τὸ Ἅγιον ... τὸ ἐκ τοῦ Πατρὸς ἐκπορευόμενον. The Fourth Oecumenical Council sanctioned the Constantinopolitan Creed, adding, Περὶ...τοῦ Πατρὸς καὶ Υἱοῦ καὶ τοῦ Ἁγίου Πνεύματος ἐκδιδάσκει τὸ τέλειον.

[2] The "Orthodox Confession" which was drawn up by the metropolitan of Kiew for the use of the Russian Church, issued in 1643 by the Patriarchs of Constantinople, Alexandria, Antioch, and Jerusalem, and sanctioned by a Synod at Jerusalem in 1672 (ὀρθόδοξος ὁμολογία τῆς καθολικῆς καὶ ἀποστολικῆς ἐκκλησίας τῆς ἀνατολικῆς), sets forth that the Holy Ghost ἐκπορεύεται ἐκ μόνου τοῦ Πατρὸς ὡς πηγῆς καὶ ἀρχῆς τῆς θεότητος ...... ἐκ μόνου τοῦ Πατρὸς αἰτιατὸν καὶ ἐκπορευτόν, διὰ δὲ τοῦ Υἱοῦ ἐν τῷ κόσμῳ ἀποστελλόμενον (Kimmel, *Mon. Fid. Eccl. Orient.* p. 142. Winer, *Confessions of Christendom*, p. 67, cf. p. 13 (Engl. Tr.).

[3] At the third Session of the Roman Co. of Trent (Feb. 4, 1546), that Synod expressly sanctioned the "Nicene" Creed, including the *Filioque:* "symbolum fidei quo S. R. Ecclesia utitur...totidem verbis quibus in omnibus ecclesiis legitur exprimendam esse censuit."

to be remembered, however, that the Eastern limitation has reference only to the essential and eternal derivation of the Holy Ghost[1]; while the Western addition has been authoritatively explained to mean that the Third Person of the Holy Trinity proceeds from the First Person and from the Second as from One Principle and by one spiration[2].

It is the purpose of these pages to examine the history of this doctrine and of the controversies which are associated with it. With this object in view, it will not be necessary to enter into the intricacies of the theological argument, or to assume as final any solution of a problem upon which the Universal Church has not yet pronounced. Our business will rather be to mark the rise and fluctuations of both Christian and heretical thought upon this subject: to trace the gradual emergence of the Catholic doctrine so far as it has already been received:

The Anglican Church also affirms (Art. VIII.) "Symbola tria Nicaenum &c. ... omnino recipienda sunt et credenda;" meaning no doubt by the *Symbolum Nicaenum* the form which is so called in the English Order for Holy Communion, and which contains the *Filioque*. Art. V. distinctly asserts the doctrine: "Sp. S... a Patre et Filio procedens."

[1] Thus in the Confession of Metrophanes Critopulus (Kimmel, p. 30) we read, Πέμπεται μὲν τὸ Ἅγιον Πνεῦμα ἐκ Πατρὸς δι' Υἱοῦ ἢ καὶ ἐξ ἀμφοῖν, καὶ χορηγεῖται καὶ γινώσκεται ἐξ ἀμφοῖν· ἔχει δὲ αἰτίαν τῆς αὐτοῦ ἀνάρχου ὑπάρξεως τὸν ἄναρχον αὐτοῦ προβολέα καὶ Πατέρα τοῦ Κυρίου ἡμῶν Ι. Χ.

[2] At Florence it was defined, Τὸ Πνεῦμα τὸ Ἅγιον ἐκ τοῦ Πατρὸς καὶ τοῦ Υἱοῦ ἀϊδίως ἐστὶ καὶ τὴν ἑαυτοῦ οὐσίαν καὶ τὸ ὑπαρκτικὸν αὐτοῦ εἶναι ἔχειν ἐκ τοῦ Πατρὸς ἅμα καὶ τοῦ Υἱοῦ, καὶ ἐξ ἀμφοτέρων ἀϊδίως ὡς ἀπὸ μιᾶς ἀρχῆς καὶ μοναδικῆς προβολῆς ἐκπορεύεται (Mansi, t. 31, p. 1029). In the Vatican Synod of 1870 it was proposed to re-affirm this interpretation for the Roman communion: *Schema de doctr. cathol.* I. "Spiritus S....... a Patre et Filio tamquam ab uno principio una spiratione aeterna procedit." The English Church, having no special teaching upon the subject, may be understood to hold by the Florentine definition.

and from the experiences of the past to seek help in the conduct of a still undetermined controversy. The subject is indeed of more than merely historical interest[1]. A question so closely connected with the central mystery of the Faith can never become obsolete, until it has received an answer in which the whole Church concurs[2]. At the present time, the instinct for re-union which is so manifestly working throughout Christendom, has again turned our thoughts to this old battle-field of East and West. It may be idle to expect that

[1] In 1861 Dean Stanley wrote (*Eastern Church*, p. 62), "It [the *Filioque* question] is an excellent specimen of the race of 'extinct controversies.'" Events have scarcely justified this verdict. Here in England the subject was brought to the front again by the visit of the late Archbishop of Syros and Tenos in 1870. In Germany, during the past year (1875) it has formed the principal matter of debate between the Easterns, Anglicans, and Old Catholics assembled at the Bonn Conference. The bitterness of the controversy is past: the controversy itself seems to be just entering on a new stage, possibly indeed the last stage, of its long life.

[2] The following are the terms of union provisionally adopted at the recent Bonn Conference. It remains to be seen whether they will find acceptance with the Eastern and Anglican communions as a whole.

"We accept the teaching of S. John Damascene on the Holy Ghost, as it is expressed in the following paragraphs, in the sense of the teaching of the ancient undivided Church:

1. The Holy Ghost issues out of the Father as the Beginning (ἀρχή), the Cause (αἰτία), the Source (πηγή) of the Godhead.

2. The Holy Ghost does not issue out of the Son (ἐκ τοῦ Υἱοῦ), because there is in the Godhead but one Beginning (ἀρχή), one Cause (αἰτία), through which all that is in the Godhead is produced.

3. The Holy Ghost issues out of the Father through the Son.

4. The Holy Ghost is the Image of the Son, Who is the Image of the Father, issuing out of the Father and resting in the Son as His revealing power.

5. The Holy Ghost is the personal production out of the Father, belonging to the Son, but not out of the Son, because He is the Spirit of the mouth of God declaratory of the Word.

6. The Holy Ghost forms the link between the Father and the Son, and is linked to the Father by the Son."

any considerable addition can now be made to the arguments which have been accumulated by theologians on either side during more than a thousand years. But it is surely not unreasonable to hope for a solution of some of the ecclesiastical difficulties by which the question is perplexed; a solution to be obtained in the calm review of the course of events which has led each of the great sections of the Church to its present conclusions. An examination of the facts may at least serve to suggest the mutual forbearance which springs from the consciousness that faults have not been wanting on either side, and which gives the fairest promise of a real and permanent reconciliation.

CHAPTER I.

FROM THE APOSTLES TO THE APOLOGISTS.

"De Spiritu Sancto verissime dicitur, 'Processionem Ejus quis enarrabit?'"

S. Augustine, *c. Maxim.* II. 14.

An essay on the history of this doctrine may fitly begin with some notice of the solitary passage in the New Testament from which the Church has derived her conception or at all events her expression of the mystery. The Gospel of S. John, to which we owe the deepest and fullest revelations of the Person of Christ, has preserved the following declaration of Our Lord with regard to the Mission and Being of the Holy Ghost:

Ὅταν ἔλθῃ ὁ Παράκλητος ὃν ἐγὼ πέμψω ὑμῖν παρὰ τοῦ Πατρὸς, τὸ Πνεῦμα τῆς ἀληθείας ὃ παρὰ τοῦ Πατρὸς ἐκπορεύεται, ἐκεῖνος μαρτυρήσει περὶ ἐμοῦ[1].

[1] S. John xv. 26. The following are the only variants of any moment. Codex Bezae, supported by the Gothic version and Epiphanius (*haer.* LXXIV. 9), exhibits πεμπω. To παρα του Πατρος D adds μου *bis*: so the Peshito Syriac (ܡܢ ܠܘܬ ܐܒܝ). In the former of the two instances this addition is supported by several cursives, including Evan. 33 and three of those collated by Mr Scrivener. On the other hand the first παρα του Πατρος is omitted altogether by the late uncial G and by Epiph. (*l. c.*).

The Vulgate gives the verse thus: "Cum autem venerit Paraclitus

In this verse the Paraclete is twice stated to be "from the Father," i. e., as the context seems to shew, to derive His essence from the Father[1]; and this derivation is further expressed by the use of

quem ego mittam vobis a Patre Spiritum veritatis qui a Patre procedit, ille testimonium perhibebit de me." In the Old Latin and Itala the following readings occur. For *mittam* Cod. Bezae and one of the Corbie MSS. (*ff*²) give *mitto*. After *a Patre*, *meo* is added in the *first* instance by Codd. Vercell., Bezae: Novatian, Ambrose (on Ps. lxi.), and Vigilius of Tapsus: in the *second*, by Codd. Veron., Colbert., Bezae: Novatian, Hilary, Ambrose, Vigilius. For *qui* one of the Codd. Sangerman. (g¹) has *quia*. For *procedit* Codex Bezae exhibits *prodit:* Jerome once [but when commenting on Is. lvii. 16 "spiritus a me egredietur"] has *egreditur* and Victorinus Afer *adveniet*. *De* Patre is read by Cod. Vercell., Novatian and Jerome *l. c.*

[1] I append a few specimens of the patristic exegesis of S. John xv. 26.

A. *Greek Fathers and Commentators.*

S. Chrysostom (*in Joann. Hom.*, Migne LIX. 417), *τὸ δὲ ‘ὃ παρὰ τοῦ Πατρὸς ἐκπορεύεται’ δηλοῖ ὅτι πάντα οἶδεν ἀκριβῶς...‘ὃν ἐγὼ πέμψω.’ ἰδοὺ οὐκ ἔτι ὁ Πατὴρ μόνος, ἀλλὰ καὶ ὁ Υἱός ἐστιν ὁ πέμπων.*

Theodore of Mopsuestia (Caten. Corderii p. 388), *ἐπιμαρτυρεῖ τὸ Πνεῦμα τοῖς λεγομένοις, ὃ ἐξ αὐτῆς τοῦ Πατρὸς τῆς οὐσίας ἔχει τὴν ὕπαρξιν...φυσικὴν ἐκεῖθεν πρόοδον ἔλεγε διὰ τοῦ ‘ἐκπορεύεται.’*

Theodoret (*haer. fab.* V. 3, Migne LXXXIII. 456), *τῷ δὲ εἰπεῖν, ‘ἐκ τοῦ Πατρὸς ἐκπορεύεται,’ ἔδειξε πηγὴν ὄντα τοῦ Πνεύματος τὸν Πατέρα· καὶ οὐκ εἶπεν ‘ἐκπορεύσεται,’ ἀλλ’ ‘ἐκπορεύεται,’ δεικνὺς καὶ τῆς φύσεως τὴν ταυτότητα καὶ τῆς οὐσίας τὸ ἄτμητον.*

S. Cyril of Alexandria (*in Joann. Comm.*, Migne LXXIV. 418—9), *ὥσπερ γάρ ἐστιν ἴδιον Πνεῦμα τοῦ Υἱοῦ φυσικῶς ἐν αὐτῷ τε ὑπάρχον καὶ δι’ αὐτοῦ προϊὸν, οὕτω καὶ τοῦ Πατρός... εἰ...οὐκ ἐκ τοῦ Πατρὸς ἐκπορεύεται, τοῦτ’ ἐστὶν ἐκ τῆς οὐσίας αὐτοῦ, ὁ Υἱὸς...πῶς οὐκ ἐν ἀμείνοσι νοοῖτο ἂν τὸ Πνεῦμα παρὰ τὸν Υἱόν;*

Theophylact (Migne CXXIV. 205), *ὅταν δὲ ἀκούσῃς ὅτι ‘ἐκπορεύεται,’ μὴ νόει ἀποστολὴν τὴν ἐκπόρευσιν...ἀλλὰ φυσικὴ ὕπαρξίς ἐστιν ἡ ἐκπόρευσις.*

Euthymius Zigabenus (Migne CXXIX. 1420), *παρὰ τοῦ Πατρὸς δὲ ἐκπορεύεται ὡς ἐκ τῆς οὐσίας αὐτοῦ ὤν. διὸ καὶ οἶδε πάντα τὰ τοῦ Πατρὸς ὥσπερ καὶ ὁ Υἱός.*

B. *Latin Fathers.*

S. Hilary of Poitiers (*de Trin.* VIII. 19, Migne X. 250), consistentis egressionem an geniti processionem; cf. XII. 55 Spiritu Tuo ex Te profecto et per Eum misso: *infr.* genitum Spiritum S. non dicturus sim.

S. Ambrose (*de Sp. S.* I. 11, Migne XVI. 762), non quasi ex loco

a verb, which has in consequence received a recognized place in the terminology of the Universal Church. Through the Latin version of the Gospels which before the end of the second century was already current in North Africa, the Western Church learnt to speak of the *Processio*[1]; whilst

mittitur Sp. aut quasi ex loco procedit...cum procedit a Patre et Filio, non separatur a Patre, non separatur a Filio.

S. Augustine (*c. Maxim.* II. 14, Migne XLII. 770), de Patre est Filius, de Patre est Sp. S.; sed ille genitus est, iste procedens...de illo Filius ait 'De Patre procedit' quoniam Pater processionis ejus est auctor. *Ib. de Trin.* IV. 29, sicut Spiritui Sancto...est a Patre procedere: ita mitti est cognosci quia ab illo procedat.

Ven. Bede (*Hom.* II. 13, Migne XCIV. 182), mittitur profecto Spiritus a Patre, mittitur et a Filio; quia et ejus missio ipsa processio est qua ex Patre procedit et Filio. [cf. Alcuin (Migne C. 949), Haymo (CXVIII. 550) &c.; Bellarmin. de Chr. II. § XXII., "missio secundum productionem"].

In later times the opposite view—that by procession no more is intended than simple mission, and that the passage in S. John has therefore no real bearing on the ecclesiastical dogma of the *productio naturalis*, seems to have been put forth first by Beza, who has been followed by a host of modern expositors, e. g. Rosenmüller, Lampe, Luthardt, Meyer, and in part by Tholuck and Alford. On the other hand the traditional interpretation has been upheld by Grotius ["qui de Patris ipsius substantia procedit et ab ipso emanat"], Stier, Olshausen; by theologians of the Latin and Greek Churches, and by the best of the Anglican divines.

[1] *Procedit* was the rendering of ἐκπορεύεται in the old Latin version as known to Novatian, S. Hilary, and S. Ambrose: see the note to p. 5 (*supr.*). Tertullian does not quote S. John xv. 26, but he uses *procedere* of the Son's generation (*adv. Prax.* 7). In the Vulgate (N. T.) *procedo* is the equivalent of ἔρχομαι προέρχομαι προσέρχομαι (of each once), ἐξέρχομαι (seven times), προβαίνω (four times), ἐκπορεύομαι (sixteen times). Other verbs by which the Vulg. renders ἐκπορ. are *ejicior* (once), *divulgor* (once), *proficiscor* (twice), *egredior* (six times), *exeo* (eight times). On the lexical and theological uses of *procedere* see Procopowicz, *de process. Sp. S.* pp. 2, 3. "Verbum *procedendi* in latino quidem sermone minime id quod in nostro negotio sonat...sed *procedere* idem est ac *progredi*, hoc est, de loco in locum moveri. ... In hac vero controversia ... abusive ... accipitur, idque dupliciter: primo idem valet ac *mitti*...secunda autem et quidem vulgatissima apud theologos verbi istius usurpatio est pro ortu Sp. Sancti ex causa seu principio suo."

the original word has long been used by the teachers of the Greek Church to represent the property which distinguishes the Holy Spirit from the Father and the Son[1].

In this dogmatic sense the verb ἐκπορεύομαι, *procedo*, is used by S. John alone among the writers of the New Testament, and by him only in this one verse of his Gospel, if we except a mystical passage in the Apocalypse of which the meaning is not equally clear[2]. But the word was in some

[1] Other terms common in the Greek fathers are ἔκπεμψις, προέλευσις, πρόοδος. For ἐκπορεύεσθαι we find προέρχεσθαι, προϊέναι, προχεῖσθαι, etc. Cf. Suicer (*s. v.* ἐκπορ.) Petav. *de Trin.* VII. X. 4. Procopowitz, p. 26, *note.*

[2] XXII. I. ἔδειξέ μοι ποταμὸν ὕδατος ζωῆς λαμπρὸν ὡς κρύσταλλον ἐκπορευόμενον ἐκ τοῦ θρόνου τοῦ θεοῦ καὶ τοῦ ἀρνίου. Cf. Gosp. of S. John vii. 38, 39 ποταμοὶ...ὕδατος ζῶντος...τοῦτο δὲ εἶπεν περὶ τοῦ Πνεύματος: and the vision of Ezekiel xlvii. to which both passages probably allude; also Zech. xiv. 8, ἐξελεύσεται ὕδωρ ζῶν ἐξ Ἱερουσαλήμ. In Cramer's *Catena* (VIII. 577) the verse in the Apocalypse is thus interpreted: τῆς ἄνω Ἱερουσαλὴμ ὁ πεπληρωμένος ὑδάτων πολλῶν ποταμὸς τοῦ Θεοῦ ἐκπορευόμενος τὸ ζωοποιὸν Πνεῦμά ἐστιν ἐκ τοῦ Θεοῦ καὶ Πατρὸς ἐκπορευόμενον καὶ διὰ τοῦ Ἀρνίου διὰ μέσου τῶν ὑπερτάτων δυνάμεων, αἳ θρόνος τοῦ Θεοῦ ὀνομάζονται, τὰς πλατείας πληροῦν τῆς ἁγίας πόλεως, δηλαδὴ τὸ πλῆθος αὐτῆς. This is the comment of the earliest Greek expositor of the entire Apocalypse, S. Andrew of Cappadocia. S. Ambrose also among the Latins interprets "Hic est utique fluvius de sede Dei procedens, hoc est Spiritus Sanctus, quem bibit qui credit in Christum." (*De Sp. S.* 101—20.) But there does not seem to be anything like a *consensus* for this view of the passage. The ποταμὸς ἐκπορευόμενος is variously explained as the symbol of Holy Baptism (Cramer *ib.* pp. 490—1); of the "grace of spiritual instruction," (Victorinus) of the blessedness of the saved, the fruit of Baptism, (Primasius, Bede, Walafrid Strabo). In a commentary which is printed among the works of Ambrose (Migne XVII. 843 sq.) the "river" of Apoc. xxii. is distinguished from the "torrent" of Ezek. xlvii. as follows: "Per torrentem scripturam divinam intelligere debemus quae de templo i. e. de ecclesia egreditur....Joannes autem non torrentem sed fluvium a sede Dei et Agni procedentem sibi ostensum fuisse docet....Per fluvium qui nullo ardore solis exsiccatur gloria sanctorum perpetua intelligitur. Qui a sede &c. procedere dicitur quia ab illo fluvius gloriae Sanctorum procedet a quo illis in carne positis processit fluvius omnium bonorum."

degree prepared for its high purpose by the uses to which it had been applied in the Septuagint. The Alexandrian translators of the Old Testament employed it to express the issue of rivers from their sources, of light from fire, of the wind from its quarter, of the offspring from the parent, of speech from the lips, and in particular, of Divine utterances from the mouth of God. It had served to describe the self-manifestations of Deity, as at the lawgiving and in judgment[1]. A word with this history was

[1] The following are examples: (*a*) Gen. ii. 10, *ποταμὸς ἐκπορεύεται ἐξ Ἐδέμ*: Deut. viii. 7, *πηγαὶ ἀβύσσων ἐκπορευόμεναι διὰ τῶν πεδίων*: Ezek. xlvii. 1, *ὕδωρ ἐξεπορεύετο ὑποκάτωθεν τοῦ αἰθρίου.* (*b*) Ezek. i. 13, *ἐκ τοῦ πυρὸς ἐξεπορεύετο ἀστραπή.* (*c*) Jer. xxxii. 18, *λαῖλαψ μεγάλη ἐκπορεύεται ἀπ' ἐσχάτου τῆς γῆς.* (*d*) Jud. viii. 30, *υἱοὶ ἑβδομήκοντα ἐκπορευόμενοι.* Job iii. 16, *ἔκτρωμα ἐκπορευόμενον ἐκ μήτρας.* (*e*) Num. xxxii. 24, *τὸ ἐκπορευόμενον ἐκ τοῦ στόματος ὑμῶν ποιήσετε.* Deut. viii. 3 [cf. S. Matt. iv. 4], *ἐπὶ παντὶ ῥήματι τῷ ἐκπορευομένῳ διὰ στόματος Θεοῦ ζήσεται ὁ ἄνθρωπος.* Ps. lxxxviii. 34, *τὰ ἐκπορευόμενα διὰ τῶν χειλέων μου οὐ μὴ ἀθετήσω.* Ezek. xxxiii. 30, *τὰ ἐκπορευόμενα παρὰ Κυρίου.* (*f*) Ps. lxvii. 8, *ὁ Θεὸς ἐν τῷ ἐκπορεύεσθαί σε.* Mic. i. 3, *Κύριος ἐκπορεύεται ἐκ τοῦ τόπου αὐτοῦ.*

In all these instances except Job iii. 16, Jer. xxxii. 18 (=xxv. 32 Hebr.) *ἐκπορεύομαι* is used to translate יָצָא (מוֹצָא), and this is the case throughout the Septuagint in the proportion of eight instances to one. In Dan. vii. 10 (*ποταμὸς πυρὸς [ἐκπορευόμενος] εἷλκεν ἔμπροσθεν αὐτοῦ*), *ἐκπορ.* is, if genuine, the representative of the Chaldee נְפַק: cf. ܢܦܩ in the Pesh. Syr. of John xv. 26. Apoc. xxii. 1.

A still more usual representative of יָצָא in the LXX. is *ἐξέρχομαι*, by which it is translated in about 500 instances (Trommius, *s. v.*). Ἐξέρχομαι is used (though not for יָצָא) in Esa. lvii. 16, a passage which in its Greek dress bears a strong likeness to John xv. 26, *πνεῦμα γὰρ παρ' ἐμοῦ ἐξελεύσεται* [*a me exiet* Vet. Lat., *a facie mea egredietur.* Vulg.]: on which S. Irenaeus comments (*haer.* v. 13, 2), *Πνεῦμα ζωοποιὸν τὸ καὶ πνευματικὸν αὐτὸν* [*sc. τὸν ἄνθρωπον*] *ἀποτελοῦν...ἰδίως ἐπὶ τοῦ Θεοῦ τάξας τοῦ ἐκχέοντος αὐτό.* The Hebr., however (כִּי־רוּחַ מִלְּפָנַי יַעֲטוֹף), gives a widely different sense, and the other Greek versions are not in agreement with the LXX.: cf. Field, *Origenis Hexapla*, II. p. 544.

With regard to the prepositions which follow *ἐκπορεύομαι*, it will be observed that *ἀπὸ*, *ἐκ*, *παρὰ* and *διὰ* are employed by the LXX., and there is a similar diversity of use in the N. T., *παρὰ* however occurring only in S. John xv. 26. It is probably chosen there to

not inappropriately chosen to signify the eternal "goings forth[1]" of a Divine Person Whose special symbols are water, wind, and light, Who "spake by the Prophets," and Whose office it is to glorify the Son and in the Son the Father also.

The adoption on the part of the Church of this expressive and divinely chosen term was however by no means immediate, or so early and general as we might have expected. No Creed or rule of faith recalls the words of S. John before the middle of the fourth century. The employment of the verb ἐκπορεύομαι, *procedo*, in reference to the Person of the Holy Spirit, is in Ante-Nicene writers, so far as I have been able to observe, exceedingly rare. Of the Generation or Procession of the Son we read much: of the Procession of the Holy Ghost, in express terms, almost nothing. In the first two centuries heresy entered more largely than Catholic Christianity into the question of the Spirit's relation to the Father and the Son. The earliest Church for the most part was satisfied with an implicit faith, and an informal and sometimes lax manner of expressing her belief[2]. At length, con-

express 'from being with' [Maldonatus: ab eo loco ubi Pater est, a sinu Patris], a sense commonly belonging to it in the theological language of S. John's Gospel: see c. i. 14, ὡς μονογενοῦς παρὰ Πατρός [cf. *infr.* 18, ὁ μονογενὴς υἱὸς ὁ ὢν εἰς τὸν κόλπον τοῦ Πατρός]: vi. 46, ὁ ὢν παρὰ τοῦ Θεοῦ οὗτος ἑώρακεν τὸν Πατέρα: vii. 29, παρ' αὐτοῦ εἰμι κἀκεῖνός με ἀπέστειλεν: xvi. 27, παρὰ [v. l. ἐκ] τοῦ Θεοῦ ἐξῆλθον: xvii. 8, παρὰ σοῦ ἐξῆλθον...σύ με ἀπέστειλας. The change of παρὰ into ἐκ in the Creed is curious, and may have been due to imperfect recollection of the original, since no variant exists in any known MS. of the Gospel. Compare, however, 1 Cor. ii. 12, τὸ Πνεῦμα τὸ ἐκ τοῦ Θεοῦ· and see ch. iv. (*infr.*).

[1] ἔξοδοι αὐτοῦ (מוֹצָאֹתָיו) ἀπ' ἀρχῆς ἐξ ἡμερῶν αἰῶνος, Mic. v. 2 [in reference to the Son].

[2] "The Church needed a long education before she was fitted to be the expositor of the true Apostolic doctrine. A conflict of more than

vinced of the necessity of defending herself against heretical perversions of the truth, and at the same time schooled to greater exactness of thought and language by the growth of culture within her own pale, she sought for a form of speech which should precisely set forth her teaching upon this subject, and found it in the very words of Our Lord as they stand recorded in the Fourth Gospel.

Between the date of S. John's Gospel and that of the earliest of sub-apostolic writings the interval is probably at the most not greater than fifteen years[1]. S. Clement of Rome was a contemporary of S. John, and, if we may believe Eusebius, barely survived the last of the Apostles[2]. But his one genuine Epistle exhibits little evidence of an acquaintance with S. John's writings and contains no certain allusion to the Gospel[3]. On the Procession of the Holy Spirit it is silent. The presence and work of the Paraclete are fully recognized; His

two centuries with Gnostics, Ebionites, Sabellians, Arians, supplied the necessary discipline. The true successors of the Apostles in this respect are not the fathers of the second century, but the fathers of the third and fourth centuries." Lightfoot, *Colossians*, p. 191. If this is true in reference to the Christology of the Church, it is true *a fortiori* with regard to the obscurer doctrine of the Holy Ghost.

[1] Dr Lightfoot places the Ep. of S. Clement "about the year 95" (*S. Clement*, p. 5). Cf. Sanday, *The Gospels in the Second Century*, p. 61. *Infr.* p. 269: "it is very possible that the Gospel was not published or barely published when Clement of Rome wrote his Epistle."

[2] Compare Euseb. III. 34 with 23, *ἔτει τρίτῳ τῆς τοῦ* [*Τραϊανοῦ*] *ἀρχῆς Κλήμης...ἀναλύει τὸν βίον.* [*ὁ Ἰωάννης*] *παρέμεινε...μέχρι τῶν Τραϊανοῦ χρόνων.*

[3] Dr Westcott (*On the Canon*, p. 25) finds indications of "the influence of S. John." Meyer (*Comm. on S. John*, E. Tr. p. 5) denies that there is "any express quotation from or sure trace of any use of the [Fourth] Gospel" in this or any other work of an Apostolical Father. The newly recovered chapters of S. Clement's Epistle do not quote S. John.

personality[1] and Deity[2] are clearly implied; but His relation to the Father and the Son does not fall within the range of the writer's teaching. He notices simply the effusion of the Holy Ghost and the effects of His grace. The Apostles, he says, μετὰ πληροφορίας Πνεύματος Ἁγίου ἐξῆλθον[3]: in the Church of Corinth, after the first preaching of the Gospel, πλήρης Πνεύματος Ἁγίου ἔκχυσις ἐπὶ πάντας ἐγίνετο[4]. The common gift of the One Spirit is regarded as the bond of Christian unity: οὐχὶ ἕνα Θεὸν ἔχομεν καὶ ἕνα Χριστὸν καὶ ἓν Πνεῦμα τῆς χάριτος τὸ ἐκχυθὲν ἐφ' ἡμᾶς[5]; The same Holy Spirit, S. Clement teaches, "spake by the Prophets:" the Holy Scriptures are His inspirations: οἱ λειτουργοὶ τῆς χάριτος τοῦ Θεοῦ διὰ Πνεύματος Ἁγίου ἐλάλησαν... ἐγκεκύφατε εἰς τὰς ἱερὰς γραφὰς τὰς ἀληθεῖς τὰς διὰ τοῦ Πνεύματος τοῦ Ἁγίου[6]. But this is all. No light is thrown as yet upon the Source from which the Divine Spirit proceeds[7].

S. Polycarp had been a hearer of S. John[8]: and the frequent use which he makes of the Apostolic

[1] Dr Donaldson (*Apostolical Fathers*, p. 164) seems to regard S. Clement as wavering between two opposite views upon this subject, because while attributing to the Holy Spirit personal properties he yet speaks of His *effusion* upon Christians. But the language of S. Peter and S. Paul is equally open to misconstruction: Acts ii. 22, ἐξέχεεν τοῦτο. Tit. iii. 6, οὗ ἐξέχεεν ἐφ' ἡμᾶς πλουσίως.

[2] The newly recovered portion of the Epistle contains (with slight variations) the words which were ascribed to S. Clement by S. Basil (*De Sp. S.* cxxix.): ζῇ γὰρ ὁ Θεὸς καὶ ζῇ ὁ Κύριος Ἰησοῦς Χριστὸς καὶ τὸ Πνεῦμα τὸ Ἅγιον, ἥ τε πίστις καὶ ἡ ἐλπὶς τῶν ἐκλεκτῶν.

[3] c. xlii. [4] c. ii. [5] c. xlvi. [6] cc. viii. xiv.

[7] The homily known as the 'Second Ep. of S. Clement,' which, whoever the author may have been, dates "probably before or about the middle of the second century," and "may have emanated from Egypt" (Lightfoot, p. 181), has nothing to tell us as to the early doctrine of the Holy Spirit. The writer uses πνεῦμα in reference to the Divine Nature in Christ; c. ix. ὢν μὲν τὸ πρῶτον πνεῦμα ἐγένετο σάρξ. See also a remarkable passage in the newly recovered c. xiv.

[8] Iren. ap. Euseb. *H. E.* v. 20.

writings shows him to have been acquainted with a large part of the New Testament Canon. It has been said that "the influence of S. Peter, S. John, and S. Paul may be traced in his doctrine[1]". Under these circumstances it is certainly singular that his Epistle to the Philippians contains no reference to the Person of the Spirit[2]. On the other hand the Epistle of Barnabas, which if wrongly ascribed to the companion of S. Paul, must yet take its place among the earliest monuments of the second century[3], opens with a passage of some interest in connection with this subject. The writer begins by congratulating his sons and daughters in the faith upon their spiritual progress, adding, Οὕτως ἔμφυτον τῆς δωρεᾶς πνευματικῆς χάριν εἰλήφατε·... ἀληθῶς βλέπω ἐν ὑμῖν ἐκκεχυμένον ἀπὸ τοῦ πλουσίου τῆς ἀγάπης Κυρίου Πνεῦμα ἐφ' ὑμᾶς[4]. Such is the reading of the Codex Sinaiticus, the only Greek MS. known to contain the opening verses of this Epistle. The Latin version, "Quia vere video in vobis infusum Spiritum ab honesto *fonte* Dei," suggests the variant πηγῆς[5]. If this conjecture be adopted, Barnabas will be the first Church writer who speaks of another Divine Person as the *Fountain* of the Holy Ghost. He uses the expression in reference

[1] Westcott, *Canon*, p. 36.

[2] Donaldson, *Ap. F.* p. 238. The letter is so brief that no inference can be based upon the fact.

[3] "Not later than the first quarter of the second century." Donaldson, p. 273.

[4] Tischendorf, *N. T. Sinaiticum*, p. 135.

[5] Hilgenfeld, *N. T. extr. Can. recept.* Barn. I. (note to l. 8, 9), "Volkm[ar] monuit vet. int., qui πλούσιος ubique vertit *honestus*, πηγῆς reperisse pro ἀγάπης." Cf. Müller, *Barnabasbrief*, p. 58.

Donaldson (*Ap. F.* p. 316—7) suggests that the Sinaitic Greek is "either a very corrupt MS. of Barnabas, or a translation based on the Latin."

to the temporal mission: the eternal ἐκπόρευσις is not in view. Yet such language seems to mark an advance upon the doctrine of S. Clement[1].

In the Ignatian letters we seem at times to be nearer to the doctrine of the Eternal Procession. The verb προέρχεσθαι, which in later Church-writers is almost a synonym of ἐκπορεύεσθαι, is twice applied to the Incarnation, if not to the Generation of the Son[2]. Concerning the Holy Ghost the shorter Greek Epistle to the Philadelphians very plainly says that He is "from God," in such a sense as to partake of Divine attributes: εἰ γὰρ καὶ κατὰ σάρκα μέ τινες ἠθέλησαν πλανῆσαι, ἀλλὰ τὸ Πνεῦμα οὐ πλανᾶται, ἀπὸ θεοῦ ὄν· οἶδεν γὰρ πόθεν ἔρχεται καὶ ποῦ ὑπάγει καὶ τὰ κρυπτὰ ἐλέγχει[3]. A singular metaphor which is found in all the recensions of the Epistle to the Ephesians, points to the work rather than

[1] Barnabas calls the Body of Christ "the vessel of [His] Spirit"—ἔμελλεν τὸ σκεῦος τοῦ Πνεύματος προσφέρειν θυσίαν (c. vii.) τὸ σκεῦος τοῦ Πνεύματος αὐτοῦ δοξάσει (c. xi.) *vas Spiritus sui=illius* in the Latin. It seems doubtful whether the πνεῦμα is here the Divine Nature in Our Lord (so Bull, *Def. fid. Nicaen.* I. ii. 5; Baur, *Chr. Dogm.* p. 508, inclines to this view), or the Holy Ghost who filled His humanity.

[2] *Magn.* 7, τὸν ἀφ' ἑνὸς Πατρὸς προελθόντα καὶ εἰς ἕνα ὄντα καὶ χωρήσαντα: *ib.* 8, ὅς ἐστιν αὐτοῦ λόγος [ἀΐδιος οὐκ] ἀπὸ σιγῆς προελθών: Cureton, *Corp. Ign.* pp. 65—8, cf. *ib.* pp. 213, 355, where the second passage is given as quoted by Severus of Antioch without the negative. Probably this was the original form of the sentence, which was altered by some officious copyist at a time when the idea of a 'procession from silence' was thought to suggest complicity with Valentinianism: see Prof. Lightfoot's remarks in *Journal of Philology*, I. ii. pp. 525, and esp. his reference to Wisd. xviii. 14, 15, ἡσύχου γὰρ σιγῆς περιεχούσης τὰ πάντα...ὁ παντοδύναμός σου λόγος...ἥλατο.

[3] *Philad.* 7 (Cureton, *Corp. Ign.* pp. 97-8). The longer Greek Epistle exhibits ἀλλὰ τὸ πνεῦμά μου οὐ πλανᾶται· παρὰ γὰρ Θεοῦ αὐτὸ εἴληφα. But even if this were the sounder text, the reference must still be to the Spirit of God dwelling in Ignatius [cf. Jacobson, *Sp. S. in corde Ignatii habitans*], the meaning being fixed by the context and by the reference to S. John iii. 8.

to the Person of the Spirit. The Holy Ghost, Ignatius says, is the rope which, attached to the Cross of Jesus Christ, lifts up the soul to its place in the Building of God: ἡτοιμασμένοι εἰς οἰκοδομὴν θεοῦ Πατρὸς, ἀναφερόμενοι εἰς τὰ ὕψη διὰ τῆς μηχανῆς Ἰησοῦ ὅς ἐστιν σταυρὸς, σχοινίῳ χρώμενοι τῷ Ἁγίῳ Πνεύματι[1]. But the prefatory matter with which this comparison is introduced by the early interpolator is remarkable, if only for the use which he makes of a passage (S. John xvi. 13, 14[2]) famous in the later history of the Procession-dogma. Τὸ δὲ Ἅγιον Πνεῦμα (he explains) οὐ τὰ ἴδια ἀλλὰ τὰ τοῦ Χριστοῦ [λαλεῖ], καὶ οὐκ ἀφ' ἑαυτοῦ ἀλλὰ ἀπὸ τοῦ Κυρίου, ὡς καὶ ὁ Κύριος τὰ παρὰ τοῦ Πατρὸς ἡμῖν κατήγγελλεν· 'ὁ λόγος γὰρ (φησὶν) ὃν ἀκούετε οὐκ ἐστὶν ἐμὸς ἀλλὰ τοῦ πέμψαντός με Πατρός·' καὶ περὶ τοῦ Πνεύματος τοῦ Ἁγίου, 'Οὐ λαλήσει (φησὶν) ἀφ' ἑαυτοῦ, ἀλλ' ὅσα ἂν ἀκούσῃ παρ' ἐμοῦ... ἐκεῖνος ἐμὲ δοξάσει ὅτι ἐκ τοῦ ἐμοῦ λαμβάνει.' In this reasoning we recognize the first indications of a tendency to represent the relation of the Holy Spirit to the Son as corresponding with the relation of the Son to the Father.

The Shepherd of Hermas is placed by the author of the Muratorian Fragment in the fifth or sixth decad of the second century[3]: but in virtue of the

[1] *Eph.* 9 (Cureton, *Corp. Ign.* pp. 25-6).

[2] I quote these verses once for all:

ὅταν ἔλθῃ ἐκεῖνος τὸ Πνεῦμα τῆς ἀληθείας ὁδηγήσει ὑμᾶς ἐν τῇ ἀληθείᾳ πάσῃ· οὐ γὰρ λαλήσει ἀφ' ἑαυτοῦ ἀλλ' ὅσα ἀκούσει λαλήσει...ἐκεῖνος ἐμὲ δοξάσει ὅτι ἐκ τοῦ ἐμοῦ λήμψεται καὶ ἀναγγελεῖ ὑμῖν. πάντα ὅσα ἔχει ὁ Πατὴρ ἐμά ἐστιν· διὰ τοῦτο εἶπον ὅτι ἐκ τοῦ ἐμοῦ λαμβάνει καὶ ἀναγγελεῖ ὑμῖν.

[3] The words are, "Pastorem vero nuperrime temporibus nostris in urbe Roma Hermas conscripsit sedente cathedra urbis Romae ecclesiae Pio episcopo:" *i.e.* between A.D. 142 and 157. The writer adds, "legi eum quidem oportet, se publicare vero in ecclesia populo neque

quasi-canonical character with which it was invested by the age in which it was written, and the primitive simplicity of its dogmatic teaching, it may conveniently be classed according to the common arrangement with the writings of the 'Apostolical Fathers.' A well-known passage in the Fifth Similitude bears indirectly upon our present subject. Hermas interprets a parable in which the leading figures are the proprietor of a vineyard, his son, and a faithful servant to whom the care of the vineyard is committed. 'This son,' he explains, 'is the Holy Spirit: the servant is the Son of God. Yet the Son of God is not to be regarded as occupying the rank of a servant: on the contrary, He is invested with great authority and power. The Body, however, into which the Holy Spirit entered served the Spirit[1].' The language is obscure, and the text uncertain: but there appears to be no sufficient reason for supposing that Hermas identifies the hypostasis of the Holy Spirit with the hypostasis of the Son, or regards the former as in any sense incarnate in the Person of Christ[2]. The exigencies of his similitude have led

inter prophetas...neque inter apostolos in finem temporum potest :" the very vehemence of his manner showing that some attempt had already been made to treat the *Shepherd* as part of the Canon. (Westcott, *Canon*, pp. 177-8, *ib.* 500.)

[1] Hilgenfeld, *N. T. extr. Can. recept.* (Hermæ Pastor, p. 89), restores the Greek text thus: *ὁ δὲ υἱὸς τὸ Ἅγιον Πνεῦμά ἐστιν· ὁ δὲ δοῦλος ὁ Υἱὸς τοῦ Θεοῦ ἐστιν...εἰς δούλου τρόπον οὐ κεῖται ὁ Υἱὸς τοῦ Θεοῦ ἀλλ' εἰς ἐξουσίαν μεγάλην κεῖται καὶ κυριότητα......τὸ Πνεῦμα τὸ Ἅγιον τὸ προὸν τὸ κτίσαν πᾶσαν τὴν κτίσιν κατῴκισεν ὁ Θεὸς εἰς σάρκα ἣν ἐβούλετο. αὕτη οὖν ἡ σὰρξ ἐν ᾗ κατῴκησεν τὸ Πνεῦμα τὸ Ἅγιον ἐδούλευσε τῷ Πνεύματι.* The moral is, *Τὴν σάρκα σου ταύτην φύλασσε καθαρὰν καὶ ἀμίαντον ἵνα τὸ Πνεῦμα τὸ κατοικοῦν ἐν αὐτῇ μαρτυρήσῃ αὐτῇ.* Hilgenfeld brackets *ὁ δὲ υἱὸς τὸ* Ἅ. Π. *ἐ.* as wanting in the Cod. Lips.

[2] Hefele, following Grotius and Bull, thinks that by the Holy Spirit in this passage Hermas means the Son : *Patr. Ap.* p. 296. Baur (see

him, however, to represent the Holy Spirit as a Son of God: and the fact that he permitted himself to do so shows that as yet no accurate discrimination had been made between the cognate ideas of generation and procession. The converse of this ambiguity is common enough in writings of the first two centuries; an instance occurs in the Ninth Similitude of the *Shepherd*, where the Spirit who conversed with Hermas is explained to be the Son: *τὸ Πνεῦμα τὸ ἅγιον τὸ λαλῆσαν μετὰ σοῦ ἐν μορφῇ τῆς ἐκκλησίας...ὁ Υἱὸς τοῦ θεοῦ ἐστίν.* But, as Bishop Bull has pointed out[1], the latter expression if ambiguous is perfectly justifiable; the Son is Spirit, inasmuch as He is God: whereas the Spirit can be represented as a Son only in virtue of a relation to the Father which the name of Son does not properly express.

Before leaving the sub-apostolic writers we may glance at the letter of the Churches of Vienne and Lyons, which, though it belongs to the year 177, emanated from a community whose Bishop, Pothinus, then but just deceased, had reached early manhood within the lifetime of S. John[2]. In this Epistle the Holy Spirit perhaps for the first time[3] bears the title

Dorner, I. i. pp. 130—4, and note, p. 388 sq.) maintains that in the *Shepherd* the conception of Christ is that of a human Body inhabited by the Holy Ghost. Hilgenfeld charges Hermas with a leaning to the Ebionite belief—"Christum vel hominem Spiritu S. plenissimum vel archangelum principem." I have ventured to adopt Dorner's view; with regard to which he candidly says (p. 129), "The explanation according to which the passage is understood as touching upon the relation of the Incarnate Son of God to the Holy Ghost is not without harshness: still as it alone harmonizes with *Sim.* IX. nay, since it alone makes *Sim.* V. consistent with itself, we feel constrained to give it the preference."

[1] *Def. fid. Nicaen.* I. ii. 5.

[2] Euseb. *H. E.* V. 1, *ὁ δὲ μακάριος Ποθεινὸς ὁ τὴν διακονίαν τῆς ἐπισκοπῆς ἐν Λουγδούνῳ πεπιστευμένος ὑπὲρ τὰ ἐνενήκοντα ἔτη τῆς ἡλικίας.*

[3] *ὁ παράκλητος* occurs in Ign. *Philad.* 5, but only in the longer Greek.

which is given to Him in the Fourth Gospel. One of the martyrs is described as ἔχων τὸν Παράκλητον ἐν ἑαυτῷ[1]. A little further on we come upon the following account of the supernatural strength by which they were animated: ἐκείνους...ἐπεκούφιζεν ἡ χαρὰ τῆς μαρτυρίας καὶ ἡ ἐλπὶς τῶν ἐπηγγελμένων καὶ ἡ πρὸς τὸν Χριστὸν ἀγάπη καὶ τὸ Πνεῦμα τὸ Πατρικόν[2]. It is difficult to avoid the supposition that these words are the echo of our Lord's, Ἐὰν ἀγαπᾶτέ με, ἐγὼ ἐρωτήσω τὸν Πατέρα καὶ ἄλλον Παράκλητον δώσει ὑμῖν...τὸ Πνεῦμα τῆς ἀληθείας ὃ παρὰ τοῦ Πατρὸς ἐκπορεύεται[3]. And thus in the latest of the early Christian writings which stand in any close connection with the Apostolic times, we seem to discover the first trace of an allusion to the words in which the Son revealed the Procession of the Holy Spirit from the Father.

Hitherto our gleanings from Church writers have been scanty and of uncertain value. The Apologists, who began to write in the third decad of the second century, supply more ample materials for the history of doctrine. In their answers to the challenge of Hellenism and Judaism, the veil with which the primitive Church was disposed to shroud the mysteries of her faith and worship is partly drawn aside, and a first attempt is made to present the Gospel to the world under a systematic form[4]. To a

[1] Euseb. *l. c.*, or Routh, *R. S.* I. 298. See the note in Routh 333 sq.

[2] Routh *R. S.* I. 308.

[3] S. John xiv. 15, 16; xv. 26.

[4] The charge of *atheism* in particular called forth a declaration of the Christian belief in the Father, Son, and Holy Ghost: cf. Justin. *Apol.* I. 6, Athenag. *Legat.* 10. When this faith had once been announced it was scarcely possible to stop short of the question "what relations do the Son and the Holy Spirit bear to God?" Cf. Baur, *Dogmengesch.* I. i. 511, "dem Athenagoras gab, wie dem Justin, die Be-

true Christian zeal the most eminent of these early defenders of the faith united a professional acquaintance with the literature and the philosophy of Greece. Aristides and Justin continued as Christians to wear the philosopher's garb[1]: the Apology of Athenagoras bears the title Ἀθηναγόρου Ἀθηναίου φιλοσόφου Χριστιανοῦ. It is no wonder if the writings of these men exhibit a tendency to adopt Platonic language which cannot always be reconciled with the maturer judgment of the Catholic Church[2]. But while the Church is not committed to these individual efforts to work out the great problems of the Faith[3], they are at least of great importance to the history of Christian dogma. We discover in them the first conscious attempt to express in harmony with the conditions of human thought the great revelation of the Baptismal words—the Name of the Father, the Son and the Holy Ghost.

The attention of the Apologists at first was necessarily directed to the doctrine of the Person of Christ. In the noble 'Epistle to Diognetus,' while the idea of the θεὸς λόγος is already apprehended, we have no mention of the Holy Ghost. The Logos

schuldigung des Atheismus Veranlassung, den heiligen Geist neben dem Vater und Sohn zu erwähnen."

[1] Neander, II. 412—3, cf. I. 381—2.

[2] On the influence of Platonism upon early Christianity, see Newman, *Arians*, p. 92 sq.

[3] "It must be observed (Dr Newman writes, *Arians*, p. 53) that the writers of these [Apologies] were frequently laymen, and so did not commit the Church as a body nor even in its separate authorities to formal statement or to theological discussion." Several of the leading Apologists belonged, in fact, to the Episcopal order (e. g. S. Melito, Claudius Apollinaris, S. Theophilus). But laymen or priests, they certainly have not entailed any responsibility upon the Church for statements which she has never sanctioned, either synodically, or by the rule of *quod semper*.

seems to fill the writer's field of vision[1]; to the power and grace of the Logos the Church owes, in his conception, all her spiritual wealth: οὗτος ὁ ἀπ' ἀρχῆς ὁ καινὸς φανεὶς...καὶ πάντοτε νέος ἐν ἁγίων καρδίαις γεννώμενος...δι' οὗ πλουτίζεται ἡ ἐκκλησία[2]. S. Justin also is deeply impressed with the magnificence of the Logos-idea[3]; and in his hands the doctrine of the Generation of the Son begins to assume something of the form which the wisdom of the Church finally impressed upon it. According to Justin, the Son is τὸ τῷ ὄντι ἀπὸ τοῦ Πατρὸς προβληθὲν γέννημα[4]. He is conceived of as generated or emitted from the Father without abscission or separation, and, as fire from fire, without diminution of the Essence from which He proceeds: οὐ κατὰ ἀποτομὴν ὡς ἀπομεριζομένης τῆς τοῦ Πατρὸς οὐσίας...ὡς τὰ ἀπὸ πυρὸς ἀναπτόμενα πυρὰ...οὐδὲν ἐλαττουμένου ἐκείνου[5]. His procession is in Justin's view closely connected with the purpose of God to create the worlds: coeternal with the Father as the Logos, as the Son He is significantly said to have been begotten 'before all creatures' (πρὸ πάντων τῶν ποιημάτων), not 'before all worlds' (πρὸ πάντων τῶν αἰώνων) as the Creeds of Caesarea and Constantinople more adequately expressed the mystery[6]. Dr Newman has shown that this notion of a 'temporal' (i. e. an economical) 'gennêsis' was held by many of the Ante-Nicene, and by some even of the earlier Post-Nicene, writers, especially by those who be-

[1] See Dorner, I. i. 263. The writer of the Epistle does not yet attempt to reconcile this Christology with the Unity of God: *ib.* 264.

[2] Migne, II. 1183.

[3] Cf. Meyer on S. John, Vol. I. 9 (E. Tr.).

[4] *Tryph.* 61, 62 (Migne, VI. 617).

[5] *Tryph.* 128 (Migne, VI. 776).

[6] See Newman, *Tracts Theological, &c.* p. 204. Kaye, *J. M.* pp. 58—61. Even Arius could use the latter formula: Socr. *H. E.* I. 26.

longed to the Asiatic and Western Schools;—without detriment however to their faith in the Eternal Deity of the Word as a distinct Person of the Holy Trinity[1]. I notice this fact here once for all, because it will prepare us to expect for some time to come a very partial and uncertain discrimination between the temporal and eternal processions of GOD the Holy Ghost.

With regard to S. Justin, he scarcely opens the question of the relation which the Holy Spirit bears to the Father and the Son. While the verbs προβάλλειν and προέρχεσθαι are freely used in reference to the Generation of the Son, the Holy Spirit is simply described by him in the *Cohortatio ad Graecos* (if that work be really his) as the Gift which descends from GOD upon the Saints (ἡ ἄνωθεν παρὰ θεοῦ κατιοῦσα ἐπὶ τοὺς ἁγίους ἄνδρας δωρεά[2].) Some idea of His subordination to the Son in the inner Life of the Holy Trinity may possibly underlie the emphatic statement that the Spirit is honoured by the Church ἐν τρίτῃ τάξει[3]. Yet this need not be more than an inference from the order in which the Persons are named in the act of Baptism, or from

[1] He finds this in Catholic fathers, Eastern and Western, down to the year 360. The initiation of a sounder doctrine is ascribed to "S. Phoebadius and S. Ambrose in the West, S. Basil and the two Gregories in the East." *Tracts*, p. 251.

[2] *Coh. ad Gr.* VIII. 32 (Migne, VI. 300). If the ἄγγελος τοῦ Θεοῦ of *Tryph.* 116 be the Holy Spirit, this divine gift is recognized by Justin as ἡ δύναμις ἡ πεμφθεῖσα ἡμῖν διὰ Ἰησοῦ Χριστοῦ. See Neander, *Hist. Dogm.* I. 173.

[3] *Apol.* I. 13 (Migne, VI. 348). Υἱὸν...ἐν δευτέρᾳ χώρᾳ ἔχοντες, Πνεῦμά τε προφητικὸν ἐν τρίτῃ τάξει. Cf. infr. p. 419, where even Plato is asserted to have recognized this order: δευτέραν μὲν γὰρ χώραν τῷ παρὰ Θεοῦ λόγῳ...δίδωσι, τὴν δε τρίτην τῷ λεχθέντι ἐπιφέρεσθαι τῷ ὕδατι Πνεύματι. On the personality of the Holy Spirit Justin is clear, notwithstanding some ambiguity in his use of the words λόγος and πνεῦμα: see Kaye, pp. 70—3.

the offices fulfilled by the Holy Spirit towards Our Lord[1] and the Church.

Justin's scholar, Tatian the Assyrian, dwells upon this last point in language which is on the verge of heterodoxy. He ventures to call the Spirit the 'minister' of the Incarnate Son (*τὸν διάκονον τοῦ πεπονθότος Θεοῦ*[2]). On the other hand, he represents Him as the ambassador and delegate of GOD in the heart of a Christian: *κατοικεῖν ἐν αὐτῷ βούλεται Θεὸς διὰ τοῦ πρεσβεύοντος Πνεύματος*[3]. Of the eternal procession of the Spirit Tatian says nothing, but like his master he speaks of the procession, i. e. the generation, of the Word, Who before the creation of the world came forth (*προελθὼν*) from the power of the Father, like torch kindled from torch, or as speech emitted from the lips[4].

[1] A remarkable passage in *Tryph.* 87, 88 (Migne, VI. 684—5) answers the objection of the Jew that the Word cannot be pre-existent because *διὰ τῶν δυνάμεων τοῦ Πνεύματος τοῦ Ἁγίου...πληροῦται ὡς ἐνδεὴς τούτων ὑπάρχων.* Justin replies in words which anticipate in part the language of S. Cyril in his controversy with Nestorius; § 87: *ταύτας τὰς κατηριθμημένας τοῦ Πνεύματος δυνάμεις οὐχ ὡς ἐνδεοῦς αὐτοῦ τούτων ὄντος...ἐπεληλυθέναι ἐπ' αὐτὸν.* infr. § 88: *οὐχ ὡς ἐνδεᾶ αὐτὸν τοῦ βαπτισθῆναι ἢ τοῦ ἐπελθόντος...Πνεύματος, οἴδαμεν αὐτὸν ἐληλυθέναι ἐπὶ τὸν ποταμόν...ἀλλ' ὑπὲρ τοῦ γένους τοῦ τῶν ἀνθρώπων.*

[2] *Orat. ad Gr.* 13 (Migne, VI. 836).

[3] *ib.* 15 (Migne, 837).

[4] *ib.* 5 (Migne, 815—7). *ὥσπερ γὰρ ἀπὸ μιᾶς δᾳδὸς ἀνάπτεται μὲν πυρὰ πολλὰ, τῆς δὲ πρώτης δᾳδὸς διὰ τὴν ἔξαψιν τῶν πολλῶν δᾳδῶν οὐκ ἐλαττοῦται τὸ φῶς· οὕτω καὶ ὁ λόγος προελθὼν ἐκ τῆς τοῦ Πατρὸς δυνάμεως οὐκ ἄλογον πεποίηκε τὸν γεγεννηκότα. καὶ γὰρ αὐτὸς ἐγὼ λαλῶ καὶ ὑμεῖς ἀκούετε καὶ οὐ δήπου...κενὸς ὁ προσομιλῶν λόγου γίνομαι· προβαλλόμενος δὲ τὴν ἐμαυτοῦ φωνὴν κ.τ.λ.* Tatian occasionally uses Spirit and Word as interchangeable terms; and once, if the reading is correct, he seems to employ *τὸ Πνεῦμα* as = *ὁ Πατήρ* (c. 5. *ἔργον πρωτότοκον τοῦ Πνεύματος* [Maranus, *Πατρός*]). Hence Dorner says that the doctrine of the Holy Ghost is the central point of Tatian's system. But this is true only if by Holy Ghost he means simply *τὸ πνεῦμα* = *τὸ θεῖον* and not the hypostatic Holy Spirit, of whom Tatian says but little.

S. Theophilus, Bishop of Antioch from A.D. 177 to 186[1], was of eastern origin like Justin and Tatian; but his life, unlike theirs, was passed at a distance from the din of opposing theologies which was rife in the capital. His Apology manifests a tendency to mysticism which renders the meaning obscure: but if we read him aright, he comes nearer than any previous father to the idea of the Holy Spirit's procession, as parallel to the generation of the Son. With the generation of the *Λόγος ἐνδιάθετος* he connects the putting forth of the *Σοφία* of GOD, which he distinguishes, as it certainly seems, from the Word: *ἔχων ὁ Θεὸς τὸν ἑαυτοῦ Λόγον ἐνδιάθετον ἐν τοῖς ἰδίοις σπλάγχνοις ἐγέννησεν αὐτὸν μετὰ τῆς ἑαυτοῦ Σοφίας ἐρευξάμενος πρὸ τῶν ὅλων*[2]. In the next few sentences it is true the Bishop vacillates between this distinction and an identification of the Logos and the Sophia: 'it was the Logos,' he says, 'Who, being the Spirit of GOD and Wisdom, came down upon the Prophets;' adding however immediately, *Οὐ γὰρ ἦσαν οἱ προφῆται ὅτε ὁ κόσμος ἐγίνετο, ἀλλὰ ἡ Σοφία ἡ ἐν αὐτῷ οὖσα ἡ τοῦ Θεοῦ καὶ ὁ Λόγος ὁ ἅγιος αὐτοῦ ὁ ἀεὶ συμπαρὼν αὐτῷ*[3]. But the well-known passage in

[1] See Neale, *Patriarchate of Antioch*, pp. 24—29. He was a native of Chaldaea; and as Bp of Antioch sixth from the Apostles.

[2] *Ad Autolycum*, II. 10 (Migne, VI. 1064—5). Compare a fine passage *ib.* I. 7 (Migne, 1034), *οὗτός μου θεὸς ὁ τῶν ὅλων Κύριος ὁ τανύσας τὸν οὐρανὸν μόνος καὶ θεὶς τὸ εὗρος τῆς ὑπ' οὐρανὸν...ὁ θεμελιώσας τὴν γῆν ἐπὶ τῶν ὑδάτων καὶ δοὺς Πνεῦμα τὸ τρέφον αὐτήν· οὗ ἡ πνοὴ ζωογονεῖ τὸ πᾶν· ὃς ἐὰν συσχῇ τὸ πνεῦμα παρ' ἑαυτῷ ἐκλείψει τὸ πᾶν...ὁ θεὸς ὁ θεραπεύων καὶ ζωοποιῶν διὰ τοῦ Λόγου καὶ τῆς Σοφίας.* The Spirit therefore is *παρὰ τῷ τῶν ὅλων θεῷ = τῷ Πατρί*: He is emitted [*παρὰ τοῦ θεοῦ*] for the quickening and preservation of the creature: He seems to be also called *ἡ Σοφία*. The whole is a good comment on the passage cited in the text. Bp Kaye, it should be added, doubts whether *τὸ πνεῦμα* in I. 7 is the hypostatic Spirit of God. (Kaye, *J. M.* p. 179.)

[3] *ib.* infr.

which for the first time in extant Christian writings S. Theophilus speaks of a Divine Triad or Trinity, seems to place beyond question the fact that he distinguished between the two, and that by the Wisdom of GOD when so discriminated from the Word he meant to express the Person of the Holy Ghost[1]. His words are, Αἱ τρεῖς ἡμέραι [πρὸ] τῶν φωστήρων γεγονυῖαι τύποι εἰσιν τῆς τριάδος, τοῦ Θεοῦ καὶ τοῦ Λόγου αὐτοῦ καὶ τῆς Σοφίας αὐτοῦ· τετάρτῳ δὲ τόπῳ ἐστὶν ἄνθρωπος ὁ προσδεὴς τοῦ φωτὸς, ἵνα ᾖ Θεὸς, Λόγος, Σοφία, Ἄνθρωπος[2]. Thus in his view GOD, the Word, and the Wisdom of GOD are conceived of as Three, to whom Man, although at an infinite distance (for Man is προσδεὴς τοῦ φωτὸς, but the Triad is ἀνενδεὴς), makes a fourth. The distinction of the hypostases seems here to be complete, and is carried almost to the extent of sacrificing the Unity of the Divine Essence. On the whole, therefore, we may conclude that when Theophilus represents the Divine Word and Wisdom as uttered together from the Heart of GOD, he regards the processions of the Son and of the Spirit as analogous and coincident but distinct. Neither however would in his view be strictly eternal: the Logos and the Sophia which were eternally immanent in GOD began to proceed from Him when He willed to create the worlds.

The *Legatio pro Christianis* of S. Athenagoras belongs to the year 177. Its author, an Athenian

[1] In the Syriac Apocryphal Acts (Wright, II. p. 190) the Holy Spirit is called "the Power of the Father and the *Wisdom of the Son.*" The expression is noteworthy as helping to connect the use of Σοφία in Theophilus with its more common application to the Second Person.

[2] *Ad Autol.* II. 15 (Migne, VI. 1077). For τόπῳ the MSS give τύπῳ.

and a philosopher, is connected by a late tradition with the Church and School of Alexandria, and his Christology has been said to exhibit traces of an affinity to Alexandrian thought[1]. It is certain that we become conscious of a marked advance in the conception of the Holy Trinity, when we pass from Justin and Theophilus to the pages of Athenagoras. The doctrine of the *circumincessio* finds a distinct place in his theology. "The Son," he teaches, "is in the Father, and the Father in the Son, by the unity and power of the Spirit[2]." "Do you ask what the Son (ὁ Παῖς) can mean in this connection? I answer briefly, that He is the First Offspring of the Father, begotten not made, Who came forth from the Father as the Archetype and the Operative Power of Creation (ἰδέα καὶ ἐνέργεια εἶναι προελθών). With regard to the Spirit, we assert Him to be the Effluence of GOD, flowing from and evermore

[1] A fragment of Philippus Sidetes (cent. V.) relates, Τοῦ διδασκαλείου τοῦ ἐν Ἀλεξανδρείᾳ Ἀθηναγόρας πρῶτος ἡγήσατο. Cf. Fabric. *Bibl. Gr.* VII. p. 95. Guerike, *Schol. Alexandr.* pp. 19 sq. Dr Newman (*Tracts*, pp. 191—3) classes him with writers who exhibit the Alexandrian tone of thought, and acquits him of the charge which he considers to be proved against the Asiatics and Westerns, that of holding the 'temporal gennêsis.' Compare Dorner, I. i. 283, who says, "The hypostatizing of the Logos at the creation is rejected utterly by the clearer and more cautious Athenagoras, who through his purer concept of God opens a way to an immanent relation between the Father and Son." The point is important to our present enquiry: for his view of the Procession of the Spirit would doubtless be affected by his view of the generation: if he held simply a temporal or economical gennêsis, he would probably also hold a merely economical procession, and *vice versâ*: see below.

[2] *Legat.* 10 (Migne, VI. 909), ὄντος τοῦ Υἱοῦ ἐν Πατρὶ καὶ Πατρὸς ἐν Υἱῷ, ἑνότητι καὶ δυνάμει Πνεύματος. Maranus annotates, "hoc loco Spiritus nomine divinitas significatur." But this is unnecessary: the hypostatic Spirit is clearly referred to a few sentences further on (θεὸν Πατέρα καὶ Υἱὸν θεὸν καὶ Πνεῦμα Ἅγιον), and is here regarded as the 'vinculum' of the Divine Unity: an idea developed at a later time by S. Augustine.

returning to the Fountain of the GODHEAD; as the Sun's rays proceed from and revert to the solar orb, or as light flashes from fire:" Ἅγιον Πνεῦμα ἀπόρροιαν εἶναί φαμεν τοῦ Θεοῦ, ἀπορρέον καὶ ἐπαναφερόμενον ὡς ἀκτῖνα ἡλίου[1]. This bold use of a philosophical term[2] may have been suggested by the memorable passage in the Book of Wisdom (vii. 25), ἀτμίς ἐστι [Σοφία] τῆς τοῦ Θεοῦ δυνάμεως, καὶ ἀπόρροια τῆς τοῦ παντοκράτορος δόξης εἰλικρινής...ἀπαύγασμα γάρ ἐστι φωτὸς αἰδίου. Applied to the Third Person of the Holy Trinity, and guarded by the explanation ἀπορρέον καὶ ἐπαναφερόμενον, the word represents the Procession of the Holy Spirit in a fairly clear and correct manner. Nor does it appear from the context that Athenagoras like Theophilus meant to limit the idea to an economical emission. In the ἀπόρροια of this early Christian Platonist we seem

[1] Comp. *ib.* 24 (Migne, 946), Θεόν φαμεν καὶ Υἱὸν τὸν Λόγον αὐτοῦ καὶ Πνεῦμα Ἅγιον ἑνούμενα μὲν κατὰ δύναμιν...ὅτι Νοῦς, Λόγος, Σοφία Υἱὸς τοῦ Πατρὸς, καὶ ἀπόρροια ὡς φῶς ἀπὸ πυρὸς τὸ Πνεῦμα. The early Vesper Hymn beginning Φῶς ἱλαρὸν ἁγίας δόξης ἀθανάτου Πατρός views the Generation of the Son in the same light.

[2] In the philosophy of Empedocles ἀπόρροιαι (ἀπορροαί) were certain hypothetical effluences by which external objects make themselves perceptible to the mind. According to his view every substance emitted such: πάντων εἰσὶν ἀπορροαὶ ὅσσ' ἐγένοντο: they proceeded even from stones and metals. Cf. Ritter and Preller, *Hist. Philos.* p. 132. Plato, *Meno*, 76 D, represents colour as an example of an ἀπορροή: ἔστι γὰρ χρόα ἀπορροὴ σχημάτων ὄψει ξύμμετρος καὶ αἰσθητός: cf. *Timaeus*, 67 C, φλόγα τῶν σωμάτων ἑκάστων ἀπορρέουσαν ὄψει ξύμμετρα μόρια ἔχουσαν πρὸς αἴσθησιν. As to its use in the language of theology, see Petav. *de Trin.* V. 8. It was applied to the Son by Origen (*de Princ.* I. 2), Theognostus (S. Athan. *de decret. N. S.* 25), Dionysius (ib. *de sent. Dionys.* 23); but rejected by Alexander, Bishop of Alexandria, in whose judgment it had a Valentinian or Sabellian sound (Theodoret, *H. E.* I. 4). S. Gregory Nazianzen also felt shy of the metaphor (*Orat. Theol.* V.), οὔτε γὰρ ἀκτὶς οὔτε φῶς ἄλλος ἥλιος ἀλλ' ἡλιακαί τινες ἀπόρροιαι καὶ ποιότητες οὐσιώδεις. Justin, without using the word ἀπόρρ., had censured the metaphor ὡς τοῦ ἡλίου φῶς, applied to the Son, preferring ὡς πῦρ ἀπὸ πυρός: cf. Kaye, *J. M.* pp. 157, 178.

to have nearly the counterpart of the later ἐκπόρευμα: his ἀπορρέον καὶ ἐπαναφερόμενον does not greatly differ in meaning from the ἐκπορευόμενον of the Catholic Creeds. But the language which the Church ultimately preferred has the advantage of being at once free from the associations of a false philosophy, and drawn from the very words of the Gospel and the lips of Christ.

CHAPTER II.

HERESY IN THE FIRST THREE CENTURIES.

Τὴν παραθήκην φύλαξον, ἐκτρεπόμενος τὰς βεβήλους κενοφωνίας καὶ ἀντιθέσεις τῆς ψευδωνύμου γνώσεως.

S. Paul, 1 *Tim.* vi. 20.

THE opposition of Hellenism and Judaism indirectly assisted the development of dogma by compelling the early Apologists to give expression to mysteries, which had found no place in the simple creed of the primitive Church. Heresy rendered even more effectual service, by appropriating and extending in opposite directions certain portions of the Catholic Faith. Such extensions sometimes indicated the line along which Christian thought might lawfully advance, and always offered a wholesome stimulus to the less speculative intellect of the Church. A glance at the heresies of the second and third centuries will show how largely they contributed to the history of the particular doctrine which is now under review.

1. It seems to have been the ambition of Gnosticism, to sweep together the unanswered questionings of Greek thinkers and Oriental theosophists, and to charge itself with the task of solving these accumulated problems. "Eadem materia," Tertullian remarks, "apud haereticos et philosophos volutatur:

idem retractatus implicantur: 'unde malum et quare;' et 'unde homo et quomodo;' et, quod proxime Valentinus proposuit, '*unde Deus*[1].' The last of these questions brought the Gnosis into direct contact with the Christian belief in the Father, the Son, and the Holy Ghost: whilst the two former almost necessarily led up to the same result. Thus the Persons of the Holy Trinity and their relations to Each Other in the life of GOD, enter more or less distinctly into all the chief Gnostic systems.

The first principles of the Gnosis, however, were opposed to the Catholic conception of the Trinity. The God of Gnosticism is an absolute, unconditioned, incomprehensible being: revelation is possible only through an act of self-limitation on the part of the Infinite[2]. Hence the doctrine of successive emanations (προβολαὶ[3]) or pairs of emanations (συζυγίαι), by which the distance between the Finite and the

[1] *De praescr.* 7.

[2] Neander, *Ch. H.* II. p. 11. Lightfoot, *Colossians*, p. 78: "This [creation] could only have been possible by some self-limitation on the part of God. God must express Himself in some way. There must be some evolution, some effluence of Deity. Thus the Divine Being germinates, as it were, and the first germination again involves a second from itself in like manner."

[3] On προβολή (prolatio, emissio, editio), see Petav. *de Trin.* V. 8, § 9; VII. 10, § 5. Newman's *Arians*, p. 195 sq., Possini, *Glossar.* s. v. (Migne, *P. Gr.* CXLIII. p. 1060). The Gnostic use of the term brought it under suspicion, and it was rejected both by Arius (Epiph. *Haer.* LXIX. 7) and by Athanasius or the Athanasian author of the *Exp. fidei*. Tertullian (as we shall see) used the word, but with an apology: Origen refused it altogether. At the later period, when the danger had passed, it was again employed as equivalent to ἐκπόρευσις: at first with some reserve and explanation, as by S. Gregory of Nazianzus (*Or. Theol.* III. ὁ μὲν γεννήτωρ καὶ προβολεὺς, λέγω δὲ ἀπαθῶς καὶ ἀχρόνως καὶ ἀσωμάτως· τῶν δὲ τὸ μὲν γέννημα τὸ δὲ πρόβλημα ἢ οὐκ οἶδ' ὅπως ἄν τις ταῦτα καλέσειεν ἀφελὼν πάντη τῶν ὁρωμένων): afterwards as belonging to the accepted terms of theology by S. John of Damascus, who (e.g. *de Fide Orth.* I. 8. 12) regularly spoke of the Father's relation to the Holy Spirit as that of προβολεύς.

Infinite was bridged over or reduced, and which therefore stood in a descending scale of relationship and likeness to the προβολεὺς from whom the primal germ was evolved.

Among these emanations we frequently meet with 'the Spirit' or 'Holy Spirit,' a distorted conception, as it seems, of the Personal Holy Ghost. The Simonian Gnosis led the way. According to S. Epiphanius, Helena was regarded by Simon as representing the Holy Spirit[1]: and though the name 'Holy Spirit' does not occur in the accounts of S. Irenaeus and Hippolytus, a somewhat corresponding idea is found in both. Irenaeus says that the father of Gnosticism styled Helena "primam mentis suae conceptionem [ἔννοιαν], matrem omnium per quam in initio mente concepit angelos facere[2]." This Primal Thought issued from its Source to create the angelic powers which in their turn created the visible universe: "hanc enim Ennoian exsilientem ex eo...generare angelos et potestates, a quibus et mundum hunc factum dixit." With the *Philosophumena* we have fortunately recovered a fragment of the "Great Announcement," which expresses in Simon's own words[3] his view upon this

[1] Epiph. *Haer.* XXI. (Migne, XLI. p. 288), τὴν δὲ σύζυγον πορνάδα Πνεῦμα Ἅγιον τετόλμηκε λέγειν, καὶ διὰ ταύτην κατεληλυθέναι φησίν· ἐν ἑκάστῳ δὲ οὐρανῷ μετεμορφούμην (φησὶ)...ἵνα...κατέλθω ἐπὶ τὴν ἔννοιαν ἥτις ἐστὶν αὕτη ἡ καὶ Προύνικος καὶ Πνεῦμα Ἅγιον καλουμένη. Another account represents him as having claimed this latter name for himself as manifested to the Gentiles: Ἰουδαίοις μὲν ὡς Υἱὸν φανῆναι πρὸς δὲ Σαμαρείτας ὡς Πατέρα κατεληλυθέναι ἐν δὲ τοῖς ἄλλοις ἔθνεσιν ὡς Πνεῦμα Ἅγιον ἐπιφοιτῆσαι (Theodoret, *Haer. fab.* I. 1, cf. Hippol. *Philos.* VI. 19). Thus he regarded the Holy Spirit as a phase of Divine self-manifestation.

[2] Iren. I. 22, § 1.

[3] Hippol. *Philos.* VI. 18, λέγει γὰρ Σίμων διαρρήδην. Bunsen assigns the authorship to Menander. On the whole passage see Mansel, *Gnostic Heresies*, p. 88.

subject. He says, *Δύο εἰσὶ παραφυάδες τῶν ὅλων αἰώνων μήτε ἀρχὴν μήτε πέρας ἔχουσαι, ἀπὸ μιᾶς ῥίζης, ἥτις ἐστι δύναμις σιγὴ, ἀόρατος, ἀκατάληπτος· ὧν ἡ μία φαίνεται ἄνωθεν...νοῦς τῶν ὅλων...ἄρσην· ἡ δὲ ἑτέρα κάτωθεν, ἐπίνοια μεγάλη, θήλεια, γεννῶσα τὰ πάντα.* Between these two, Simon proceeds, is the Father, Who sustains all finite being and is Himself immutable—*ὁ ἑστὼς, στὰς, στησόμενος*: an *ἀρσενόθηλυς δύναμις*, originally illimitable and solitary. From the solitude of this Infinite Power in which she dwelt, Thought proceeded forth and so made two: *προελθοῦσα ἡ ἐν μονότητι ἐπίνοια ἐγένετο δύο.* Thus by a process of self-manifestation the One became a Second and acquired the name of Father, and revealed Himself to Himself: *αὐτὸς ἑαυτὸν ὑπὸ ἑαυτοῦ προαγαγὼν ἐφανέρωσεν ἑαυτῷ τὴν ἰδίαν ἐπίνοιαν.* On the other hand the emanating Thought received the Father within herself, and though originally a *θήλεια δύναμις*, became in her turn *ἀρσενόθηλυς*. The passage is bewildering; nor is it easy to judge whether Simon's conception of the *ἐπίνοια* comes nearer to the *Λόγος* or to the *Πνεῦμα* of Christianity. The *θήλεια δύναμις* points however to the latter, which is constantly represented in the Gnosis under this aspect. But independently of this question, the idea of a Divine procession appears to have been grasped by Simon with greater clearness than by some of the later Gnostics. It will be noticed that the issue of the Divine Thought does not in his view interfere with her immanence in God: it is a procession without separation, which is so far the Catholic view of the *ἐκπόρευσις*.

In some of the early Ophite systems on the other hand, we have a nearer approach to the Christian Trinity, but a less distinct theory of procession. The

Ophite first principle is at once Father of All and First Man: the Adam Kadmon of the Kabbala. As in the Simonian system, this Being is ἀρσενόθηλυς[1]: and from It proceeds a Second, an 'Ennoia,' strangely converted into a male principle and styled the Son, the Son of Man, the Second Man...After these two comes a third, which bears the name of the Holy Spirit[2]. This third power is female and is represented as the Mother of all living[3]. M. Matter thinks that the Second Man was regarded as being together with the First Man the προβολεὺς of the Ophite Holy Spirit[4]. Such a fact would obviously be of high interest in our present enquiry if it were supported by ancient testimony: but I cannot find it reflected in any of the early accounts of the Ophite Gnosis. In the *Pistis Sophia*, a work which is now attributed to the later Ophites, the Spirit asks "Ubi est Jesus meus frater[5]?" A συζυγία seems to be implied here, but one which would represent Christ and the Holy Spirit as being alike προβολαὶ of the Father.

The Syrian Basilides, who appears to have

[1] Hippol. *Philos.* v. 6, ἐστὶ δὲ ἄνθρωπος οὗτος ἀρσενόθηλυς...ὕμνοι δὲ εἰς αὐτὸν γεγόνασι πολλοὶ καὶ ποικίλοι· οἱ δὲ ὕμνοι...λέγονται...τοιοῦτόν τινα τρόπον, Ἀπὸ σοῦ πατὴρ καὶ διὰ σὲ μήτηρ τὰ δύο ἀθάνατα ὀνόματα, αἰώνων γονεῖς πολῖτα οὐρανοῦ, μεγαλώνυμε ἄνθρωπε.

[2] Iren. I. 30. 1, "sub his [Patre, Ennoia] Spiritum Sanctum esse." Theodoret, *Haer. fab.* I. 14, μετα δὲ τοῦτον ὑπάρχειν τὸ Ἅγιον Πνεῦμα.

[3] Baur (*die Christliche Gnosis*, p. 171 sq.): "der heilige Geist ist das erste weibliche Princip und wird daher auch die Mutter alles Lebendigen gennannt (die Urmutter)." Cf. Harvey, p. lxxxiv. note. Manes seems to have distinguished the "Mother of life" from the Holy Spirit: see Routh, *R. S.* v. 50.

[4] *Hist. Crit. du Gnosticisme*, II. p. 135, "la pensée considerée comme la compagne (syzygos) de Dieu donne l'existence au Pneuma." According to Irenaeus the Barbeliotae held that the Holy Spirit was produced from the First Angel, *Haer.* I. 29. 4.

[5] ed. Petermann, p. 77.

flourished at Alexandria during the reign of Hadrian[1], struck out an independent course. Irenaeus credits him with inventing a series of heavens as numerous as the days of the solar year[2]; and this certainly formed a leading feature in the gnosis of his followers. But Basilides himself, if we may believe Hippolytus, discarded the theory of emanation and sought to refer all finite existences to the *fiat* of the Supreme First Cause[3]. God, whom he regarded as absolute non-existence, made the world out of the non-existent: ἦν ἄπορον εἰπεῖν προβολήν τινα τοῦ μὴ ὄντος Θεοῦ γεγονέναι τι οὐκ ὄν. For the προβολαὶ of other Gnostic teachers he substituted the idea of a πανσπερμία wrapped up in a primal germ (τὸ σπέρμα τὸ κοσμικὸν), itself deposited by God. In the working out of this cosmogony, Basilides discloses his conception of the Holy Spirit's relation to God, and to the world. The germ possesses, he proceeds, a tripartite sonship, consubstantial with the non-existent God (υἱότης τριμερὴς κατὰ πάντα τῷ οὐκ ὄντι Θεῷ ὁμοούσιος). That which is of a finer nature mounts up at once to its Author, the οὐκ ὢν Θεός: the second, which is of grosser character, ascends only when it is winged by the Holy Ghost[4]. But the Holy Spirit,

[1] Mansel, *Gnostic Heresies*, p. 145.

[2] Iren. I. 24. 3, "in immensum extendit sententiam doctrinae suae, ostendens Nun primo ab innato natum Patre, ab hoc autem natum Logon, &c. &c....et deinceps secundum eum modum alteros et alteros principes et angelos factos esse dicunt et caelos CCCLXV. quapropter et tot dies habere annum secundum numerum caelorum."

[3] Hippol. VII. 22: φεύγει γὰρ πάνυ καὶ δέδοικε τὰς κατὰ προβολὴν τῶν γεγονότων οὐσίας ὁ Βασιλείδης· ποίας γὰρ προβολῆς χρεία ἢ ποίας ὕλης ὑπόθεσις ἵνα κόσμον θεὸς ἐργάσηται καθάπερ ὁ ἀράχνης τὰ μηρύματα; His alternative was, οὐκ ὢν θεὸς ἐποίησε τὸν κόσμον οὐκ ὄντα ἐξ οὐκ ὄντων.

[4] *ib.* ἐπτέρωσεν οὖν αὐτὴν ἡ υἱότης ἡ παχυμερεστέρα τοιούτῳ τῷ πτερῷ ὁποίῳ...Πλάτων...τὴν ψυχὴν πτεροῖ· καὶ καλεῖ τὸ τοιοῦτο ὁ Βασιλείδης

though it can assist the *υἱότης* to mount up to God, cannot itself attain to Him: the presence of the Ineffable and Non-existing would be uncongenial and even fatal to it, as air is to the fishes of the sea. The Spirit is therefore parted from the Sonship as soon as the latter attains to God: yet it preserves, so to speak, an odour of sonship derived from its past connection with the *υἱότης*; and occupying henceforth a position intermediate between the earth and the supermundane, it diffuses this fragrance upon our lower and disordered world[1]. There is of course no hypostatization of the Spirit in such a system: but the idea of a *ἅγιον πνεῦμα* which is not consubstantial with the First Cause, and which occupies a position inferior to that of sonship[2], is not far removed from the Macedonian conception of the Person of the Holy Ghost.

Valentinus, who also belonged to the Alexandrian school of Gnosticism, abandoning the *οὐκ ὢν Θεὸς* of Basilides, was content to postulate the unknowableness of the Supreme First Cause, whom he styles *Βύθος*, *Ἄρρητος*, or *Πατήρ*. Returning to the *προβολαὶ* and *συζυγίαι* of the earliest Gnostics, he developed beyond any previous Gnostic teacher the doctrine of a *pleroma* of Aeons prolated from the primal cause. The pleroma, he said, was already made up to the number of twenty-eight, when the misfortunes of the youngest of the Aeons led to the projection of two more, to whom he gives the name of Christ and Holy Spirit. This *συζυγία* was put forth latest

οὐ πτερὸν ἀλλὰ Πνεῦμα Ἅγιον...τοιοῦτόν τινα τὸν λόγον ἔσχεν ἡ υἱότης πρὸς τὸ Πνεῦμα τὸ Ἅγιον καὶ τὸ Πνεῦμα πρὸς τὴν υἱότητα.

[1] Hippol. *l. c.* *τὸ δὲ μεταξὺ τοῦ κόσμου καὶ τῶν ὑπερκοσμίων μεθόριον Πνεῦμα τοῦτο...τῆς υἱότητος ἔχει μένουσαν ἐν ἑαυτῷ τὴν ὀσμήν.*

[2] *ib.* *ἦν γὰρ οὐχ ὁμοούσιον [τὸ Πνεῦμα] οὐδὲ φύσιν εἶχε μετὰ τῆς υἱότητος.* Cf. Mansel, p. 151, note.

in time, but from the first pair of Aeons and by the special command of the Supreme Father: ἐλεήσας ὁ Πατὴρ τὰ δάκρυα τῆς Σοφίας...ἐπιπροβαλεῖν κελεύει—οὐ γὰρ αὐτὸς (φησὶ) προέβαλεν ἀλλὰ ὁ νοῦς καὶ ἡ ἀλήθεια—Χριστὸν καὶ Πνεῦμα Ἅγιον εἰς μόρφωσιν καὶ διαίρεσιν τοῦ ἐκτρώματος καὶ παραμυθίαν καὶ διανάπαυσιν τῶν τῆς Σοφίας στεναγμῶν[1]. The temporal mission of the Son and the Holy Spirit for the redemption of the world and the sanctification of the Church is evidently the groundwork of this myth: the mission being confused with the eternal generation and procession. It is important to observe that the Holy Spirit of Valentinus is the σύζυγος of his Christ: they are projected together at the Father's bidding, and a procession or emission from the Son finds no reflection in his system[2], unless we may see it in the prolation of both the Christ and the Spirit from Nous or Monogenes, the immediate offspring of Bythos[3].

2. A few words must be devoted in passing to the Montanistic movement, which has been characterized by Neander as "the extreme of the antignostic position[4]." Montanism set itself to deal primarily with the mission of the Paraclete. But the

[1] Hippol. VI. 31, cf. Iren. I. 2. 5, τὸν Μονογενῆ πάλιν ἑτέραν προβαλέσθαι συζυγίαν κατὰ προμήθειαν τοῦ Πατρὸς...Χριστὸν καὶ Πνεῦμα Ἅγιον εἰς πῆξιν καὶ στηριγμὸν τοῦ πληρώματος ὑφ' ὧν καταρτισθῆναι τοὺς Αἰῶνας. *ib.* II. I, καὶ τὸ Πνεῦμα τὸ Ἅγιον ὑπὸ τῆς ἐκκλησίας [a veritate] φησὶ προβεβλῆσθαι εἰς ἀνάκρισιν καὶ καρποφορίαν τῶν Αἰώνων, ἀοράτως εἰς αὐτοὺς εἰσιόν· δι' οὗ τοὺς Αἰῶνας καρποφορεῖν τὰ φυτὰ τῆς ἀληθείας.

[2] Marcus, a disciple of Valentinus, taught that the Spirit which descended on Jesus at the Baptism was the σπέρμα τοῦ Πατρὸς [Iren.—τοῦ πληρώματος Hipp.] ἔχον ἐν ἑαυτῷ καὶ τὸν Πατέρα καὶ τὸν Υἱόν (Iren. I. 15. 3, Hippol. V. 51). Was this meant to express the relation of the Spirit to the Father and the Son as the Spirit of Both, and the 'vinculum amoris'?

[3] See *Early History of the doctrine of the Holy Spirit*, p. 11.

[4] *Ch. H.* II. p. 199.

great emphasis which it laid upon the operations of the Spirit could scarcely fail to give prominence to the doctrine of His Person and to the whole Trinitarian teaching of the Church. Tertullian distinctly attributes to this cause the fuller exhibition of the Catholic Faith which he initiated in the West. The light which had been thrown upon the baptismal Creed was in his view almost a new revelation, although upon the lines of the traditional belief: 'nos vero et semper (he writes) et nunc magis ut instructiores per Paracletum deductorem scilicet omnis veritatis, unicum quidem Deum credimus, sub hac tamen dispensatione quam *οἰκονομίαν* dicimus"—upon which follows the rest of the Rule of faith as it was held by the Church of North Africa[1]. Theodoret therefore hardly does justice to the earlier Montanists when he admits that the sect did not corrupt the doctrine of the Holy Trinity[2]: the probability is that they realized the doctrine more fully than most of the Catholics of their time, and led the way to a more complete exposition of the mystery. At a later date the tendency to doctrinal degeneration which is inherent in sectarianism triumphed over the traditions of primitive Montanism; we find Socrates and Sozomen agreeing to class Montanus with Sabellius as guilty of 'confounding the Persons[3].' Theodoret

[1] *Adv. Prax.* c. 2 (Migne, II. 156). Cf. infr. c. 8, and *de Res. Carn.* c. 63, "omnes ambiguitates...aperta atque perspicua totius sacramenti prædicatione discussit per novam prophetiam de Paracleto inundantem."

[2] *Hær. fab.* III. 2 (Migne, LXXXIII. 403), *τὸν δὲ περὶ τῆς θείας* Τριάδος *οὐκ ἐλυμήνατο λόγον.* Epiphanius (*Haer.* XLVIII.) says expressly, *περὶ δὲ* Πατρὸς καὶ Υἱοῦ καὶ Ἁγίου Πνεύματος ὁμοίως φρονοῦσι τῇ ἁγίᾳ καθολικῇ ἐκκλησίᾳ. On the other hand, see Bp Montagu's note on Phot. *Ep.* 2.

[3] Socr. I. 23 (Soz. II. 18), *οἱ μὲν γὰρ τοῦ ὁμοουσίου τὴν λέξιν ἐκκλίνοντες τὴν Σαβελλίου καὶ Μοντανοῦ δόξαν εἰσηγεῖσθαι τοὺς αὐτὴν προσδεχομένους ἐνόμιζον.*

supplies the key: a Sabellian school had arisen within the body: τινὲς δὲ αὐτῶν τὰς τρεῖς ὑποστάσεις τῆς θεότητος...ἠρνήσαντο, τὸν αὐτὸν εἶναι λέγοντες καὶ Πατέρα καὶ Υἱὸν καὶ Ἅγιον Πνεῦμα[1]. But even toward the middle of the fifth century this error was only partial among them, and it was certainly altogether absent from the system which was so warmly espoused by Tertullian.

3. In connection with the doctrine of the Holy Spirit, the heretical and semi-heretical developments of Jewish Christianity deserve attention. It is unnecessary to enter here upon the history of the early Judaeo-Christian Church, or to attempt a discrimination of its various schools. For our purpose we may be content with the common classification under the heads of Nazarene and Ebionite, adding perhaps a subdivision of the latter party into the earlier Pharisaic Ebionites, and those of Essene or Gnostic tendencies[2].

The Nazarene view of the Holy Spirit is represented by (1) two fragments of their recension of the First Gospel, and (2) the book known as the 'Twelve Testaments,' now assigned by the best judges to this school. From the former we learn that the Holy Ghost was regarded as the Mother of Christ—an expression which Origen illustrates rather than explains by a reference to S. Matt. xii. 50[3]. Another

[1] *Haer. fab.* III. 2.

[2] See Prof. Lightfoot, *St Paul and the Three*, (*Galatians*, p. 298 sq.).

[3] Orig. *in Joann.* ii. 6, ἐὰν δὲ προσίεταί τις τὸ καθ' Ἑβραίους εὐαγγέλιον, ἔνθα αὐτὸς ὁ Σωτήρ φησιν 'ἄρτι ἔλαβέ με ἡ μήτηρ μου τὸ ἅγιον Πνεῦμα ἐν μιᾷ τῶν τριχῶν μου καὶ ἀπήνεγκέ με εἰς τὸ ὄρος τὸ μέγα Θαβώρ,' ἐπαπορήσει πῶς μήτηρ Χριστοῦ τὸ διὰ τοῦ Λόγου γεγενημένον [see below, ch. iii.] Πνεῦμα Ἅγιον εἶναι δύναται. ταῦτα δὲ καὶ τοῦτο οὐ χαλεπὸν ἑρμηνεῦσαι· εἰ γὰρ ὁ ποιῶν τὸ θέλημα τοῦ Πατρὸς...μήτηρ ἐστὶν αὐτοῦ...

fragment describes the *Fons omnis Spiritus Sancti* as descending on the Lord at His Baptism and addressing Him thus: "Fili mi, in omnibus prophetis exspectabam te ut venires et requiescerem in te. Tu es enim requies mea: tu es filius meus primogenitus[1]." The simplest view of this passage seems to be that which regards the Father as the speaker. It will then assert at least the economical procession of the Holy Spirit from the First Person. That the Holy Spirit thus emitted from the Father becomes the 'Mother' of the Son, implies a somewhat confused Christology, but not of necessity any Gnostic conception of the Spirit as a θήλεια δύναμις; the name is sufficiently explained by the gender of the Hebrew noun[2]. It is impossible to decide from these extracts, whether the Nazarenes held in any manner the distinct personality of the Holy Spirit, or regarded Him simply as the sanctifying and life-giving power of God. His relation to the Son does not appear to be carried back further than the Baptism. The 'Testaments' do not materially add to our knowledge[3]. They represent the Holy Spirit as poured out on our Lord at His Baptism, that He in turn might pour It forth upon the world and become

οὐδὲν ἄτοπον...τὸ Πνεῦμα τὸ Ἅγιον εἶναι μητέρα. Cf. Westcott, *Study of the Gospels*, p. 459 note. Neander *Ch. H.* I. 484.

[1] S. Hieron. *Comm. in Esa.* IV. [c. xi. 2] (Migne, XXIV. 145). Cf. Schliemann, *die Clementinen*, p. 454.

[2] A mediaeval writer in Pitra (*Spic. Solesm.* II. 47) remarks, 'Spiritus S. dicitur πνεῦμα græce, et tunc est neutri generis: רוּחַ hebraice, et tunc est femininum: Spiritus latine, et tunc masculini generis. ecce tres linguae et tria genera.'

[3] Mr Sinker (*Introd.* p. 114 sq.) says, "The notions scattered throughout the *Testaments* as to the nature and office of the Holy Spirit are exceedingly few and vague." He is of opinion "that the writer of the *Testaments* entertained a vague, general sort of idea of the Holy Spirit as a manifestation or phase of the Godhead, but not a person with proper attributes and functions of His own."

the πηγὴ εἰς ζωὴν to all mankind. To the question, 'Whence this outpouring of grace upon the Christ,' they answer distinctly enough, 'From the Father:' it is the special εὐλογία Πατρός: it came forth from the sanctuary of the Shechinah accompanied by the Father's voice[1]. If the Nazarene Holy Spirit could safely be regarded as hypostatical, these expressions would be almost in advance of the Church teaching of the times. But the hypostatization is more than doubtful[2].

The Ebionite school has left larger materials for determining its doctrine of the Holy Spirit. With the earliest Ebionites, who succeeded to the Judaizing ψευδάδελφοι of S. Paul's day[3], the Spirit was probably no more than the Divine power which descended on Jesus and raised Him to the dignity of Christ and Son of God. Their recension of S. Matthew iii. 16, as given by S. Epiphanius, laid stress upon the entrance of the Holy Spirit into the Body of the Lord at Baptism: εἶδε τὸ Πνεῦμα τοῦ Θεοῦ τὸ Ἅγιον ἐν εἴδει περιστερᾶς κατελθούσης καὶ εἰσελθούσης εἰς αὐτόν[4]. But the Gnostic element very shortly supervened upon this purely Judaic form: and in the teaching of Cerinthus, the Holy Ghost of the Baptism was identified with the Christ[5], who, de-

[1] *Jud.* 24, ἀνοιγήσονται ἐπ' αὐτὸν οἱ οὐρανοὶ ἐκχέαι Πνεύματος [*v. l.* Πνεῦμα] εὐλογίαν Πατρὸς ἁγίου· καὶ αὐτὸς ἐκχεεῖ Πνεῦμα χάριτος ἐφ' ὑμᾶς...οὗτος ὁ βλαστὸς Θεοῦ ὑψίστου, καὶ αὕτη ἡ πηγὴ εἰς ζωὴν πάσης σαρκός. *Benj.* 9, μεταβήσεται [*v. l.* καταβ.] τὸ Πνεῦμα τοῦ Θεοῦ ἐπὶ τὰ ἔθνη ὡς πῦρ ἐκχυνόμενον. *Lev.* 18, ἐκ τοῦ ναοῦ τῆς δόξης ἥξει ἐπ' αὐτὸν ἁγίασμα μετὰ φωνῆς πατρικῆς...καὶ δόξα Ὑψίστου ἐπ' αὐτὸν ῥηθήσεται καὶ Πνεῦμα συνέσεως καὶ ἁγιασμοῦ καταπαύσει ἐπ' αὐτὸν ἐν τῷ ὕδατι...καὶ δώσει τοῖς ἁγίοις φαγεῖν ἐκ τοῦ ξύλου τῆς ζωῆς καὶ πνεῦμα ἁγιωσύνης ἔσται ἐπ' αὐτοῖς.

[2] Cf. Dorner, I. i, pp. 194 sq., 430.

[3] Lightfoot, *Galatians*, p. 301.

[4] *Haer.* XXX. 13 (Migne XLI. 438).

[5] Cerinthus taught (acc. to Epiph. *Haer.* XXVIII. 4) ἄνωθεν ἐκ τοῦ

scending on Jesus at the Jordan, left Him before the Passion and returned to the *pleroma* from which he came. Epiphanius describes an Ebionite party who thus interpreted the language of their Gospel: Εἰς αὐτὸν ἦλθε τὸ Πνεῦμα ὅπερ ἐστὶν ὁ Χριστὸς, καὶ ἐνεδύσατο αὐτὸν τὸν Ἰησοῦν καλούμενον. Thus, they added, He was called Son of GOD κατ' ἐκλογήν, ἀπὸ τοῦ ἄνωθεν εἰς αὐτὸν ἥκοντος Χριστοῦ ἐν εἴδει περιστερᾶς[1]. They denied that the Christ-Spirit was begotten of GOD the Father, holding Him to be a creature, like one of the Archangels, although greater than they (φάσκουσι...ἐκτίσθαι ὡς ἕνα τῶν ἀρχαγγέλων, μείζονα δὲ αὐτῶν ὄντα). In the Elchasaite speculations a distinction is again drawn between the Son and the Spirit, who are represented as a pair or syzygy of mighty and gigantic Angels: τὸν μὲν ἄρσενα υἱὸν εἶναι τοῦ Θεοῦ, τὴν δὲ θήλειαν καλεῖσθαι ἅγιον πνεῦμα[2]. On the other hand the 'Clementine Homilies' seem to identify the Spirit with the Son. GOD is conceived of as a Monad Who by self-extension becomes a Dyad: His Wisdom in which He delights as in His own spirit, which is united to Him as His own soul, is put forth, hand-wise, to create man and the world: εἷς ἐστὶν ὁ τῇ αὐτοῦ σοφίᾳ εἰπὼν

ἄνω Θεοῦ...κατεληλυθέναι τὸν Χριστὸν εἰς αὐτὸν [Ἰησοῦν], τουτέστι τὸ Πν. τὸ ἅγιον ἐν εἴδει περιστερᾶς...καὶ ἀποκαλύψαι αὐτῷ καὶ δι' αὐτοῦ τοῖς μετ' αὐτοῦ τὸν ἄγνωστον Πατέρα. Cf. Iren. III. 2. § 1, "iterum revolasse in suum pleroma," and Dr Lightfoot's remarks, *Colossians*, pp. 111, 330.

[1] *Haer.* XXX. 3, 16. Cf. Dorner, I. i. p. 434 sq.

[2] Hippol. *Philos.* IX. 14. The female is of the same proportions as the male: εἶναι δὲ σὺν αὐτῷ καὶ θήλειαν ἧς τὰ μέτρα κατὰ τὰ προειρημένα εἶναι λέγει. Compare the account given by Epiphanius, *Haer.* XIX. 4, εἶναι δὲ καὶ τὸ Ἅγιον Πνεῦμα καὶ αὐτὸ θήλειαν ὅμοιον τῷ Χριστῷ ἀνδρίαντος δίκην ὑπὲρ νεφέλην, κ.τ.λ. *ib.* LIII. 1 (adv. Sampsaeos), εἶναι τὸ ἅγιον Πνεῦμα ἀδελφὴν αὐτοῦ θηλυκῷ σχήματι ὑπάρχουσαν, ἐνενηκονταὲξ μιλίων τὸ ὕψος ἕκαστον αὐτῶν ἔχον, ὅ τε Χριστὸς καὶ τὸ Ἅ. Πν., καὶ τὸ πλάτος εἰκοσιτεσσάρων. Cf. Hilgenfeld, *N. T. extr. Can.* p. 157.

'ποιήσωμεν ἄνθρωπον.' ἡ δὲ σοφία, ᾗ ὥσπερ ἰδίῳ πνεύματι αὐτὸς ἀεὶ συνέχαιρεν, ἥνωται μὲν ὡς ψυχὴ τῷ Θεῷ· ἐκτείνεται δὲ ἀπ' αὐτοῦ ὡς χείρ, δημιουργοῦσα τὸ πᾶν[1]. A parallel to this ἔκτασις is found in the production of Eve from Adam: διὰ τοῦτο δὲ καὶ εἷς ἄνθρωπος ἐγένετο· ἀπ' αὐτοῦ δὲ προῆλθε καὶ τὸ θῆλυ[2]. In this theogony there is no room for a Divine υἱὸς Θεοῦ as personally distinct from a Divine Spirit: although it would seem that Ebionites of this class did not find it necessary to abandon the Trinitarian formulae of the Church: the 'Homilies' ascribe glory to Father, Son, and Holy Ghost, and speak of the τρισμακαρία ἐπονομασία as essential to the act of Baptism[3].

The 'Recognitions' take up a very distinct line with regard to the Holy Spirit. Rejecting the identification of the Spirit with the Son[4], they regard the former as the creature of the latter, and anticipate to a remarkable degree the language of the modified Arianism which was prevalent in the latter part of the fourth century. The following extracts will illustrate this phase of Ebionite belief. *Recogn.* I. 24. "Erat semper et est et erit a quo prima voluntas genita sempiternitate constat; et ex prima voluntate iterum voluntas. Post hoc mundus: ex mundo

[1] *Hom.* XVI. 12 (Migne, II. 376), cf. Schliemann, p. 139 sq. "Sofern sie in Gott verborgen ruht, heisst sie σοφία: sofern sie aus Gott heraustritt, υἱὸς Θεοῦ." *ib.* infr. note 21, "dass πνεῦμα ἅγιον in den Clementinen identisch ist mit υἱὸς Θεοῦ in der ersten Bedeutung folgt einmal daraus &c."......"der Verfasser mit allen diesen Ausdrücken πν. ἅγ., σοφία, υἱὸς θ.,...dasselbe Wesen bezeichnet welches vor der Weltschöpfung aus Gott hervorgegangen das medium der Schöpfung gewesen ist und in Christo erschien." See also Dorner, I. i. p. 205.

[2] It is added, Καὶ μονὰς οὖσα τῷ γένει δυάς ἐστιν· κατὰ γὰρ ἔκτασιν καὶ συστολὴν ἡ μονὰς δυὰς εἶναι νομίζεται.

[3] *Hom.* III. 72, IX. 19, 23, XI. 26, XIII. 4, 19. The references are from Schliemann, p. 144.

[4] Schliemann, p. 310. Dorner, I. i. 446.

tempus: ex hoc hominum multitudo[1]." *Ib.* III. 11. "Spiritus autem Sanctus pignus ad conservationem eorum quae a Domino data sunt nobis...habet quod est ab Unigenito, plenissima declaratio virtutis Ejus, sicut Unigenitus...imago est immutabilis ingenitae Virtutis...Cum ergo unus sit Ingenitus et unus Genitus, Spiritus Sanctus Filius dici non potest nec primogenitus; factus est enim per factum, subconnumeratur autem Patre et Filio[2]." It was precisely against this teaching that the Church, a century and a half later, produced from the Gospel of S. John the long latent formula ὃ παρὰ τοῦ Πατρὸς ἐκπορεύεται. Thus the heretical *a Filio* is traced to an Ebionite source. It is scarcely necessary to remark that it bears no real affinity whatever to the *Filioque* or *et a Filio* of the West, which apart from all question of its truth or propriety is as far as possible removed from connection with this form of heresy.

4. In the neighbourhood of Thyatira about the year 180, an obscure sect arose whom Epiphanius for want of a better name describes as the Alogi, from the circumstance of their dislike to the Logos doctrine of S. John[3]. They rejected, as it appears, both the Apocalypse and the Fourth Gospel[4], and for S. John's doctrine of the Incarnation[5] they pro-

[1] Migne, I. 1220. On 'ex prima voluntate iterum voluntas' see the note of Cotelier, *l. c.*

[2] Migne, 1288. The genuineness of ch. 2—12 has been doubted.

[3] *Haer.* L. I, 3, ταύτην γὰρ αὐτοῖς τίθημι τὴν ἐπωνυμίαν...ἐπεὶ τὸν Λόγον οὐ δέχονται τὸν παρὰ Ἰωάννου κεκηρυγμένον, Ἄλογοι κληθήσονται. Cf. Heinichen's monograph *de Alogis Theodotianis* (Lips. 1829).

[4] S. Aug. *de Haeres.* xxx. "Deum Verbum recipere noluerunt Johannis Evangelium respuentes: cuius nec Apocalypsim accipiunt, has videlicet scripturas negantes esse ipsius." They attributed both (Epiph.) or at least the latter (Philastr.) to Cerinthus.

[5] Epiph. *ib.* 28, τὸν Λόγον τοῦ Θεοῦ ἀποβάλλονται τὸν διὰ Ἰωάννου κηρυχθέντα πατρικὸν Θεὸν Λόγον ἀπ' οὐρανοῦ κατεληλυθότα. Cf. *Anaceph.*

bably substituted the idea of a union between a purely human Christ, and the Deity of the Father. S. Irenaeus mentions, though not under this or any other special name, a party which nearly about the same time rejected the Gospel of S. John, but on other grounds. His words are: "Alii vero ut donum Spiritus frustrentur quod in novissimis temporibus secundum placitum Patris effusum est in humanum genus, illam speciem non admittunt quae est secundum Joannis Evangelium in qua Paracletum se missurum Dominus promisit; sed simul et Evangelium et propheticum repellunt Spiritum[1]." Whether this sect was one and the same with the Epiphanian Alogi[2] may fairly be open to question; but the fact remains that in the second half of the second century, the Fourth Gospel was attacked on two grounds; for its doctrine of the Eternal Word, and for its doctrine of the Holy Ghost. We may see in this double attack the beginnings of a revolt on the one hand against the growing Christology of the Catholic Church to which the Apologetic writings of the second century bear witness: and on the other, against the emphasis which Montanism had just begun to lay upon the Person and Office of the Paraclete. These nameless sectarians are the forerunners of the reactionary Monarchianism which for the next century continued to disturb the peace of the Church[3].

(Migne, XLII. p. 865), τὸν...ἄνωθεν ἀπὸ Πατρὸς ἀεὶ Θεὸν Λόγον παραβάλλοντες. See Dorner, II. i. p. 5.

[1] *Haer.* III. xi. 9 (Migne, VII. 890). Cf. Neander, *Ch. H.* II. 223, and *Dictionary of Sects and Heresies*, art. *Alogi.*

[2] Heinichen denies the identity (p. 93), nor does it seem easy to demonstrate it from our present sources of information.

[3] Dorner, I. ii. 4, "The *Alogi*...opposed to Cerinthus on the one side and to the Montanists on the other, appear from the indefiniteness which they sought to maintain in reference to the doctrine of the Holy

Neither of the two great branches into which the Monarchian heresy developed itself was able to admit any true procession of the Holy Spirit from the Father or from the Son. The earlier or Ebionite Monarchianism which saved the Unity by sacrificing the Deity of the Son, must have logically denied also the Deity of the Holy Ghost. But the Holy Spirit appears to have scarcely entered into the teaching of Theodotus and his successors, except as the agent of the supernatural birth[1] which they seem to have claimed for their otherwise purely human Christ. Allied however to the Theodotians, disciples, it is said, of the younger Theodotus[2]—was an offshoot of the Monarchian party[3] which saw in Melchizedek a sort of incarnation of the Holy Ghost. They did not indeed expressly name the Holy Spirit, but their description as preserved by Hippolytus points distinctly enough towards Him: *δύναμίν τινα τὸν Μελχισεδὲκ εἶναι μεγίστην· καὶ τοῦτον εἶναι μείζονα τοῦ Χριστοῦ, οὗ κατ' εἰκόνα φάσκουσι τὸν Χριστὸν τυγχάνειν*[4]. At a later date and under another name the sect completed this identification. Hierax[5], or

Spirit and the Logos and from the latitudinarian movement which they initiated to form the point of departure for the two possible forms of Monarchianism."

[1] Ps.-Tertullian, *adv. o. Haer.* 23, "ex Spiritu quidem sancto natum et Virgine, sed hominem solitarium atque nudum nulla alia prae ceteris nisi sola iustitiae auctoritate."

[2] Hippol. *Philos.* VII. 36, *διαφόρων δὲ γενομένων ἐν αὐτοῖς ζητήσεων ἐπεχείρησέ τις καὶ αὐτὸς Θεόδοτος καλούμενος τραπεζίτης τὴν τέχνην λέγειν κ.τ.λ.*

[3] Epiph. *Hær.* LV. I, *ἀποσπασθέντες τάχα ἀπὸ τῶν Θεοδοτιανῶν καλουμένων.*

[4] *ib.* infr.

[5] Epiph. *Hær.* LXVII. 2, 3 (Migne, XLII. p. 176. Cf. *ib.* XLI. p. 980). Cf. Fabric. *Bibl. Gr.* (ed. Harles), IX. p. 246. Cave, *h. l.* a. 302. Hieracas seems to have written a lengthy defence of his doctrine of the Holy Spirit. Epiph. *l. c.* *διεξῆλθε περὶ τούτου πολλὴν πραγματείαν.* He

Hieracas, at the beginning of the fourth century, taught that the wondrous personage who made like unto the Son of GOD abideth a Priest continually is none other than the Spirit Which 'maketh intercession for us with groanings which cannot be uttered,' Who, he added, is like the Son in that, though not begotten, He is yet 'of the Father:' περὶ τοῦ Πνεύματος Ἁγίου [πιστεύει] ἐκ Πατρὸς εἶναι. But in the earlier form of the Melchizedekian heresy these refinements were wanting, and the simple object of those who first propounded the view was that of depreciating the Person of Christ by exalting another supernatural being to an eminence superior to His.

The Patripassian Monarchians were ultimately able to admit into their view of the life of GOD a principle of self-evolution which bore some resemblance to the Catholic doctrine of Divine Processions. Praxeas indeed, who began his course by an emphatic opposition to Montanism[1], seems to have paid no attention to the question of the Holy Spirit's relation to GOD. So far as he recognized the existence of a Holy Spirit, he identified Him with the Father[2].

quoted in support of his view the "Ascents of Isaiah"—an apocryphal vision in which two persons, closely resembling each other, and appearing respectively on the right hand and on the left hand of the Throne of God, are interpreted to be the Son and Spirit of God. The Spirit, he argued, is the ἀφωμοιωμένος τῷ Υἱῷ τοῦ Θεοῦ ἱερεύς. He taught that the Son is from the Father as light from light, but expressed himself so as to suggest a division of the Divine Essence: οὐδ' ὡς Ἱέρακας λύχνον ἀπὸ λύχνου ἢ ὡς λαμπάδα εἰς δύο. (Arius, *ap.* Ath. *de Synod.*)

[1] In Tertullian's eyes he was guilty of two almost equally heinous offences: "duo negotia diaboli Praxeas Romae procuravit—prophetiam expulit et haeresim intulit: Paracletum fugavit Patrem et crucifixit." (*Prax.* I.)

[2] *Prax.* 9, "eundem Patrem et Filium et Spiritum contenderat adversus οἰκονομίαν monarchiae adulantes." *Ib.* 27, "Spiritum Patrem ipsum vis haberi quia Deus spiritus; *quasi non et Dei Spiritus,* sicut et Sermo Deus et Dei Sermo."

He charged the Church with tritheism: "duo et tres," Tertullian complains, "iam iactitant a nobis praedicari, se vero unius Dei cultores praesumunt[1]." Noetus appears to have made no advance upon this shallow unitarianism. But Sabellius, or the school which took its name from him, saw that the Father, Son, and Spirit could not be merely synonymous names of God. An attempt was made to restore the doctrine of the Trinity upon the basis of an economical self-revelation of God: it was taught that God *ἐν μὲν τῇ παλαιᾷ ὡς Πατέρα νομοθετῆσαι, ἐν δὲ τῇ καινῇ ὡς Υἱὸν ἐνανθρωπῆσαι, ὡς Πνεῦμα δὲ Ἅγιον τοῖς ἀποστόλοις ἐπιφοιτῆσαι*[2]. As the Homoousion became the watchword of the Church, so the Monoousion was the formula of the Sabellians: the term *υἱοπάτωρ* was in use among them[3], and had occasion required, a similar compound might have been devised to express the relation of the Spirit to the Father or to the Son. Another, probably a later, phase of Sabellianism explained this Divine self-revelation by a process which it called *πλατυσμὸς*—the *ἔκτασις* of the Clementine Homilies: *λέγει* [*Σαβέλλιος*] *υἱὸν τὸν λόγον ἐν τῷ Πατρὶ μένοντα καὶ κατὰ καιρὸν τῆς δημιουργίας φαινόμενον, ἔπειτα μετὰ τὴν πάντων πλήρωσιν τῶν πραγμάτων εἰς θεὸν ἀνατρέχοντα· τὸ αὐτὸ δὲ καὶ περὶ τοῦ Πνεύματος λέγει*[4]. In support of

[1] *Prax.* 3.

[2] Theodoret, *Haer. fab* II. 9. Cf. Ps.-Hieron. *de Haer.* 26, "trinitas in officiorum nominibus." Epiph. *Hær.* LXII. *ἐν μιᾷ ὑποστάσει τρεῖς ὀνομασίας.* A real distinction of the Persons was still denied. Thus the Sabellian 'Gospel acc. to the Egyptians', represented our Lord as teaching *τὸν αὐτὸν εἶναι Πατέρα, τὸν αὐτὸν εἶναι Υἱὸν, τὸν αὐτὸν εἶναι Ἅγιον Πνεῦμα.* (Hilgenfeld, *libror. deperd. fragm.*)

[3] Athan. *Exp. fid.* (Migne, XXV. p. 204), *οὔτε γὰρ υἱοπάτορα φρονοῦμεν ὡς οἱ Σαβέλλιοι λέγοντες μονοούσιον καὶ οὐχ ὁμοούσιον.*

[4] [Ps.] Greg. Thaum. (*ἡ κατὰ μέρος πίστις*). Migne, X. 1109. It is not certain whether Sabellius regarded the *πλατυσμὸς* which led to the

this theory it was usual to cite the analogous relation of light and heat to the Sun: *εἶναι μὲν τὸ θάλπον εἴτουν θερμὸν καὶ ζέον, τὸ Πνεῦμα· τὸ φωτιστικὸν τὸν Υἱόν. τὸν δὲ Πατέρα αὐτὸν εἶναι τὸ εἶδος πάσης τῆς ὑποστάσεως· τὸ δὲ Ἅγιον Πνεῦμα πέμπεσθαι εἰς τὸν κόσμον καὶ καθεξῆς καὶ καθ' ἕκαστα εἰς ἕκαστον τῶν καταξιουμένων· ἀναζωογονεῖν δὲ τὸν τοιοῦτον καὶ ἀναζέειν, θάλπειν τε καὶ θερμαίνειν ὡς εἰπεῖν διὰ τῆς τοῦ Πνεύματος δυνάμεώς τε καὶ συμβάσεως*[1]. Epiphanius has preserved another Sabellian illustration, which seems intended to represent the internal relations of the Trinity: *ὡς ἐν ἀνθρώπῳ σῶμα καὶ ψυχὴ καὶ πνεῦμα...... τὸ πνεῦμα ὡς ἀνθρώπου, οὕτως καὶ τὸ Ἅγιον Πνεῦμα ἐν τῇ θεότητι*[2]. We learn from the author of the *Praedestinatus* that this heresy drew forth by way of protest one of the earliest statements of the Catholic doctrine of the Procession. He says: "His occurrit Dositheus episcopus Seleuciae, docens eam totam trinitatem negare dum se aestimat unitatem defendere; Pater enim ingenitus, Filius genitus, *Spiritus Sanctus procedens ex Patre* coaequalis per omnia Patri et Filio[3]." Other testimonies to the faith of the Church, called forth by the Sabellian movement, will be given hereafter.

manifestation of the Holy Spirit as having begun under the O. T.: see Neander, II. 324 sq. With the *πλατυσμὸς* he compared the *διαιρέσεις χαρισμάτων* (Ath. *or. c. Ar.* IV 25).

[1] S. Epiph. *Haer.* LXXII. I (Migne, XLI. 1052). [2] *ib.* supra.

[3] *Praedest.* I. 41 (Migne, LIII. p. 599). It is not clear from this account which of the Patripassian sects was the object of Dositheus's attack, for he regards Sabellians Praxeans and Hermogenians as identical ("Sabelliani...sunt qui et Praxeani dicuntur...dicuntur et Hermogeniani"). Le Quien, *Oriens Christ.* II. p. 778, places this Dositheus in the third century: "saeculo ni fallor tertio iam adulto Seleuciae Syriae episcopus sedebat Dositheus qui contra Sabellianos Praxeanos et [?] Hermogenianos calamum strinxit utpote tunc nascentes haereticos." The Seleucia of which he was bishop was Sel. Pieria, at the mouth of the Orontes. Its bishops were suffragans of Antioch: Wiltzsch, I. p. 50.

In this way, rather than by direct contribution, Sabellianism may claim a place in the history of the Procession-dogma.

We must not forget Paulus of Samosata, whose somewhat singular heresy completes the cycle of third century Monarchianism. Paulus found a place for the Holy Spirit in his conception of the inner life of God; but of this part of his theology we have very imperfect knowledge, if indeed it was ever developed by its author. The account of Epiphanius is as follows: *φάσκει δὲ οὗτος Θεὸν Πατέρα καὶ Υἱὸν καὶ Ἅγιον Πνεῦμα ἕνα Θεόν· ἐν Θεῷ δὲ ἀεὶ ὄντα τὸν αὐτοῦ Λόγον καὶ τὸ Πνεῦμα αὐτοῦ ὥσπερ ἐν ἀνθρώπου καρδίᾳ ὁ ἴδιος λόγος......εἷς ἐστὶν ὁ Θεὸς καὶ οὐχὶ Πατὴρ ὁ Πατὴρ καὶ Υἱὸς ὁ Υἱὸς καὶ Ἅγιον Πνεῦμα τὸ Ἅγιον Πνεῦμα*[1], i.e. the Son and the Spirit are impersonal attributes. The Logos was capable of being united to the Man Jesus, and the Holy Spirit could in some sense be emitted from God, since He was the Agent of the miraculous conception[2]. But the system of Paulus excluded belief in an essential procession; and we know in fact that he rejected the idea of such a procession as inconsistent with the Unity of the Divine Essence, arguing thus; *εἰ μὴ ἐξ ἀνθρώπου γέγονεν ὁ Χριστὸς Θεὸς, οὐκοῦν ὁμοούσιός ἐστι τῷ Πατρὶ καὶ ἀνάγκη τρεῖς οὐσίας εἶναι, μίαν μὲν προηγουμένην, τὰς δὲ δύο ἐξ ἐκείνης*[3]. In answer to this cavil, the Church withdrew for a time the term ὁμοούσιος, but reasserted in other words the true Deity of our Lord. The relation of the Holy

[1] S. Epiph. *Haer.* LXV. 1 (Migne, XLII. p. 13).

[2] Routh, *R. S.* p. 300, *συνῆλθεν ὁ λόγος τῷ ἐκ Δαβὶδ γεγεννημένῳ ὅς ἐστιν Ἰησοῦς Χριστὸς, ὁ γεννηθεὶς ἐκ Πνεύματος Ἁγίου. καὶ τοῦτον μὲν ἤνεγκεν ἡ παρθένος διὰ Πνεύματος Ἁγίου.* Cf. Leont. *de Sect.* 3.

[3] Athan. *de Syn.* (Routh, III. p. 315).

Spirit to the Father, which had held a secondary place at the most in Paul's theology, is not touched upon in the Synodical Epistle of the Council of Antioch.

A glance at the foregoing chapter will show the difficulty which Ante-Nicene heresy found in dealing with the doctrine of the Holy Ghost. In some systems the Spirit is but a synonym of the Father and the Son, or a particular manifestation of the Divine life. In others He is a person, but distinct from GOD: an Aeon or an Angel, produced or made by the Supreme. Of this latter class of hypotheses, some represent Him as the *σύζυγος* and co-equal of the Son: whilst others regard Him as subordinate and the creature of a created Logos. But amidst these contending voices, none was heard to anticipate the judgement of the Church. No heresiarch, no leader of a sect, Gnostic or Montanist, Ebionite or Patripassian, stumbled upon the simple expression of the truth, which the Catholic Church already possessed in her canonical Gospels, and which in due time she brought forth out of her treasury—"the Holy Ghost Whom I will send unto you from the Father ...proceedeth from the Father."

CHAPTER III.

THE ANSWER OF THE ANTE-NICENE CHURCH.

"Non aliunde quam a Patre per Filium."
TERTULLIAN, *Prax.* 4.

OUR examination of Catholic writers was broken off in order to take the measure of the work accomplished by the heretical leaders of the second and third centuries in reference to the doctrine of the Holy Ghost. We now return to the progress made during the same period within the Church.

M. Matter, the historian of Gnosticism, has rightly rejected the idea that Christian doctrine owes anything of its essence to the speculations of the Gnosis[1]. But he freely grants that the indirect influence of the latter upon the scientific expression of the Faith was incalculable[2]. If its effects upon thought and language were chiefly visible in Syria and Egypt, the opposition which it excited in the West endowed the Church with a new literature. To the anti-gnostic reaction we owe the great

[1] *Histoire critique du gnosticisme*, III. p. 4 sq.: "nous n'admettons pas d'influence dans ce sens."

[2] *Ib.* p. 10: "il est certain que les théories jetées dans le sein du christianisme par les gnostiques ont entraîné les docteurs de l'Église dans une série d'études spéciales...études dont l'influence sur les écoles chrétiennes de Syrie et d'Égypte sinon de Rome et de Carthage est incalculable. Il est certain aussi que plusieurs des ouvrages les plus importants que nous ont laissés les meilleurs écrivains des premiers siècles ont été provoqués par le gnosticisme."

work of Irenaeus, and an important part of the writings of Tertullian. Montanism and Monarchianism were equally fruitful in results; and it is not too much to say that in this way heresy introduces us to a fresh stage in the history of Catholic dogma.

I. S. Irenaeus, who to the originality of a Christian thinker adds the authority of a hearer of S. Polycarp, the disciple of the Apostle S. John, opens his Ἀνατροπὴ τῆς ψευδωνύμου γνώσεως with a vigorous attack upon the Valentinian system of emanations. He sees that the προβολαὶ, by means of which Valentinus replenished his Pleroma, involved a separation of the Divine Essence wholly inconsistent with the incorporeal Unity of God. "Si enim sensum [i. e. νοῦν] emisit, ipse qui emisit sensum secundum eos compositus et corporalis intelligitur, ut sit separatim quidem qui emisit Deus, separatim autem qui emissus est sensus...... Si autem non emissum extra Patrem illum dicant sed in ipso Patre, primo quidem superfluum erit etiam dicere emissum esse eum; quemadmodum enim emissus est si intra Patrem erat [1]?" Furthermore, he is indignant at the inferior and adventitious place which was assigned amongst the Valentinian Aeons to Christ and the Holy Ghost: "Quis enim sensum habens et veritatis vel modicum attingens sustinebit dicentes....alterum quidem esse Monogenem, alterum autem Christum quem et posteriorem reliquis Aeonibus cum Spiritu Sancto factum esse dicunt ?...ut nisi in ignorantia et deminoratione fuissent Aeones, secundum eos nec Christus emissus fuisset nec Spiritus Sanctus.... Non solum itaque in fabricatorem tantum irreligiosi sunt, labis eum dicentes fructum, sed et in Christum et in Spiritum Sanctum propter

[1] *Haer.* II. 13, § 5. 6 (Migne, VII. 745).

labem dicentes eos emissos[1]." Yet in his zeal against this false emanation-theory, Irenaeus does not forget that the Faith itself reveals the existence of processions in God. Thus, of the Son's Eternal generation he says, "Si quis...nobis dixerit, Quomodo ergo Filius prolatus a Patre est? dicimus ei quia prolationem [προβολὴν] istam sive generationem sive nuncupationem sive adapertionem aut quolibet quis nomine vocaverit generationem, nemo novit...nisi solus qui generavit Pater et qui natus est Filius[2]." And if he has no explanation to offer of that which is ineffable, more than one fresh illustration of the mystery is attempted. The Son is described as the *progenies* Patris, the Spirit as His *figuratio* i.e. His Image[3]. The Son and the Spirit are the Hands of God: "homo...per Manus Eius plasmatus est, hoc est per Filium et Spiritum, quibus et dixit, 'Faciamus hominem[4]'." The latter is a favourite simile with Irenaeus. Rejecting the notion of a creation of man by created angels, he exclaims, "Quasi ipse suas non haberet manus! adest enim ei semper Verbum et Sapientia, Filius et Spiritus, per quos et in quibus omnia...fecit, ad quos et loquitur dicens, 'Faciamus hominem ad imaginem et similitudinem nostram.'" The fifth book has two other passages

[1] *ib.* II. 19 § 9 Migne, 776.

[2] *ib.* II. 28. § 6 (Migne, 809).

[3] *ib.* IV. 7. § 4 (Migne, 993), "ministrat enim ei ad omnia sua progenies et figuratio sua, id est, Filius et Sp. S., Verbum et Sapientia." Fathers of the 4th cent. speak of the Holy Spirit as the εἰκὼν (S. Basil) or σφραγὶς (S. Athan.) of the Son; hence it has been inferred that *figuratio sua* represents μόρφωσις or διατύπωσις αὐτοῦ, i. e. τοῦ Υἱοῦ. Cf. the note in Migne *l. c.*, and Harvey's *S. Iren.* II. p. 164. But it seems precarious to interpret Irenaeus by the practice of a later age. Dorner is probably right: "he calls the Spirit Figuratio Patris." Cf. Hippol. *Philos.* VI. 14. τὸ Πνεῦμα...εἰκὼν τῆς ἀπεράντου δυνάμεως (cited from Simon's ἀπόφασις).

[4] *Haer.* IV. *praef.* *ib.* 20 § 1 (Migne, 975 sq.).

of the same character[1]. Such a figure, whilst it maintained the equality of the Spirit and the Son, and Their consubstantiality with the Father and inseparableness from Him, set forth also a doctrine of Divine Processions. It taught that the Son and the Holy Spirit alike proceed from the Father. Nor did it necessarily connect the act of procession with the creation of the world. A man has hands before he uses them to build or to construct. God was never without His Hands; His Word and Spirit were ever with Him.

It is not so easy to determine what relation Irenaeus supposes the Son and the Spirit to bear to Each Other in the life of the Holy Trinity. The metaphor of the Hands suggests consubstantiality coupled with inferiority of order and office in the case of the Holy Spirit. Mr Harvey sees the Western view of the Procession in a passage where Irenaeus writes, "Pater enim conditionem simul et Verbum suum portans et Verbum portatum a Patre praestat Spiritum omnibus quemadmodum vult Pater[2]." A more striking passage is that in which Christians are regarded as "per Spiritum imaginem et inscriptionem Patris et Filii accipientes[3]." The Holy Spirit is, moreover, described as the "communicatio Christi," the "scala ascensionis ad Deum[4];" and the

[1] viz. V. 16 § 1, 28 § 4. See Newman, *Tracts*, p. 171.

[2] *Haer.* V. 18 § 2 (Migne, 1173). "The Holy Spirit therefore (Mr Harvey annotates) proceedeth from the Father and the Son. Only the Spirit is said to stand in the same ratio to the Son that the Son bears to the Father...Therefore the processions of the Spirit from the Son could never have been denied in the theology of S. Irenaeus." (*S. Irenaeus*, II. p. 373.) On *Haer.* V. 13 § 2 see p. 9 (note) *supr.*

[3] *ib.* III. 17 § 3 (Migne, 930).

[4] *ib.* III. 24 § 1 (Migne, 966). "Communicatio Christi id est Spiritus Sanctus, arrha incorruptelae et confirmatio fidei nostrae et scala ascensionis ad Deum." *Infr.* "qui non participant eum...neque

latter idea seems to have been received by tradition from the Apostolic age: "hanc esse adordinationem et dispositionem eorum qui salvantur, dicunt presbyteri Apostolorum discipuli, et per huiusmodi gradus proficere, et per Spiritum quidem [ad] Filium, per Filium autem ascendere ad Patrem." In a fragment probably belonging to the lost treatise 'On Knowledge,' the same truth is expressed still more distinctly: *εἰ μὲν οὐκ ἔχει [τις] Ἅγιον Πνεῦμα, οὐκ ἔχει γνῶσιν τοῦ κτίσαντος· οὐ παρεδέξατο τὴν ζωὴν Ἰησοῦ Χριστοῦ· οὐκ οἶδε τὸν Πατέρα τὸν ἐν τοῖς οὐρανοῖς*[1]. Such language does not directly teach the eternal procession from or through the Son: but it certainly implies a relation of the Spirit to the Son deeper than that of simple mission, and such that the Spirit receives of the Son and is in His Essence the Spirit of the Son as he is the Spirit of the Father.

2. Tertullian, the earliest of Latin Church writers properly so called, takes up a much bolder position. It is hardly too much to say that he is the first to formulate the floating belief of the Church as to Divine Processions, and that in his writings we also find the first distinct approximation to the Western doctrine of the Procession of the Holy Ghost. His encounter with the school of Praxeas led him to see

percipiunt de corpore Christi procedentem nitidissimum fontem." Mr Harvey refers to Jer. ii. 13, *ἐμὲ ἐγκατέλιπον πηγὴν ὕδατος ζωῆς*. But is not the allusion rather to Apoc. xxii. 1, *ποταμὸν...λαμπρὸν... ἐκπορευόμενον*?

[1] Iren. *fragm.* XXXVI (Migne, 1244). The fragment numbered XXI. in Massuet's collection (Migne, VII. 1242) would be of the greatest value if certainly genuine, but the reasons for ascribing it to Irenaeus are of the slightest: see Massuet's note in Migne *l. c.* and Stieren, I. p. 838 n. 4. It runs, *Δίδωσι δὲ [Μωϋσῆς] οὐκ ἐμφυσήσει καθάπερ, ὁ Χριστός· ὅτι μὴ ἔστι πηγὴ τοῦ Πνεύματος.* A Syriac fragment printed by Pitra (*Spic. Solesm*, I. p. 6), cites among many other indications of Our Lord's Deity His power to give the Holy Ghost by insufflation.

more clearly than Irenaeus the elements of truth which the Valentinian system contained. If the Son and the Holy Ghost were not, as Praxeas asserted them to be, mere alternative names of the One Supreme God, or, at most, as Sabellius maintained, successive manifestations of His inner life, then the Divine Nature must, in some sense, be generative and productive: and the formula 'God of God'[1] must find place in the Catholic Creed. Tertullian applies this principle in the first instance to the Second Person: "unicum quidem Deum credimus sub hac tamen dispensatione quam *οἰκονομίαν* dicimus, ut unici Dei sit et Filius, sermo ipsius qui ex ipso processerit[2]." This is probably the earliest instance, outside the Canon, of the theological use of *procedere;* but it is doubtful whether the eternal procession, i.e. the Generation of the Son, is more than in the background of the word as Tertullian understands it. To express the essential relation of the Son and the Spirit to the Father, he boldly wrests out of the hands of the Gnosis the terminology which it had contrived to make its own, and which Irenaeus had been disposed to surrender to the enemy. Such words as *προβολὴ*[3], *prolatio, producere, emittere,* are capable in his judgment of a true and orthodox sense as well as of a false. Thus, arguing that the Word of the Lord, by which the heavens were made, must be a *person,* he

[1] *Prax.* 15 (Migne, II. 173) "nam etsi Deus Sermo, sed apud Deum, quia ex Deo Deus." Cf. Hippolyt. *c. Noet.* (ed. Lagarde, p. 51). *οὕτως παρίστατο αὐτῷ ἕτερος· ἕτερον δὲ λέγων οὐ δύο θεοὺς λέγω. ἀλλ' ὡς φῶς ἐκ φωτὸς κ.τ.λ.* Hippolytus, however, stops short at the generation of the Son.

[2] *ib.* 2 (Migne, 156). Cf. S. John viii. 42, *ἐκ τοῦ Θεοῦ ἐξῆλθον, ex Deo processi.* Tertullian however read *ex Deo exivi:* see Rönsch, *das N. T. Tertullian's*, p. 270.

[3] Cf. Kaye's *Tertullian*, p. 504 sq.

writes[1]: "Quid est enim, dices, sermo nisi vox et sonus oris...vacuum nescio quid et inane et incorporale? At ego nihil dico de Deo inane et vacuum prodire potuisse, ut non de inani et vacuo prolatum nec carere substantia quod de tanta substantia processit et tantas substantias fecit." 'But is not this sheer Gnosticism?' Tertullian anticipates the objection. "Hoc si quis putaverit me προβολὴν aliquam introducere (id est prolationem rei alterius ex altera) quod facit Valentinus alium atque alium Aeonem de Aeone producens: primo equidem dicām tibi non ideo non utatur et Veritas vocabulo isto et re ac cursu eius quia et haeresis utitur; immo haeresis potius ex veritate accepit quod ad mendacium suum strueret." The simple question remains, Does the Word of God derive His Essence from the Father, or not? If He does, there is a true προβολὴ of which the Gnostic emanations are counterfeits. The Valentinian πρόβλημα was cut off and separate from its source; the true is consubstantial with and immanent in its προβολεύς. "Protulit enim Deus Sermonem...sicut radix fruticem et fons fluvium et sol radium...Nam et radix et frutex duae res sunt sed conjunctae: et fons et flumen duae species sunt sed indivisae: et sol et radius duae formae sunt sed cohaerentes." But Tertullian recognises another Divine προβολὴ; there is a Third Person in the Godhead, and, therefore, a second procession from God. He extends his illustrations so as to embrace this procession of the Spirit, and thus admits us to a view of his doctrine of the Holy Ghost. "Omne quod prodit ex aliquo, secundum sit eius necesse est de quo prodit...... secundus autem ubi est, duo sunt; et tertium ubi est, tres sunt. Tertius enim est Spiritus a Deo

[1] *Prax.* 7, 8 (Migne, 162 sq.).

et Filio sicut tertius a radice fructus ex frutice et tertius a fonte rivus ex flumine et tertius a sole apex ex radio." It cannot fairly be objected that Tertullian deals here simply with the order of the Persons: his illustrations carry him into the ground and reason of that Divine order[1]. The Son is second, because He proceeds from the Father immediately: the Spirit is third, because He derives His existence immediately from the Son. The 'fructus' is 'ex frutice' in more than the order of nature: the 'rivus' is 'ex flumine' by a real process of derivation: although the 'frutex' is not the 'radix' nor the 'flumen' the 'fons'. If any doubt could be left as to Tertullian's meaning, it is removed by other passages. Thus his exposition of S. John xvi. 14 implies a relation of the Spirit to the Son analogous to the relation of the Son to the Father: "de Meo sumet, inquit, sicut ipse de Patre. Ita connexus Patri in Filio et Filii in Paracleto tres efficit cohaerentes alterum ex altero[2]." And the following is explicit in support of an essential emission through the Son: "Filium non aliunde deduco sed de substantia Patris...Spiritum non aliunde puto quam a Patre per Filium. Vide ergo ne tu potius monarchiam destruas[3]." If Tertullian would have dissented from the *Filioque* of the Latin Creed, his dissent could have been grounded only on the inexactness of the

[1] Cf. Van der Moeren *de process. Spiritus Sancti* (Lovanii, 1864), p. 41, "non me latet sat multos esse auctores inter quos ipse Petavius, qui existimant Tertullianum hoc loco non agere de Sp. S. origine, sed tantum de personarum divinarum ordine...Verum illi satis non attenderunt ad totum contextum sermonem...fructus...non tantum dicitur et est tertius a radice et frutice; sed ita tertius ut sit *ex frutice* adeoque ex radice, cum ipsa frutex sit ex radice."

[2] *Prax.* 25 (Migne, 188). Cf. Baur, *Dreienigkeit*, II. p. 260.

[3] *ib.* 4 (Migne, 159).

expression or its want of adequate authority. The dogma which is meant to be conveyed by the *Filioque* is not appreciably different from the dogma which Tertullian expresses by his *per Filium*[1].

3. While heresy was being opposed by Irenaeus in Gaul and by Tertullian in North Africa, Egypt witnessed the rise at Alexandria of the first great Christian school of theology. In that home of Neoplatonism and the Gnosis the Church made its earliest effort to set forth in human words the treasures of wisdom and knowledge which are hid in Christ. By the Apologists the doctrine of the Holy Trinity had been regarded as offering the best answer to the Pagan charge of Atheism, whilst the writers against heresy contrasted it with the Gnostic and Monarchian perversions of the Faith. The Alexandrians for the first time approached the doctrine in the character of scientific theologians, or rather, perhaps, as earnest and devout, but free and cultivated enquirers after truth.

Pantaenus, the first in our list of Alexandrian catechists[2], has left nothing of doctrinal importance[3]. His successor, the Alexandrian Clement, in his extant writings deals largely with the relation of the Logos to God. The Divine Nature in Christ is defined as the *δύναμις τοῦ Θεοῦ*, the *ἀρχικώτατος λόγος τοῦ Πατρὸς καὶ σοφία*, the *φωτὸς ἀρχέτυπον φῶς*, the *ἄχρονος καὶ ἄναρχος ἀρχὴ* of Creation. The Generation of the Son is thus expressed: *ἓν μὲν τὸ ἀγέννητον...ἓν δὲ καὶ τὸ προγενηθὲν δι' οὗ τὰ πάντα ἐγένετο*[4]. An Arian interpretation of this language is

[1] *Per Filium* exceeds the teaching of Tertullian's own 'Rule of Faith' (Hahn, p. 69 sq.).

[2] See, however, p. 25 (note) *supr.*

[3] The fragments are collected in Routh, *R. S.* I. pp. 378—383.

[4] I take these instances from Guerike, *Schol. Alex.* p. 131 sq.

excluded by the fact that Clement repeatedly ascribes to Christ the name and attributes of Deity[1]. With regard to the Holy Spirit he speaks in a vague and undogmatic manner. The Spirit is the holy anointing oil prepared by the Christ for His friends, a fragrant unguent compounded of celestial spices: *τοῦτο σκευάζει Χριστὸς ἀνθρώποις γνωρίμοις εὐωδίας ἄλειμμα ἐκ τῶν οὐρανίων συντιθεὶς ἀρωμάτων τὸ μύρον*[2]. The beauty of the truly Gnostic soul is deemed meet by the Holy Spirit to become His temple, since it is the earthly image of the power and excellence of God: *ἐπίγειος εἰκὼν θείας δυνάμεως ἡ γνωστικὴ ψυχὴ τελείᾳ ἀρετῇ κεκοσμημένη...τοῦτο τὸ κάλλος τῆς ψυχῆς νεὼς γίνεται τοῦ Ἁγίου Πνεύματος*[3]. The Platonists hold that the human mind is an effluence from the Deity: we teach that the soul of the believer is inspired by the Holy Ghost. But this must not be understood to imply a division of the Spirit's essence as if a part of God were in each of us: *ἡμεῖς μὲν τῷ πεπιστευκότι προσεπιπνεῖσθαι τὸ Ἅγιον Πνεῦμά φαμεν· οἱ δὲ ἀμφὶ Πλάτωνα νοῦν μὲν ἐν ψυχῇ θείας μοίρας ἀπόρροιαν ὑπάρχοντα, ψυχὴν δὲ ἐν σώματι κατοικίζουσιν...ἀλλ' οὐχ ὡς μέρος θεοῦ ἐν ἑκάστῳ ἡμῶν τὸ Πνεῦμα· ὅπως δὲ ἡ διανομὴ αὕτη, καὶ ὅ τι ποτέ ἐστι τὸ Ἅγιον Πνεῦμα, ἐν τοῖς περὶ προφητείας κἀν τοῖς περὶ ψυχῆς ἐπιδειχθήσεται ἡμῖν*[4]. Whether Clement fulfilled the promise of these last words is not certainly known. Fabricius has collected from his extant writings a long list of such promises[5], many of which, it is probable, were

[1] Cf. Kaye's *Clement of Alexandria*, pp. 332—3, notes.

[2] *Paedag.* II. 8 (Migne, VIII. 471).

[3] *Strom.* VII. 11 (Migne, IX. 490).

[4] *Strom.* V. 13 (Migne, IX. 129). Cf. *Strom.* VI. 24, ἀμερῶς μεριζόμενον Πνεῦμα Κυρίου (Kaye, p. 353).

[5] *Bibl. Graec.* ed. Harles. pp. 133—4. Among the *opera deperdita* of Clement Fabricius mentions a book entitled ὅροι διάφοροι, from

never redeemed. A fragment, however, first printed by Cotelier under the name of Clement of Rome, may possibly belong to one or other of the works in which the Alexandrian Clement undertook to deal with the doctrine of the Holy Spirit. If so, we can only regret the loss of a treatise which, in the few words that remain, has so much to teach. It will be observed that this fragment, of which the most important part is subjoined, borrows for the first time the terminology of S. John's Gospel. Μακάριος ἀνὴρ ὁ γινώσκων τὴν τοῦ Πατρὸς δόσιν δι' ἐκπορεύσεως τοῦ παναγίου Πνεύματος· μακάριος ὁ γινώσκων καὶ λαβὼν ὅτι τὸ Ἅγιον Πνεῦμά ἐστιν ἡ δόσις αὐτοῦ. Καὶ τοῦτο ἐν τύπῳ περιστερᾶς παρέσχε· τὸ γὰρ ζῶον ἀκακίαν ἔχει καὶ ἄχολόν ἐστιν· ἄκακος δὲ ὁ πατὴρ πνεῦμα ἔδωκεν ἄκακον...ἀπὸ σπλάγχνων ἰδίων προϊέμενος...ἔστιν οὖν τοῦτο ἅγιον καὶ εὐθὲς τὸ ἀπ' αὐτοῦ προελθὸν καὶ δύναμις αὐτοῦ καὶ θέλημα αὐτοῦ εἰς πλήρωμα δόξης αὐτοῦ φανερωθέν[1]. The passage is of a practical character: it deals with the mission and work of the Paraclete: yet the eternal procession is clearly in the background of the thought; the ἐκπόρευσις of which the writer speaks is an issuing forth from the Heart, i.e. from the inner Life of God.

We are in some measure consoled for the loss of Clement's work περὶ προφητείας by the full and

which Veccus (*de process. Sp. S.*) quotes the following definition of the Spirit: ἐστὶ λεπτὴ καὶ ἄϋλος καὶ ἀσχημάτιστος ἐκπορευτικὴ ὕπαρξις.

[1] Migne, I. 459. Cotelier extracted it from Cod. 1026 in the Royal Library at Paris, where it was headed τοῦ ἁγίου Κλήμεντος ἐπισκόπου Ῥώμης...εἰς τὸ Ἅγιον Πνεῦμα. Dr Lightfoot, who follows Bp. Jacobson in appending it to the works of the Roman Clement, writes (p. 220), "I am disposed myself to believe...that the fragment belongs not to the Roman but to the Alexandrian....It accords entirely with his tone of thought, and even resembles extant passages where he speaks on this subject." Gebhardt thinks it not earlier than cent. iv.

interesting treatment which the doctrine of the Holy Spirit receives in the extant writings of Origen. Dorner indeed states that this doctrine was "but little developed by Origen[1]": little, that is, in proportion to the extent of his Christology. But in comparison with other writers of the Ante-Nicene period, the great Alexandrian is diffuse and explicit upon this subject. If we do not find in his works the solution of a problem which still perplexes the Church, the elements of the problem are at least for the first time clearly recognized.

Origen's theology starts from the conception of God as a simple and indivisible because incorporeal Unity: "intellectualis natura simplex...ut sit ex omni parte *μονὰς* et ut ita dicam *ἑνάς*...fons ex quo initium totius intellectualis naturae vel mentis est[2]." He turns with peculiar aversion from the Valentinian system of emanations, refusing to use the word which Valentinus had abused: *εἰ γὰρ προβολή ἐστιν ὁ Υἱὸς τοῦ Πατρὸς καὶ γεννᾷ μὲν ἐξ αὐτοῦ ὁποῖα τὰ τῶν ζώων γεννήματα, ἀνάγκη σῶμα εἶναι τὸν προβάλλοντα καὶ τὸν προβεβλημένον*[3]. He conceives that a juster analogy is to be found in the mystery of the human spirit: "sicut voluntas procedit e mente...neque ab ea separatur aut dividitur[4]." On the other hand he is equally opposed to the false Monarchianism of Praxeas. It was by the arguments of Origen that Beryllus of Bostra, who regarded the life of the Incarnate Son as a *περιγραφὴ* of

[1] Dorner, I. ii. 123.

[2] *de princip.* I. 6 (Migne, XI. 126).

[3] *de princip.* IV. 28 (Migne, 401).

[4] *ib.* I. 2, § 6 (Migne XI. 135): *infr.* (Migne, 402) "absque ulla corporali passione velut si voluntas procedat e mente." Yet (*Comm. in Joann.* XIII. 25) the Son is an *ἀπαύγασμα, ἀπόρροια, εἰκὼν τῆς δόξης τοῦ Πατρός*: see next page.

the Father's Godhead, was induced to retract[1]. In the extant writings of Origen the Patripassians—*οἱ συγχέοντες* as he calls them—are repeatedly attacked: "We," he emphatically says, "believe that there are three hypostases, the Father, the Son, and the Holy Ghost[2]." With regard to the Second Person he finds a resting place in the doctrine of an eternal generation, a process timeless and endless: *οὐχὶ ἐγέννησεν ὁ Πατὴρ τὸν Υἱὸν καὶ ἀπέλυσεν αὐτὸν ὁ Πατὴρ ἀπὸ τῆς γενέσεως αὐτοῦ, ἀλλὰ ἀεὶ γεννᾷ αὐτόν*—just as the *ἀπαύγασμα* streams forth continuously and indivisibly from the source of light[3]. Thus the Father was always Father, the Son always Son: *πότε γὰρ ὁ θεὸς ἀπαύγασμα οὐκ εἶχε τῆς ἰδίας δόξης*[4];...*Οὐ γὰρ ὁ θεὸς Πατὴρ εἶναι ἤρξατο κωλυόμενος ὡς οἱ γενόμενοι πατέρες ἄνθρωποι ὑπὸ τοῦ μὴ δύνασθαι*[5]. The same, he significantly adds, must be said concerning the Holy Ghost[6]. Like the Generation of the Son the Procession of the Holy Spirit is an eternal fact in the Life of God, expressing the relation of a derived but coeternal Person to the Source of Deity. "Filium generat Pater et Spiritum Sanctum profert, non quasi qui ante non erat, sed quia origo et fons Filii vel Spiritus Sancti Pater est, et nihil in his anterius posteriusve intelligi potest[7]."

[1] Euseb. *H. E.* VI. 33.

[2] *in Joann.* II. 6 (Migne, XIV. 128).

[3] *in Jeremiam* IX. 4 (Migne, XIII. 357).

[4] fragm. ap. Athan. *de decr. S. N.* 27.

[5] fragm. *in Genesin* ap. Euseb. *c. Marcell.* I. 22.

[6] τὸ αὐτὸ μέντοιγε καὶ περὶ τοῦ Ἁγίου Πνεύματος λεκτέον.

[7] *de princip.* II. 1. (Migne, XI. 186.) Cf. *ib.* I. 2, "principalis bonitas in Deo sentienda est Patre, ex quo vel Filius natus vel Spiritus Sanctus procedens sine dubio bonitatis eius naturam in se refert quae est in eo fonte de quo vel natus est Filius, vel procedit Spiritus Sanctus." *Hom. in Num.* XVII. 4 (Migne, XII. 708); "quamvis et Salvator noster fluvius sit qui laetificat civitatem Dei; et

There are two passages in which we get a nearer view of Origen's teaching on the relation of the Holy Spirit to the Son. (*a*) His exposition of Rom. viii. 9—11[1] seems to anticipate a line of argument which is common in Western theologians of a later age. "Requirendum est (he writes) utrum diversum sit Spiritum Dei esse in aliquo an Spiritum Christi...Sed quantum vel consequentiam loci praesentis intueor vel illud quod Salvator in Evangelio de Spiritu Sancto dicit quia 'a Patre procedit' et 'de meo accipiet'—cum, inquam, tantam hanc unitatis inter Patrem et Filium aspicio rationem, Spiritus Dei et Spiritus Christi unus atque idem mihi Spiritus dici videtur[2]." (*b*) Writing on S. John, i. 2[3], Origen raises

Spiritus Sanctus non solum ipse fluvius sit, sed et iis quibus datus fuerit, flumina ventre eorum procedant; et Deus Pater dicat, 'Me dereliquerunt fontem aquae vivae, ex quo scilicet fonte flumina ista procedunt.'" The Father is the *fons Spiritus Sancti:* and the only point upon which Origen hesitates is the distinction between Generation and Procession: *de princ.* I. *Praef.* § 4, "honore ac dignitate Patri ac Filio sociatum tradiderunt [apostoli] Spiritum Sanctum. In hoc non iam manifeste discernitur utrum natus an innatus [γενητὸς ἢ ἀγένητος (? 'factus an infectus.' Jerome)], vel Filius etiam Dei ipse habendus sit necne [*v. supr* pp. 16, 17]."

[1] εἰ δέ τις Πνεῦμα Χριστοῦ οὐκ ἔχει, κ.τ.λ.

[2] *Comm. in Ep. ad Roman.* VI. 12 (Migne, XIV. 1098). Origen mentions, however, other solutions, and hastens to a practical conclusion. The latter is so beautiful and true that I cannot refrain from giving it a place here. "Sic unus quisque habere in se probatur Spiritum Christi. Christus Sapientia est: si sit quis sapiens secundum Christum...habet in se per sapientiam Spiritum Christi. Christus pax est: si quis habeat in se pacem Christi, per Spiritum pacis habet in se Spiritum Christi. Sic et caritatem, sic et sanctificationem, sic et singula quaeque quae Christus esse dicitur qui habet, hic Spiritum Christi in se habere credendus est, et sperare quod mortale corpus suum vivificabitur propter inhabitantem in se Spiritum Christi."

[3] πάντα δι' αὐτοῦ ἐγένετο καὶ χωρὶς αὐτοῦ ἐγένετο οὐδὲ ἓν ὃ γέγονεν. Cf. S. Ambrose *de Sp. S.* I. 2 (Migne, XVI. 740), "Omnia per Filium Scriptura dicit esse quae facta sunt: cum autem factus non doceatur Sp. S., utique nec inter omnia probari potest." Origen placed the full

the question whether the Holy Spirit is to be included among "things that were made" by the Logos. Since 'without Him was not anything made,' there appear to him to be only two possible modes of escape from this conclusion: the pseudo-monarchian hypothesis, which destroys the distinct personality of the Spirit; and the equally erroneous tritheistic view, which regards Him as ingenerate (ἀγέννητος). Accordingly, Origen decides that the Holy Spirit had in some sense a γένεσις[1]: that He derived His existence through the Word. This Genesis of the Spirit seems to him to imply the dependence of His Person on the Person of the Son, οὗ χρήζειν ἔοικε διακονοῦντος αὐτοῦ τῇ ὑποστάσει. Lastly, regarding the Holy Spirit in His relation to the Church, Origen holds τὴν ὕλην τῶν ἀπὸ θεοῦ χαρισμάτων παρέχειν τοῖς ἁγίοις, τῆς εἰρημένης ὕλης τῶν χαρισμάτων ἐνεργουμένης μὲν ἀπὸ τοῦ θεοῦ, διακονουμένης δὲ ὑπὸ τοῦ Χριστοῦ, ὑφεστώσης δὲ κατὰ τὸ Ἅγιον Πνεῦμα[2].

If this passage stood by itself, it would be hard to acquit Origen of having held an unworthy view of the Person of the Holy Spirit, and thus having been led to resolve His Procession from the Father into a production by the Son. But, as elsewhere he distinctly refuses to call the Holy Ghost a creature, and asserts His timeless procession from the Father, it is fair to suppose that in this place by

stop after ἐν, connecting ὃ γέγονεν ἐν αὐτῷ, ζωὴ ἦν. Was it this punctuation which led him to overlook the true solution?

[1] ἀγέννητον μηδὲν ἕτερον τοῦ Πατρὸς εἶναι πιστεύοντες...τὸ Πνεῦμα γενητὸν ὂν διὰ τοῦ Λόγου γεγονέναι.

[2] *in Joann.* II. 6 (Migne, XIV. 128). Cf. *ib.* XX. 23. τὸ μὲν οὖν Ἅγιον Πνεῦμα...ὅταν λαλῇ, οὐκ ἐκ τῶν ἰδίων λαλεῖ ἀλλ' ἀπὸ τοῦ Λόγου (citing ἐκ τοῦ ἐμοῦ λήμψεται). He says the same however of the created Angels. See *Early History*, &c. pp. 21—23.

the γένεσις of the Spirit he means no more than His ἐκπόρευσις, the derivation of His Essence from an ἀγέννητος ἀρχή. On the whole we conclude that Origen held substantially the Eternal Procession of the Holy Spirit from the Father through the Son; a view which we shall find supported by the great Greek theologians of the next century, and which differs in little more than expression from the present doctrine of the Western Church.

Dionysius of Alexandria had been Origen's pupil, and one of his successors in the Catechetical School. His view of the Procession may be gathered from a fragment of his Epistle to Dionysius of Rome[1]. Speaking of the indivisibility of the Divine Essence, and of the doctrine known as the *circumincessio*, he says, Τῶν ἀπ' ἐμοῦ λεχθέντων ὀνομάτων ἕκαστον ἀχώριστόν ἐστι καὶ ἀδιαίρετον τοῦ πλησίον...Ἅγιον Πνεῦμα προσέθηκα· ἀλλ' ἅμα καὶ πόθεν καὶ διὰ τίνος ἧκεν ἐφήρμοσα. The Holy Spirit came, he means to say, *from* the Father and *through* the Son—the view we have seen cause to ascribe to Origen. Dionysius adds, Οὔτε ὁ Υἱὸς ἀπῴκισται τοῦ Πατρὸς...ἔν τε ταῖς χερσὶν αὐτῶν ἐστὶ τὸ Πνεῦμα μήτε τοῦ πέμποντος μήτε τοῦ φέροντος δυνάμενον στέρεσθαι. He is speaking of the Spirit's mission, but the eternal relations of the Persons are present to his mind; for 'shortly after this,' as S. Athanasius witnesses[2], 'he adds' Οὕτω μὲν ἡμεῖς (we Catholics in contrast to the followers of Sabellius) εἴς τε τὴν τριάδα τὴν μονάδα πλατύνομεν ἀδιαίρετον, καὶ τὴν τριάδα πάλιν ἀμείωτον εἰς τὴν μονάδα

[1] Routh, *R. S.* III. p. 395. Of the Son he taught (*ib.* p. 394) that He is ποταμὸς ὑπ' [*fors.* ἀπ'] αὐτοῦ [τοῦ Θεοῦ] προχεόμενος = Tertullian's *fontis fluvius*. The fragments are preserved by S. Athanasius (*de sentent. Dionysii*).

[2] Athan. *l. c.* (ap. Routh, III. p. 395).

συγκεφαλαιούμεθα: i.e. our πλατυσμός neither divides the substance nor confounds the Persons: it is a process which does not depend upon the wants of the creature, but which is immanent in the eternal Life of God.

Of the other Alexandrian Catechists of the third century, Pierius, we are informed by Photius, subordinated the Spirit to the Father and the Son[1]. Probably this means that Pierius, like Origen, asserted the production, i.e. the procession of the Holy Ghost from the Father through the Son. Theognostus may be supposed to have held the same view. In a fragment of his work 'On the Blasphemy against the Holy Ghost,' he labours to prove that the unpardonableness of that sin is not due to any superiority of the Spirit over the Son: οὐ διὰ τὴν ὑπερβολὴν τοῦ Πνεύματος πρὸς τὸν Υἱὸν ἄφυκτός ἐστι καὶ ἀσύγγνωστος ἡ εἰς τὸ Πνεῦμα βλασφημία[2]. Photius says that in his *Hypotyposes* Theognostus set himself to establish the ὕπαρξις of the Spirit: i.e. His distinct personal existence[3]. The subject must have led him across the question of the Procession, upon which Photius hints that he expressed the views of Origen[4].

S. Gregory Thaumaturgus, though not a successor of Origen, had been his disciple: and if we

[1] Routh, p. 430. *Early History*, &c. p. 25.

[2] Routh, p. 410. Theognostus accounts for the fact thus: 'Ο μὲν Υἱὸς συγκαταβαίνει τοῖς ἀτελέσι, τὸ δὲ Πνεῦμα σφραγίς ἐστι τῶν τελειουμένων...ἐπὶ μὲν τοῖς ἀτελέσιν ἐστὶ συγγνώμη, ἐπὶ δὲ τοῖς...τελειωθεῖσιν οὐδεμία περιλείπεται συγγνώμης ἀπολογία καὶ παραίτησις.

[3] *Biblioth.* Cod. CVI. (ap. Routh, p. 413) ἐν τῷ τρίτῳ λόγῳ [τῶν ὑποτυπώσεων] περὶ τοῦ Ἁγίου Πνεύματος διαλαμβάνων τίθησι μὲν ἐπιχειρήματα τὴν τοῦ παναγίου Πνεύματος δεικνύειν ὕπαρξιν ἀποπειρώμενος.

[4] *ib.* τὰ δὲ ἄλλα ὥσπερ Ὠριγένης ἐν τῷ περὶ ἀρχῶν οὕτω καὶ αὐτὸς ἐνταῦθα παραληρεῖ. On the Generation of the Son Theognostus was sound: ἐκ τῆς τοῦ Πατρὸς οὐσίας ἔφυ (ap. Athan. *de decr. S. N.* 25).

may regard as genuine the shorter confession which from the days of S. Basil has borne his name, his view of the Procession nearly coincided with Origen's. "There is one Holy Spirit," so this Ante-Nicene ecthesis teaches, *ἐκ θεοῦ τὴν ὕπαρξιν ἔχον καὶ διὰ Υἱοῦ πεφηνὸς [δηλαδὴ τοῖς ἀνθρώποις], εἰκὼν τοῦ Υἱοῦ τελείου τελεία...οὔτε οὖν ἐνέλιπέ ποτε Υἱὸς Πατρὶ οὔτε Υἱῷ τὸ Πνεῦμα*[1]. The bracketed words are open to suspicion; their form suggests the *glossator*: and there is nothing which corresponds to them in the version of Rufinus[2]. Moreover, if the *ἔκφανσις* of the Spirit by the Son had been in Gregory's view merely temporal and economical[3], it is difficult to see why he should have regarded the Spirit as the Perfect Image of the Son, or as cohering to the Person of the Son as the Son coheres to the Father. It is doubtful whether the longer Confession (*ἡ κατὰ μέρος πίστις*) which bears the name of S. Gregory of Neo-Caesarea belongs, in its present form, to so early a writer: but its fuller statement of the Procession-dogma may be given here as a fair comment upon the language of the briefer ecthesis: *ὁμολογοῦμεν ὁμοούσιον εἶναι τῷ Πατρὶ...τὸ Πνεῦμα...τοῦ Πνεύματος ἐκ τῆς οὐσίας τοῦ Πατρὸς δι' Υἱοῦ ἀϊδίως ἐκπεμφθέντος*[4].

[1] Migne X. 986.

[2] Le Quien, *diss. Damasc.* I. 53: "In codicibus Graecis in quos hactenus incidi additur *δηλαδὴ τοῖς ἀνθρώποις*...Quas voculas Gregorianae istius confessionis simplicitas pati non videtur...porro falsatam Thaumaturgi expositionem coarguit vetus interpretatio Latina historiae ecclesiasticae Eusebii quam Ruffinus Aquileiensis adornavit... Eas [voces] etiam non legebat Adrianus I."

[3] *Ib.* "Patribus Graecis tritissimum est quamlibet personae divinae processionem *ἐκφάνσεως* et *ἐκλάμψεως* vocabulo enuntiare: quocirca Gregorius Theologus alicubi ait (*Orat.* XXX. 9) personas divinas ab invicem discriminari ratione *τῆς ἐκφάνσεως ἢ τῆς πρὸς ἄλληλα σχέσεως*."

[4] The larger *ἔκθεσις* has recently been edited by Lagarde in Syriac

One other writer, more distantly related to the school of Origen, must not here be overlooked. S. Methodius, Bishop of Tyre, who flourished in the last years of the third century and was martyred A.D. 311, has much to say about the relation of the Holy Spirit to God, to Christ, and to the Church. His language, however, is so charged with metaphor that it is not easy to determine his precise view of the Procession. He calls the Holy Spirit an *ἐκπορευτὴ ὑπόστασις*, likening Him to Eve, who proceeded from the side of Adam[1]: yet, in another passage, the Church is Eve, and the Spirit is the rib of the Second Adam: *τοῦτο γὰρ κυρίως ἂν ἡ πλευρὰ λέγοιτο τοῦ Λόγου τὸ Πνεῦμα...ἀφ' οὗ λαμβάνων ὁ Θεὸς μετὰ τὴν ἔκστασιν τοῦ Χριστοῦ (ὃ δή ἐστι μετὰ τὴν ἐνανθρώπησιν καὶ τὸ πάθος) τὴν βοηθὸν αὐτῷ κατασκευάζει*[2]. Again, the Spirit is symbolized by the result of two perfect numbers, *καθὸ τῆς γνώσεώς ἐστι τοῦ Υἱοῦ τοῦτο καὶ τοῦ Πατρὸς περιεκτικόν*[3]. Lastly, Methodius regards the Son and the Holy Ghost as personally distinct and as coordinate sources of Grace. They are the Vine and the Fig-tree of the spiritual husbandry[4]. They correspond to the two Olive-trees of Zechariah's vision: *εἶπεν ὁ ἄγγελος, Οὗτοι οἱ δύο υἱοὶ τῆς πιότητος*

from a MS. in the Brit. Mus. dated A.D. 569. On its genuineness see Dorner, I. ii. 480. To the passage quoted above may be added the following: *ὁ προσερχόμενος οἰκείως διὰ Χριστοῦ ἔρχεται. προσελθεῖν δὲ ἀδύνατον τῷ Υἱῷ χωρὶς τοῦ Πνεύματος· τὸ Πνεῦμα γὰρ καὶ ἡ ζωὴ καὶ ἡ ἁγία μόρφωσις τῶν ὅλων· καὶ τοῦτο ἐκπέμπων δι' Υἱοῦ τὴν κτίσιν ὁμοιοῖ πρὸς ἑαυτόν...πρωτότυπος τοῦ Πνεύματος ὁ Κύριος...Ὁμολογοῦμεν οὖν ἕνα Θεὸν ἀληθινὸν μίαν ἀρχὴν, καὶ ἕνα Υἱὸν...καὶ ἓν Πνεῦμα Ἅγιον...ἐκ τῆς οὐσίας τοῦ Θεοῦ ὑπάρχον.*

1 *Fragm.* V. (ed. Jahn, p. 119), *τῆς ἐκπορευτῆς Εὔας σημαινούσης τὴν τοῦ Ἁγίου Πνεύματος ἐκπορευτὴν ὑπόστασιν.*

2 *Conviv.* III. 8 (Migne XVIII. 73).

3 *ib.* VIII. 11 (Migne, 156).

4 *ib.* X. 5 (Migne, 201).

...τὰς δύο λέγων ἀρχεγόνους δυνάμεις εἶναι τὰς δορυφορούσας τὸν Θεόν[1]. On the whole it appears that Methodius, like Origen, derived the Holy Spirit from the Father through the Son, whilst on the other hand he refrained from the dangerous language of his master upon this subject, and once at least anticipated the terminology of the Church.

4. In the West, theological thought was still comparatively dormant. A few Latin writers, chiefly of the North African school, shared the field with teachers of Greek extraction or education. Among the latter are S. Hippolytus, the disciple of S. Irenaeus, and Pope Dionysius; the Latin theologians of the period include S. Cyprian, Novatian and Lactantius.

Neither class of writers has contributed largely to the history of this doctrine. Something indeed might have been expected from Hippolytus, who succeeded Irenaeus as the antagonist of Gnosticism, and Tertullian as the exponent of the Catholic truth of the *monarchia*. But his allusions to the Person of the Holy Spirit are few and meagre; he is content to unfold the relation of the Son to the Father: and this he does by the help of the old theory of an economical gennêsis[2]. 'God, being Alone and having nothing coeval with Himself, willed to create the world: and so willing, He begat the Word to be His Counseller and Agent in the work of Creation—that Word which dwelling within Him unseen He manifests to the world in the

[1] *ib.* x. 6.

[2] Dorner, I. ii. 87—8: "[Hippolytus] assigns the precise moment when the understanding or Word of God was begotten as His Son... Eternal as to His essence, He [the Son] was not eternal as to His Personality...His Sonship was a growing one, and first attained completion at the Incarnation."

creative act. Thus GOD had Another by His side: not as though there were henceforth two gods, but as light streaming from light, as water welling from its source, as the ray beaming from the sun. All things were made by Him: He Alone was from the Father' (*αὐτὸς δὲ μόνος ἐκ τοῦ Πατρός*)[1]. Then, anticipating the Monarchian objection, *Δύο λέγεις θεούς*, he replies, *Δύο μὲν οὐκ ἐρῶ θεοὺς ἀλλ' ἢ ἕνα· πρόσωπα δὲ δύο, οἰκονομίᾳ δὲ τρίτην τὴν χάριν τοῦ Ἁγίου Πνεύματος. Πατὴρ μὲν γὰρ εἷς, πρόσωπα δὲ δύο, ὅτι καὶ ὁ Υἱός· τὸ δὲ τρίτον τὸ Ἅγιον Πνεῦμα...οἰκονομίᾳ συμφωνία συνάγεται εἰς ἕνα Θεόν*[2]. How the existence of the Third Person consists with the Unity, Hippolytus does not undertake to explain: but a hint is dropped which leads the reader to connect the Holy Spirit with the Father, through the Word. The words however are obscure: *δύναμις γὰρ μία ἡ ἐκ τοῦ παντὸς, τὸ δὲ πᾶν Πατὴρ, ἐξ οὗ δύναμις Λόγος...οὗτος [ὁ εἷς] δὲ ἔδωκεν νόμον καὶ προφήτας καὶ δοὺς διὰ Πνεύματος Ἁγίου ἠνάγκασεν τούτους φθέγξασθαι, ὅπως τῆς Πατρῴας δυνάμεως τὴν ἀπόπνοιαν λαβόντες τὴν βουλὴν καὶ τὸ θέλημα τοῦ Πατρὸς καταγγείλωσιν. ἐν τούτοις τοίνυν πολιτευόμενος ὁ Λόγος ἐφθέγγετο περὶ ἑαυτοῦ*[3]. His meaning appears to be that the Spirit, even before the Incarnation, was the *ἀπόπνοια* of the

[1] *c. Noetum* 9 sq. (ed. Lagarde, p. 50): *Θεὸς μόνος ὑπάρχων καὶ μηδὲν ἔχων ἑαυτῷ σύγχρονον ἐβουλήθη κόσμον κτίσαι...αὐτὸς δὲ μόνος ὢν πολὺς ἦν· οὔτε γὰρ ἄλογος οὔτε ἄσοφος οὔτε ἀδύνατος οὔτε ἀβούλευτος ἦν. πάντα δὲ ἦν ἐν αὐτῷ, αὐτὸς δὲ ἦν τὸ πᾶν. ὅτε ἠθέλησεν, καθὼς ἠθέλησεν, ἔδειξε τὸν λόγον αὐτοῦ...πάντα γὰρ τὰ γενόμενα διὰ λόγου καὶ σοφίας* [cf. Theophil. *ad Autolycum* I. 7. I, II. 10] *τεχνάζεται, λόγῳ μὲν κτίζων σοφίᾳ δὲ κοσμῶν...τῶν δὲ γενομένων ἀρχηγὸν καὶ σύμβουλον καὶ ἐργάτην ἐγέννα Λόγον. ὃν Λόγον ἔχων ἐν ἑαυτῷ ἀόρατόν τε ὄντα τῷ κτιζομένῳ κόσμῳ ὁρατὸν ποιεῖ...καὶ οὕτως παρίστατο αὐτῷ ἕτερος...ὡς φῶς ἐκ φωτὸς ἢ ὡς ὕδωρ ἐκ πηγῆς ἢ ὡς ἀκτῖνα ἀπὸ ἡλίου.*

[2] *ib.* 14. (*v. l. οἰκονομία συμφωνίας*). Cf. *infr.* p. 78.

[3] *ib.* 11, 12.

Word: the Word alone is immediately from the Father. On the other hand the Roman Dionysius seems to regard the Holy Ghost only in His relation to the ἀρχὴ θεότητος: 'We must refer the Divine Triad to One Person as Its Head: the Word is one with God in essence, and so must be the Holy Spirit': ἐμφιλοχωρεῖν τῷ Θεῷ καὶ ἐνδιαιτᾶσθαι δεῖ τὸ Ἅγιον Πνεῦμα[1].

The relation of the Spirit to the Son might have been expected to come more clearly into view in the teaching of Tertullian's successors, the Latin writers of the Western Church. Novatian devotes to the Person of the Holy Ghost an entire chapter of his book *On the Trinity*[2]. After laying stress upon the identity of the Paraclete with the Spirit of Old Testament prophecy—"non est in Evangelio novus sed nove datus"—he quotes S. John xv. 26 ("cum venerit Advocatus ille quem ego missurus sum vobis a Patre meo Spiritum veritatis, qui de Patre meo procedit") and after a little continues thus: "Hic est qui in modum columbae super eum venit et mansit habitans in solo Christo plenus et totus...ut ex illo delibationem quandam gratiarum ceteri consequi possint, totius Sancti Spiritus in Christo fonte remanente ut ex illo donorum atque operum venae ducerentur." But this language has only an indirect bearing upon the Eternal Procession; and Novatian offers no comment on the words of Christ. Like Tertullian, he uses *procedere* in reference to the generation of the Son[3].

[1] Routh, *R. S.* III. p. 374. On the other hand since the ἕνωσις is ascribed only to the Word, ἡνῶσθαι ἀνάγκη τῷ Θεῷ τῶν ὅλων τὸν θεῖον Λόγον (*bis:* Routh, pp. 374, 377), Dionysius may have conceived of the Spirit as receiving the Divine Essence through the Son.

[2] c. 29 (Migne III. 943 sq.).

[3] c. 31, "Quando Pater voluit, processit ex Patre."

S. Cyprian enters but slightly upon the doctrine of the Holy Trinity. But the conception and the term are perfectly familiar to him[1]. Thus in the three Apostolical hours of prayer he sees a symbol of the mystery, working out the comparison in a manner which reminds us of Tertullian's view of the Son as intermediate between the Father and the Holy Ghost: "et prima hora in tertiam veniens consummatum numerum Trinitatis ostendit; itemque ad sextam quarta procedens declarat alteram trinitatem; et quando a septima nona completur, per ternas horas trinitas perfecta numeratur. . . Super discipulos hora tertia descendit Spiritus Sanctus, qui gratiam Dominicae promissionis implevit[2]." Elsewhere he rejects as absurd the notion that Christ can be separated from the Holy Spirit, or the Spirit from Christ[3].

Arnobius and Minucius Felix are altogether silent upon the doctrine of the Spirit[4]. Lactantius hardly alludes to it in his extant works. But S. Jerome distinctly affirms that Lactantius denied the personality of the Holy Ghost[5], regarding the Spirit as the sanctifying grace of the Father and the Son, which might be referred to either Person indifferently. Assuming that this writer expressed himself as Jerome declares, we may view his opinion as the

[1] Thus he speaks of the "unitas Patris et Filii et Spiritus Sancti" (*de Dominica orat.* 23), and of the "sacramentum trinitatis quae in novissimis temporibus manifestari habebat" (*ib.* 34).

[2] *de Domin. orat.* l. c. (ed. Hartel, I. p. 292).

[3] *Ep.* LXXIV. 5 (Hartel, II. 803) "quasi possit aut sine Spiritu Christus aut a Christo Spiritus separari."

[4] Dorner, I. ii. p. 193. "Neither Arnobius nor Minucius Felix allude to the Holy Spirit and the Trinity."

[5] S. Hieron. *Ep.* LXXXIV. (Migne XXII. 748), "Lactantius in libris suis et maxime in epistolis ad Demetrianum Spiritus Sancti omnino negat substantiam et more Judaico dicit eum *vel ad Patrem*

attempt of a thoughtful mind, working apart from the guidance of the Church, to express the twofold relation of the Spirit—His relation to the Father and to the Son. Missing the truth which the West has attempted to express by its *Filioque*, he sought to solve the mystery by reducing the personal Holy Spirit of Scripture and of the Creeds into an energy, a virtue or a power, which might easily be conceived of as common to Both[1].

We have now reached the fourth century and the borders of the Arian age without encountering any distinct conflict of opinion within the Church upon the Procession of the Holy Ghost. But the elements of the controversy have been seen to be already at work. The Church has begun to seek an answer to the question, 'Whence is the Spirit of GOD and of Christ? how is He related to the Father? how to the Son?' Already from North Africa and Alexandria the answer has been substantially given, 'He is from the Father; He is through the Son.' But no Church, no individual teacher has yet ventured to say 'He is from Both.'

referri vel filium et sanctificationem utriusque Personae sub eius nomine demonstrari."—On the Person of the Son Lactantius goes far to anticipate Arius: Dorner, I. ii. 212—3.

[1] Among the Latin Church writers of this period Dorner (I. ii. 187 sq.) claims a place for Zeno of Verona, who is usually regarded as Post-Nicene. Zeno deals chiefly with the doctrine of the Son. When he touches upon the Holy Spirit, it is to represent Him as the *vinculum* of the Father and the Son. The following passage is of no little interest: *Tractat.* I. 2, "Alter in altero exsultat cum Spiritus Sancti plenitudine una originali coaeternitate renitens. Quemadmodum, si dicere dignum est, duo maria quae in semet recumbunt, ficto aestu alternos in unum conferente connexa: quae licet sui proprietate locis vocabulisque distincta sint, tamen tunc profundi vaporis una virtus, una substantia, una est fluendi natura." (Migne XI. 389.)

Nor on the other hand have we heard as yet the faintest mutterings of the retort, 'He is from the Father, and from the Father Alone[1].'

[1] The following passages from the *Apostolical Constitutions* may claim a place here. I owe the references to Bunsen (*Analecta Ante-Nicaena*, II.). *Const.* II. 26, οὐδὲ ὁ Παράκλητος ἀφ' ἑαυτοῦ τι λαλεῖ ἢ ποιεῖ· ἀλλὰ δοξάζων τὸν Χριστὸν περιμένει τὸ ἐκείνου θέλημα. VI. 11, καταγγέλλομεν...ἕνα Θεὸν, ἑνὸς Υἱοῦ Πατέρα οὐ πλειόνων, ἑνὸς Παρακλήτου διὰ Χριστοῦ [προβολέα] τῶν ἄλλων ταγμάτων ποιητήν. VII. 41, βαπτίζομαι καὶ εἰς τὸ Πν. τὸ Ἅ., τουτέστι τὸν Παράκλητον, τὸ ἐνεργῆσαν ἐν πᾶσι τοῖς ἀπ' αἰῶνος ἁγίοις, ὕστερον δὲ ἀποσταλὲν καὶ τοῖς ἀποστόλοις παρὰ τοῦ Πατρὸς, κατὰ τὴν ἐπαγγελίαν τοῦ Σωτῆρος ἡμῶν Κ. Ι. Χ. VIII. 37, ὁ ἄναρχος Θεὸς, ὁ τῶν ὅλων ποιητὴς διὰ Χριστοῦ καὶ κηδεμὼν, πρὸ δὲ πάντων αὐτοῦ Θεὸς καὶ Πατὴρ, ὁ τοῦ Πνεύματος Κύριος, καὶ τῶν νοητῶν καὶ αἰσθητῶν βασιλεύς. There is perhaps nothing in these passages which implies Macedonian doctrine. So far as the Procession is in view, it seems to be regarded from Origen's platform.

CHAPTER IV.

THE FOURTH CENTURY IN THE EAST.

Πνευματικῆς ἀληθῶς χρεία τῆς χάριτος ἵνα περὶ Πνεύματος Ἁγίου διαλεχθῶμεν· οὐχ ἵνα τὸ ἄξιον εἴπωμεν, ἀδύνατον γάρ· ἀλλ' ἵνα τὰ ἀπὸ τῶν θείων γραφῶν εἰπόντες ἀκινδύνως διέλθωμεν.

S. Cyrill. Hieros., *Catech.* XVI.

THE Fourth Century is an age of Creeds. Theologians, Catholic and heterodox, have learnt the need of definite and authoritative expressions of belief. The Church has begun to expound the One Faith: heresy is busy with the work of formularizing its many guesses at truth[1].

The Council which condemned Paulus of Samosata had set the example of guarding the deposit of the faith by a synodical ἔκθεσις[2]. Sixty years after

[1] The 'acatholic' Creeds of the 4th century are collected by Hahn, *Bibliothek der Symbole*, pp. 148—174. Twelve forms are given, of which however several are mere recensions. Almost all dwell upon the mission of the Paraclete, neglecting His procession. His mission is regarded as due to the Son. The 2nd Sirmian Creed says, "Spiritus *per Filium est* qui missus venit juxta promissum"; but the Greek version in S. Athan. *de Synodis* runs τὸ Πν. τὸ Ἅ. δι' Υἱοῦ ἀποσταλὲν ἦλθε. For further particulars as to the teaching of these Creeds, see *Early History*, &c. pp. 36—44.

[2] The synodical letter of the Council began, Ἤδη μὲν εἰς λόγους ἀλλήλων ἀφικόμενοι τὴν ἑαυτῶν πίστιν ἐδείξαμεν· ἵνα δὲ φανερώτερα ἅπερ ἕκαστος φρονεῖ γένηται καὶ πέρας ἀσφαλέστερον τὰ ἀμφισβητούμενα λάβῃ, ἔδοξεν ἔγγραφον τὴν πίστιν ἣν ἀπ' ἀρχῆς παρελάβομεν...ἐκθέσθαι. Routh, *R. S.* III. p. 289: or Hahn, p. 91.

this beginning, the First Œcumenical Council followed with its great Catholic Creed, which restored to the Church the *Homoousion*, and fixed the doctrine of the Son's eternal generation ἐκ τῆς οὐσίας τοῦ Πατρός. Before the end of the century an enlarged recension of the Nicene Faith was already in extensive use[1], and had in all probability obtained the sanction of a second Council of Œcumenical authority[2]. This fuller Creed completed the exposition of the Catholic Faith touching the Holy Trinity. As the Son is of the Essence of the Father, so (it was now ruled) is the Holy Ghost[3];

[1] Epiphanius writing in 373—4 thus introduces a Creed substantially the same as the 'Constantinopolitan': Οὕτως ἕκαστον τῶν κατηχουμένων...οὐ μόνον ἀπαγγέλλειν ὀφείλετε τὸ πιστεύειν...ἀλλὰ καὶ διδάσκειν ῥητῶς ὡς πάντων ἡ αὐτὴ μήτηρ ὑμῶν τε καὶ ἡμῶν, τὸ λέγειν, κ.τ.λ. Dr Swainson (*Nicene and Apostles' Creeds*, pp. 80, 86) suggests that this may have been the πίστεως γραφὴ ἑτέρα πλατυτέρα μὲν τῆς ἐν Νικαίᾳ, φυλάττουσα δὲ τὴν αὐτὴν διάνοιαν καὶ οὐ παρὰ πολὺ διαλλάττουσα τῶν ἐκείνης ῥημάτων (Sozom. III. 12), which was accepted by the Western Catholic Bishops at the Council of Sardica in 347.

[2] This is doubted by Mr Lumby (*Hist. of the Creeds*, pp. 68—83), and Prof. Swainson (*N. and A. Creeds*, pp. 120—125). The fact, however, is distinctly affirmed in the Synodical definition of the 4th Œcumenical Council (κρατεῖν δὲ καὶ τὰ παρὰ τῶν ρν' ἁγίων πατέρων ἐν Κωνσταντινουπόλει ὁρισθέντα): and it is difficult to believe that the Council was hoodwinked by Aetius upon so important a matter. In a dissertation just published, Dr Hort maintains that the 'Constantinopolitan' Creed was formed, probably by S. Cyril, *on the basis of the Creed of Jerusalem*. But he admits that the revised Creed may have been produced at the Council of 381 and approved.

[3] There seems no reason to doubt that ἐκ τοῦ Πατρὸς was understood in the sense of ἐκ τῆς οὐσίας τοῦ Πατρός. Reverence for the words of Scripture and tenderness for the scruples of weak brethren may have forbidden the use of the latter phrase. It is remarkable that in all copies of the Creed ἐκ is substituted for the παρὰ of S. John (cf. *supr.* p. 10, note). Can this be due to a desire to represent the Procession of the Spirit as parallel to the Generation of the Son, both being ἐκ τοῦ Πατρός? Dr Hort (*On the 'Constantinopolitan' Creed*, p. 86 sq.) traces the phrase through Athanasius to the Origenists, and ultimately to Tertullian.

with this difference, that the Son is begotten, the Holy Ghost proceeding: [πιστεύομεν] εἰς τὸ Πνεῦμα τὸ Ἅγιον...τὸ ἐκ τοῦ Πατρὸς ἐκπορευόμενον.

We have now to examine the history of this period, so far as it bears upon the doctrine of the Procession.

It will be remembered that Paulus of Samosata implicitly denied the derivation of the Second and Third Persons from the Father[1]. The Council of Antioch found no difficulty in reasserting the Generation of the Son; for had not the Son been declared by the old baptismal symbols of Palestine to be Θεὸς ἐκ Θεοῦ and ἐκ τοῦ Πατρὸς γεννηθείς[2]? But on the derivation of the Holy Ghost the Creeds were silent; and the Antiochene Synod forbore or forgot to enter upon this ground.

The leaven of Paulus, which was a sophistical temper in relation to the truths of revelation rather than a systematic heresy[3], continued to work after the deposition and death of the heresiarch. Lucian, a priest of the Church of Antioch, who was excommunicated along with his chief, remained without the Church during the episcopates of three succeeding Bishops. In later life his views seem to have undergone a reaction: and a Creed which bears his name[4], and possibly formed part of his lost treatise 'On the

[1] See p. 48 *supr.*

[2] Cf. Hahn, pp. 47, 49.

[3] Newman's *Arians*, pp. 4—6. Compare some pertinent remarks on "underground communications" between opposite heresies, *Tracts Theological*, &c. p. 258 sq.

[4] Sozomen will not undertake to assert its genuineness: *H. E.* III. 5, ἔλεγον δὲ ταύτην τὴν πίστιν ὁλόγραφον εὑρηκέναι Λουκιανοῦ τοῦ ἐν Νικομηδείᾳ μαρτυρήσαντος...πότερον δὲ ἀληθῶς ταῦτα ἔφασαν...λέγειν οὐκ ἔχω. See however Bp. Bull, *Def. F. N.* II. xiii. § 6. Bull's defence of Lucian's orthodoxy seems less satisfactory: *ib.* 8. Cf. Neale, *Patriarch. of Antioch*, p. 72.

Faith[1],' discriminates between the Persons of the Trinity in a distinctly anti-Sabellian tone. 'The Father is truly Father, the Son truly Son, the Holy Ghost truly Holy Ghost. The names are not otiose or synonymous: they represent in each case a separate hypostasis which has an order and a glory peculiar to itself[2].' So far all is capable of an orthodox construction; but Lucian adds, *ὡς εἶναι τῇ μὲν ὑποστάσει τρία τῇ δὲ συμφωνίᾳ ἕν*. If the Divine unity consists simply in a perfect harmony, no place is left for the idea of eternal processions in GOD; and thus, starting from a different point of view, the theology of Lucian tends to the same result as that of his master and fellow-countryman, the Samosatene heresiarch.

Dr Newman has not scrupled to say that Lucian, saint[3] and martyr though he was, 'may almost be considered as the author of Arianism[4].' Certain it is that Arius himself and Eusebius of Nicomedia, with half a dozen of the other Arian leaders, prided themselves upon being disciples of Lucian[5]: whilst the Eusebian Council of Antioch (341) adopted his Creed as its own. Thus it seems to have been

[1] Cave, *Hist. liter.* I. p. 155.

[2] Hahn, p. 103: τῶν ὀνομάτων οὐχ ἁπλῶς οὐδὲ ἀργῶς κειμένων ἀλλὰ σημαινόντων ἀκριβῶς τὴν οἰκείαν ἑκάστου τῶν ὀνομαζομένων ὑπόστασιν καὶ τάξιν καὶ δόξαν.

[3] He is commemorated in the Greek Menaea on Oct. 15: see Neale's *Antioch*, l. c. Dr N. adds that S. Lucian is commemorated by the Roman Church on Jan. 7, and by the English Church on the day following. But the Saint commemorated on Jan. 8 is said to have been a different person—a bishop and martyr of the Gallican Church (Blunt, *Annotated Book of C. P.*, p. 39; and see the *Acta Sanctorum*: Jan. 7, 8).

[4] *Arians*, p. 6.

[5] Philostorg., *H. E.* II. 14: τούτου τοῦ μάρτυρος πολλοὺς μὲν καὶ ἄλλους μαθητὰς ἀναγράφει, οἷς καὶ Εὐσέβιον τὸν Νικομηδείας καὶ Μάριν τὸν Χαλκηδόνος καὶ τὸν Νικαίας Θέογνιν συντάττει, καὶ Λεόντιον...καὶ Ἀντώνιον καὶ Μηνόφαντον καὶ Νεομήνιον καὶ Εὐδόξιον· οὐ μὴν ἀλλὰ καὶ Ἀλέξανδρον καὶ Ἀστέριον.

through Lucian that the false method of Paulus made its way into the Churches of Egypt and Asia Minor. Moreover the Arian denial of the Eternal Generation and of the Eternal Procession is but the logical outcome of Lucian's own attempt to discriminate between the Persons by sacrificing the Unity of the Essence.

Seven years after Lucian's martyrdom, the hint which he had dropped was suddenly expanded by Arius into a full-blown heresy (318). The Trinity of Arius is one in which an infinite distance divides the Second Person from the First, and a distance all but infinite the Third from the Second: τὸν γοῦν Λόγον φησὶν εἰς ὁμοιότητα δόξης καὶ οὐσίας ἀλλότριον εἶναι παντελῶς ἑκατέρων τοῦ τε Πατέρος καὶ τοῦ Ἁγίου Πνεύματος[1]. The inference was clear, if Arius did not stop to draw it[2]; the relation of the Spirit to the Father must be that of a creature to the Creator; the relation of the Spirit to the Son that of the second of created beings to the First-begotten. Thus for an eternal procession from the Father Arianism from the first practically substituted *creation by the Son*[3]. The followers of Arius were not slow to draw this conclusion: τολμῶσι λέγειν (S. Epiphanius tells us) κεκτίσθαι ὑπὸ τοῦ Υἱοῦ [τὸ Ἅγιον Πνεῦμα]· ὅπερ ἐστιν ἄκτιστον, ἐκ Πατρὸς ἐκπορευόμενον καὶ τοῦ Υἱοῦ λαμβάνον[4]. There was in fact no other

[1] Athan. *Or. c. Arian.* I. 6.

[2] The confession which Arius and Euzoius presented to Constantine (Socr. *H. E.* I. 26, Hahn, p. 193) went no further into the doctrine of the Holy Ghost than the Nicene Creed had gone: πιστεύομεν...καὶ εἰς τὸ Ἅγιον Πνεῦμα.

[3] Cf. e.g. Athan. *Or. c. Arian.* II. 24: ποιεῖ καὶ κτίζει πρώτως μόνος μόνον ἕνα καὶ καλεῖ τοῦτον Υἱὸν καὶ Λόγον· ἵνα τούτου μέσου γενομένου οὕτω λοιπὸν καὶ τὰ πάντα δι' αὐτοῦ γενέσθαι δυνηθῇ.

[4] *Haer.* LXIX. § 52 (Migne, XLII. 281). Cf. *ib.* § 18, οὗτοι δὲ βούλονται

alternative: the Holy Ghost must be a *κτίσμα* if He were not, as the Gospel of S. John asserted, the *ἐκπόρευμα τοῦ Πατρός.*

Contemporary with Arius, but, although born and bred in Syria, less Antiochene in his theological standpoint than the Alexandrine presbyter, was the cultivated, laborious, yet unsatisfactory Eusebius of Caesarea.

That Eusebius at one time regarded Arius with a tenderness approaching to sympathy is clear from a fragment of his letter to Alexander, which has been preserved among the records of the second Council of Nicaea[1]. If he was induced to subscribe the anathema pronounced against Arius at Nicaea, it was on the ground that in promulgating his views Arius had used certain strange and unscriptural terms[2]. Moreover the Bishop of Caesarea shared the excessive antipathy of the Arian party to quasi-Sabellian language, and its inability to reconcile the doctrine of a coequal and coeternal Triad with the *μοναρχία* which belongs to the Father. His conceptions had been moulded in early life by the ancient Creed of his Church, to which he clung with an affection which led him to

αὐτὸ εἶναι κτίσμα κτίσματος· φασὶ γὰρ ὅτι πάντα δι' αὐτοῦ γέγονε...ἄρα, φασί, καὶ τὸ Πνεῦμα ἐκ τῶν ποιημάτων ὑπάρχει.

[1] *Act.* vi. § 4. "Athanasius," writes Dean Stanley (*Eastern Church*, p. 118), "was convinced that he was at heart an Arian." The Dean cites *de Syn.* c. 17, ὁ δὲ ἀπὸ Καισαρείας τῆς Παλαιστίνης Εὐσέβιος...οὐκ ἐφοβήθη φανερῶς εἰπεῖν ὅτι ὁ Χριστὸς οὐκ ἔστιν ἀληθινὸς θεός. On the other hand see Socr. *H. E.* II. 21, οὔτε ἔχουσι δεῖξαι ὅτι Εὐσέβιος ἀρχὴν τῆς ὑπάρξεως δίδωσι τῷ Υἱῷ τοῦ Θεοῦ, κἂν ταῖς τῆς οἰκονομίας λέξεσι ἐν τοῖς βιβλίοις εὑρίσκωσιν αὐτὸν καταχρώμενον.

[2] Socr. I. 8, καὶ τὸν ἀναθεματισμὸν ... ἄλυπον εἶναι ἡγησάμεθα διὰ τὸ ἀπείργειν ἀγράφοις χρήσασθαι φωναῖς. With a happy inconsistency he accepted the *Homoousion:* ἀλλά γε τὰς λέξεις οὐκ ἠρνήσατο. Ath. *de Syn.* 13.

propose it at Nicaea as the basis of a Catholic Creed. And this Caesarean symbol is of the same general type as the Creed of Lucian: not very definite as to the Eternal Generation, silent upon the Eternal Procession, emphatic in its use of anti-Sabellian language[1]. Nevertheless between Eusebius and Arius there was an impassable gulf. With his Syrian creed Eusebius united an admiration for Origen[2] which preserved him from the presumptuous dialectics of the Arian school. The minute discussion of relations interior to the Nature of GOD was distasteful to the Bishop's religious instincts. He shrank from religious controversy. "Brothers, brothers," he exclaims, "seek not for adversaries to combat: seek rather for souls to save[3]." But the times did not admit of reticence upon the abstruser questions of theology: and in the later writings of Eusebius we have the outline of a theological system which strives to hold the balance between heresy and the Church; and which, in the hands of the Semiarians, nearly succeeded in undoing the work of the Nicene Council, whilst it represented itself to be both 'scriptural' and Catholic.

By Eusebius, as by Origen, the Holy Spirit is regarded as *γενητόν*, but not *κτιστόν*: inferior to the Son, yet Divine. If, as the Church teaches, the Only Begotten is 'Light of Light,' or 'the Sun of Righteousness,' as the Scripture speaks; the Holy Ghost may be likened to the moon, whose light is derived from the sun, but vastly exceeds the bright-

[1] Hahn, p. 48. Τούτων ἕκαστον εἶναι καὶ ὑπάρχειν πιστεύοντες... Πν. Ἅ. ἀληθῶς Πν. Ἅ.—unless this is a comment by Eusebius himself.

[2] Socr. II. 21, ζηλωτὴς καὶ θαυμαστὴς τῶν Ὠριγένους βιβλίων ἐστὶν, ἐν οἷς πανταχοῦ τὸν Υἱὸν ἐκ τοῦ Πατρὸς γεννηθέντα εὑρίσκουσιν οἱ τῶν Ὠριγένους βιβλίων τὸ βάθος κατανοῆσαι δυνάμενοι.

[3] *de fide adv. Sabellium* II. (Migne, XXIV. 1076).

ness of the other luminaries: *τρίτης μετὰ τὴν δευτέραν οὐσίαν ἐν χώρᾳ σελήνης καθισταμένης τοῦ Ἁγίου Πνεύματος, ὃ καὶ αὐτὸ ἐν τῇ πρώτῃ καὶ βασιλικῇ τῆς τῶν ὅλων ἀρχῆς ἀξίᾳ καὶ τιμῇ καταλέγουσιν εἰς ἀρχὴν τῶν μετὰ ταῦτα γενητῶν......οὐ μὴν ἀλλὰ καὶ ἀντιλαμβάνει παρ' ἑτέρου του ἢ παρὰ Θεοῦ Λόγου τοῦ δὴ καὶ ἀνωτέρω καὶ κρείττονος· ὃν δὴ δευτερεύειν ἔφαμεν τῆς ἀνωτάτω καὶ ἀγεννήτου φύσεως Θεοῦ τοῦ παμβασιλέως*[1]. Yet if classed on the one hand with the *γενητά* as the link between God and the world, on the other hand the Holy Spirit is clearly distinguished from the creature by being included in the Divine Triad. The number *three*, Eusebius argues in Platonic style, is *πρώτη τῶν ἐξ ἀρτίων καὶ περιττῶν ἀριθμῶν συνισταμένων· ἄρτιος γὰρ ὁ δύο μονάδα προσλαβὼν τριάδος πρώτην περιττὴν ἐγέννησε φύσιν· πρώτη δὲ τριὰς δικαιοσύνην ἀνέδειξεν ἰσότητος καθηγησαμένη, ὡς ἂν ἀρχὴν καὶ μεσότητα καὶ τελευτὴν ἴσην ἀπολαβοῦσα· εἰκὼν δὲ ταῦτα μυστικῆς καὶ παναγίας καὶ βασιλικῆς Τριάδος*[2]. Thus the Holy Spirit is what He is through the Son: the Holy Scriptures number Him *μετὰ τὸν περὶ Πατρὸς καὶ Υἱοῦ λόγον ἐν τρίτῃ τάξει...ὡς ἂν τῆς τρίτης δυνάμεως πᾶσαν ὑπερβεβηκυίας γεννητὴν φύσιν, οὔσης τε πρώτης μὲν τῶν διὰ τοῦ Υἱοῦ συστασῶν νοερῶν οὐσιῶν, τρίτης δὲ ἀπὸ τοῦ πρώτου αἰτίου*. This is substantially the doctrine of Origen's commentary on S. John. But where Origen falters and hesitates, Eusebius speaks with the confidence of one who has worked out his view into a definite and tangible form.

During the last years of his life Eusebius had occasion to state his doctrine of the Procession still more explicitly. After the Nicene Council,

[1] *Praep. Evang.* VII. 16 (Migne, XXI. 550).
[2] *de laud. Constantini* (Migne, XX. 1348).

one Asterius, a sophist of Cappadocia, who had been a disciple of Lucian and was intimate with Arius and Eusebius of Nicomedia, overran the dioceses of Syria, sowing broadcast a doctrine more Arian than that of Arius himself[1]. The extracts of his 'Syntagma' which are preserved by Athanasius refer to the Person of the Son: but if pressed to their legitimate results, they are subversive of all faith in a Divine Trinity. One of the Bishops who had sat at Nicaea, Marcellus of Ancyra, undertook to answer Asterius. In the heat of his zeal against Arianism and Origenism, Marcellus himself was betrayed into the use of language which, it was said, savoured of Sabellianism or something worse[2].

To refute Marcellus was no distasteful task to Eusebius, to whom it was committed by the Constantinopolitan Synod of 336. In the interval between that Council and his own death, which occurred in 340, the veteran Bishop of Caesarea composed two important treatises on the controversy, his *Contra Marcellum* and *De ecclesiastica theologia*. Marcellus's book, it appears, was 'on the subor-

[1] S. Athan. *de Syn.* 18. 19. His teaching upon the Person of the Son was, Εὐεργετικῇ φιλοτιμίᾳ ἐκτίσθη ὁ Υἱὸς καὶ περιουσίᾳ δυνάμεως ἐποίησεν αὐτὸν ὁ Πατήρ. Yet Asterius acknowledged the procession of the Holy Ghost from the Father (*De eccl. theol.* III. 4, τὸ Πνεῦμα τὸ Ἅγιον, ὡς καὶ Ἀστέριος ὡμολόγησε παρὰ τοῦ Πατρὸς ἐκπορεύεται), understanding the ἐκπόρευσις, no doubt, of simple mission.

[2] Even S. Basil writes (*Ep.* 263 A.D. 377), Πάσης ἡμῶν τῆς ἐλπίδος ἀθέτησιν ἔχει τὸ Μαρκέλλου δόγμα, οὔτε Υἱὸν ἐν ἰδίᾳ ὑποστάσει ὁμολογοῦν ἀλλὰ προενεχθέντα καὶ πάλιν ὑποστρέψαντα εἰς τὸν ὅθεν προῆλθεν, οὔτε τὸν Παράκλητον ἰδίως ὑφεστηκέναι συγχωροῦν. Theodoret (*Haer. fab.* II. § 10) charges him with having called the Third Person παρέκτασιν τῆς ἐκτάσεως. See Montfaucon's *diatr. de causa Marcelli* (Migne, XVIII. 1282 sq.): Newman, *Tracts*, pp. 18 sq., Dorner, I. ii. pp. 271—286. Neale, *Patriarch. of Antioch*, pp. 105—107. Marcellus declared that he had been misunderstood—μὴ νενοῆσθαι αὐτοῦ τὰ συγγράμματα: Socr. I. 36.

dination of the Son.' But he had found it impossible to avoid the cognate subject, and in the passages quoted by Eusebius we have perhaps the first instance of a free use of the theological term ἐκπόρευσις and the earliest formal discussion of the doctrine which it symbolizes. It will be instructive to read the language of Marcellus as it stands in the pages of Eusebius, accompanied by the comments of the latter[1].

The Holy Trinity, Marcellus argued, implies a πλατυσμός of the Unity without separation of the Essence. Πῶς γὰρ, εἰ μὴ ἡ Μονὰς ἀδιαίρετος οὖσα εἰς Τριάδα πλατύνοιτο, ἐγχωρεῖ αὐτὸν [τὸν Σωτῆρα] περὶ τοῦ Πνεύματός ποτε μὲν λέγειν ὅτι ἐκ τοῦ Πατρὸς ἐκπορεύεται· ποτὲ δὲ λέγειν, ''Ἐκεῖνος ἐκ τοῦ ἐμοῦ λήψεται καὶ ἀναγγελεῖ ὑμῖν'· αὖθίς τε ἐμφυσήσαντα τοῖς μαθηταῖς 'Λάβετε Πνεῦμα Ἅγιον' εἰρηκέναι; i. e. If the Divine Essence be not strictly indivisible, how can the Holy Ghost, who proceeds from the Father, be said to receive from that which is the Son's, and to be breathed forth by the Son? Πῶς γὰρ (he continues) εἰ ἐκ τοῦ Πατρὸς ἐκπορεύεται, παρὰ τοῦ Υἱοῦ τὴν διακονίαν ταύτην διακονεῖν ἐπαγγέλλεται; ἀνάγκη γὰρ εἰ δύο διαιρούμενα (ὡς Ἀστέριος ἔφη) πρόσωπα εἴη, ἢ τὸ Πνεῦμα ἐκ τοῦ Πατρὸς ἐκπορευόμενον μὴ δεῖσθαι τῆς παρὰ τοῦ Υἱοῦ διακονίας (πᾶν γὰρ ἐκ τοῦ Πατρὸς ἐκπορευόμενον τέλειον εἶναι ἀνάγκη, μηδαμῶς προσδεόμενον τῆς παρ' ἑτέρου βοηθείας)· ἢ εἰ παρὰ τοῦ Υἱοῦ λαμβάνει καὶ ἐκ τῆς ἐκείνου δυνάμεως διακονοίη τὴν χάριν, μηκέτι ἐκ τοῦ Πατρὸς ἐκπορεύεσθαι. Marcellus sees that the effusion of the Spirit by the Son implies an essential dependence of the Spirit upon the Son which he is at a loss to distinguish from the ἐκπόρευσις. Our

[1] *De eccl. theol.* III. 4—6. (Migne, XXIV. 1002 sq.)

Lord breathed the Spirit upon the Apostles: ἐκ τοῦ Λόγου τὸ Πνεῦμα ἐξῆλθε· πῶς οὖν εἰ ἐκ τοῦ Λόγου τὸ Πνεῦμα προῆλθε πάλιν τὸ αὐτὸ ἐκ τοῦ Πατρὸς ἐκπορεύεται; if the Father and the Son were distinct existences, the procession of the same Spirit from Both would be an impossibility. It will be seen that his own solution of the difficulty approaches very nearly to the present Western belief. The Spirit proceeds from Both as from One ἀρχή, because the Father and the Son are One[1].

The length and elaborate character of Eusebius's reply shew how formidable he felt this argument to be. He begins by denying that the procession either of the Son or of the Spirit implies more than simple mission. The procession[2] of the Son has reference to His Incarnation: ἐπὶ σωτηρίᾳ τοῦ τῶν ἀνθρώπων γένους πρὸς τοῦ Πατρὸς ἐκπεμπόμενος, ἐκ τοῦ Πατρὸς ἐξεληλυθέναι ἑαυτὸν ἔλεγεν. In like manner the Holy Ghost was sent forth to rest upon the Christ at His Baptism and to inspire the Prophets and Apostles; and this is what is meant by His proceeding from the Father: διὸ ἐκ τοῦ Πατρὸς ἐκπορεύεσθαι καὶ αὐτὸ εἴρηται. Even the Evil Spirit and his legions are said in Scripture to "go forth from the Lord[3]." This may not be an exact parallel, but it sufficiently illustrates the general meaning

[1] If from the Western point of view Marcellus erred, it was only in his attempt to explain how the Father and the Son are One.

[2] Eusebius uses ἐκπορεύεσθαι of the Son and of the Spirit indifferently: καὶ ὁ Υἱὸς ἐκ τοῦ Πατρὸς ἐκπορεύεσθαι λέγεται καὶ τὸ Ἅγιον Πνεῦμα ὁμοίως: supporting this application of the term by a reference to Mark iv. 3 (ἐξῆλθεν ὁ σπείρων τοῦ σπεῖραι).

[3] ὁπότε καὶ περὶ τοῦ διαβόλου λέλεκται, Καὶ ἐξῆλθεν ὁ διάβολος παρὰ τοῦ Κυρίου [Job i. 12]· καὶ δεύτερον πάλιν εἴρηται, Ἐξῆλθε δὲ ὁ διάβολος ἀπὸ τοῦ Κυρίου [*ib.* ii. 7]. The Alexandrian MS. of the LXX. gives ἀπὸ προσώπου in the former passage, παρὰ in the latter. The Hebr. is מֵעִם [מֵאֵת] פְּנֵי־יְהוָֹה: cf. the Latin versions, *e facie Domini*.

of a procession from GOD. Procession from GOD implies no more than the original nearness to GOD of the Person who proceeds; *ὁ μονογενὴς Υἱὸς τοῦ Θεοῦ ἐκ τοῦ Πατρὸς ἐξεληλυθέναι ἑαυτὸν διδάσκει διὰ τὸ συνεῖναι αὐτῷ πάντοτε· καὶ τὸ Ἅγιον δὲ Πνεῦμα ὁμοίως.* As for the Spirit's 'receiving from' the Son, such language shews still more clearly the distinctness of His personality: *τὸ γὰρ παρ' ἑτέρου λαμβάνον τι ἕτερον παρὰ τὸν διδόντα νοεῖται.* Nor can the identity of the hypostases of the Father and the Son be inferred from the fact that the Holy Spirit is sent by Both. The Son doeth whatsoever He seeth the Father do: Both, therefore, send the Holy Ghost, *τοῦ μὲν Πατρὸς αὐθεντοῦντος καὶ δωρουμένου τὴν χάριν, τοῦ δὲ Υἱοῦ ταύτῃ* [*fors.* *ταύτην*] *διακονουμένου.* Yet the Person of the Holy Ghost is doubtless dependent on the Son: the Son alone receives a direct communication of the Father's deity: the Spirit derives from the Son all that He is and has: *ὁ δὲ Υἱὸς μόνος Πατρικῇ θεότητι τετιμημένος ποιητικὸς ἂν εἴη καὶ δημιουργικὸς τῆς τῶν γενητῶν ἁπάντων...καὶ δὴ καὶ τῆς τοῦ Παρακλήτου Πνεύματος ὑπάρξεως.* The Son is the Only Begotten GOD, Who is in the Bosom of the Father: the Paraclete Spirit is neither GOD [i. e. the Father], nor Son, since He has not, like the Son, received His origin [immediately] from the Father, but is one of the things which were made by the Son. Such, says Eusebius, is the Catholic faith: such the teaching of Holy Scripture and of the Church concerning the mystery of the Holy Trinity[1].

[1] *De eccl. theol.* III. 6 (Migne, XXIV. 1013), *καὶ μόνος μὲν αὐτὸς εἷς Θεὸς καὶ Πατὴρ...χρηματίζοι ἄν, ὁ δὲ Υἱὸς μονογενὴς Θεὸς...τὸ δὲ παράκλητον Πνεῦμα οὔτε Θεὸς οὔτε Υἱός· ἐπεὶ μὴ ἐκ τοῦ Πατρὸς ὁμοίως τῷ Υἱῷ καὶ αὐτὸ τὴν γένεσιν εἴληφεν ἓν δέ τι τῶν διὰ τοῦ Υἱοῦ γενομένων τυγχάνει...Ταῦτα μὲν οὖν τῆς καθολικῆς καὶ ἁγίας ἐκκλησίας ὧδέ πη διὰ τῶν*

In this controversy between Marcellus and Eusebius the question of the Procession is collateral only, but the subject is worked out far enough to throw light upon the opinions which were held on either side. Marcellus maintains the essential derivation of the Holy Ghost from the Father and the Son[1], although he does not venture to speak of an *ἐκπόρευσις* from the Son. Eusebius anticipates the modern view of the Procession, as being simple mission. But when pressed for an answer to the question 'Whence then is the Holy Ghost?' he replies with Origen, 'He was produced by the Son.' On both sides it is held that the Third Person stands in some essential relation to the Son; but whilst Eusebius carries this idea to the extent of explaining away the essential procession from the Father, Marcellus lays himself open to the charge of merging the distinct personality of the Son and the Spirit in the Oneness of Their Divine Life.

From Eusebius of Caesarea we pass to another influential Bishop of Palestine, who, like Eusebius, but with less reason, has fallen under the suspicion of heterodoxy. The Catechetical Lectures of S. Cyril were delivered in A. D. 347—8, some ten years after the publication of Eusebius's reply to Marcellus. Of these lectures, the 16th and 17th form the earliest of the many patristic treatises upon the doctrine of the Holy Ghost. We turn to them eagerly, hoping to learn the view of the Procession

θείων φωνῶν παραδίδοται τὰ μυστήρια. Of Marcellus Eusebius adds, *μίαν ὑπόστασιν τριπρόσωπον ὥσπερ καὶ τριώνυμον εἰσάγει, τὸν αὐτὸν εἶναι λέγων τὸν Θεὸν καὶ τὸν ἐν αὐτῷ Λόγον καὶ τὸ Ἅγιον Πνεῦμα.*

[1] Baur, *Dogmengesch.* I. ii. p. 205: "in der griechischen Kirche sprach zuerst Marcell von Ancyra von einem Ausgehen des Geistes sowohl vom Vater als vom Sohn." Cf. however, Langen, *die Trinitarisches Lehtdifferenz*, p. 23.

which the Church of Palestine had reached by the middle of the fourth century. This expectation, however, is disappointed. Of the office and work of God the Holy Ghost S. Cyril seems to have spoken with especial delight, reminding his catechumens that on the very spot where they stood, the Spirit had first descended upon the Church[1]. But he shrinks with a proportionate dread from handling so awful a subject in the spirit of an investigator. He cannot forget the warning of the Gospel concerning blasphemy against the Holy Ghost: he determines to confine himself in this matter to the very words of Holy Scripture: *λεγέσθω τοίνυν ὑφ' ἡμῶν περὶ Ἁγίου Πνεύματος μόνα τὰ γεγραμμένα· εἰ δέ τι μὴ γέγραπται, μὴ πολυπραγμονῶμεν*[2]. His most dogmatic passage is one in which he strings together the teachings of Our Lord upon the subject, adding the remark, *Αὐτοῦ τοῦ Μονογενοῦς νῦν ἀνέγνων σοι τὰς φωνάς, ἵνα μὴ προσέχῃς ἀνθρωπίνοις ῥήμασιν*[3]. It is satisfactory to find such a mind thoroughly made up upon the Deity of the Spirit, and equally removed from the Origenistic notion of a *γένεσις* of the Third Person, and from that which frittered away the fact of His distinct personality[4]. A few casual expressions point to a more or less definite belief in His procession from the Father, and from or through the Son: as when he says that the Spirit of God is *ζῶν καὶ ὑφεστὼς*

[1] *Catech.* XVI. 4 (Migne, XXXIII. 924), *οἴδαμεν τὸ Πνεῦμα τὸ Ἅγιον τὸ λαλῆσαν ἐν προφήταις, καὶ ἐν τῇ Πεντηκοστῇ κατελθὸν...ἐνταῦθα ἐν Ἱερουσαλὴμ...Πάντων γὰρ παρ' ἡμῖν ἔστι τὰ ἀξιώματα.*

[2] *ib.* 2 (Migne, 920).

[3] *Catech.* XVII. 11 (Migne, 984).

[4] Cf. *Catech.* IV. 16, *τὴν αὐτὴν ἔχε περὶ αὐτοῦ δόξαν ἣν παρέλαβες ἔχειν περὶ Πατρὸς καὶ Υἱοῦ.* VI. 6, *τῆς θεότητος τῆς πατρικῆς ἐστὶ σὺν τῷ Πνεύματι τῷ Ἁγίῳ κοινωνὸς ὁ Υἱός.* XVII. 2, *τῶν ὑπὸ Θεοῦ διὰ Χριστοῦ γενομένων ἁπάντων λογικῶν καὶ ἀγγέλων καὶ ἀνθρώπων ἐστὶν ἁγιαστικόν.*

καὶ πάντοτε Πατρὶ καὶ Υἱῷ συμπαρὸν, οὐκ ἀπὸ στόματος καὶ χειλέων Πατρὸς ἢ Υἱοῦ λαλούμενον ἢ ἀναπνεόμενον[1], i. e. not parted, after the analogy of human breath, from Either of the Persons by Whom He is breathed forth. Or again, when he suffers himself to write, Καὶ Πατὴρ μὲν δίδωσιν Υἱῷ, καὶ Υἱὸς μεταδίδωσιν Ἁγίῳ Πνεύματι, citing S. John xvi. 13, 14[2]; although, as if to avoid being drawn further into this question, he immediately turns the subject with the customary remark, Αὔταρκες ἡμῖν εἰδέναι ταῦτα...εἰ γὰρ ἦν γεγραμμένον ἐλέγομεν· ὃ οὐ γέγραπται μὴ τολμήσωμεν· αὔταρκες ἡμῖν εἰδέναι πρὸς σωτηρίαν ὅτι ἔστι Πατὴρ καὶ Υἱὸς καὶ Ἅγιον Πνεῦμα. Nor must we altogether blame S. Cyril for this unwillingness to discuss the mystery of the Holy Spirit's relation to God, seeing that the Church, the witness and keeper of God's word, had as yet advanced no further in her Creed than to express belief in the Person of the Holy Ghost[3].

From Palestine we proceed to Egypt, where for nearly half a century the battle of the Faith raged round the person of a single orthodox champion. From 326 to 373 the history of the Alexandrian Patriarchate is the history of the sufferings and triumphs, the exiles and restorations, of 'Athanasius the Great[4].'

[1] *Catech.* XVII. 5 (Migne, 973). [2] *ib.* XVI. 24 (Migne, 952).

[3] The Coislin MS. (after *Catech.* XVI. 3), adds *inter alia*, Τοῦτο οὖν ἐστὶ τὸ Πνεῦμα εἰς ὃ πιστεύομεν...τὸ ἐκ τοῦ Πατρὸς ἐκπορευόμενον· τὸ ἐκ θεότητος Πατρὸς καὶ Υἱοῦ ὑπάρχον. In Migne's *Patrologia* this fragment is rejected as supposititious, with the comment, "cuius sit auctoris reperire non potuimus...vetustiorem Graecorum theologiam omnino sapere videntur et Graecorum contra Latinos disputationibus antiquiora." Theodorus Lascaris (*de proc. Sp. S.* p. 14) cites the passage against the Latins as S. Cyril's, but with the reading τὸ ἐκ τῆς θεότητος τοῦ Πατρὸς ὑπάρχον.

[4] Stanley, *Eastern Church*, p. 269: "not only in name and office,

S. Athanasius was before all things a Teacher[1]; and it is happy for the Church that periods of enforced absence from his flock afforded him leisure for committing to writing his conceptions of the mystery which he lived to expound and defend. In his earlier writings the particular point of doctrine with which we are concerned is regarded merely in its bearing on the great dogma of the *Homoousion*. Thus the *Exposition of the Faith*[2], while dealing at length with the Deity and Incarnation of the Word, dismisses the Procession of the Spirit in these few words: τὸ Ἅγιον Πνεῦμα ἐκπόρευμα ὂν τοῦ Πατρὸς ἀεί ἐστιν ἐν ταῖς χερσὶ τοῦ πέμποντος Πατρὸς καὶ τοῦ φέροντος Υἱοῦ[3]. In the *Orations against the Arians* the relation of the Spirit to the Son comes more distinctly into view; but it is approached from its Christological side. The Son, Athanasius argues, must be of one substance with the Father; for equally with the Father, He possesses the Spirit as His very own. When He says, Ἐγὼ ἁγιάζω ἐμαυτόν, what is this but to say, Ἐγὼ Λόγος ὢν τοῦ Πατρὸς αὐτὸς ἐμαυτῷ ἀνθρώπῳ γενομένῳ δίδωμι τὸ Πνεῦμα[4]? The same Person being God and Man both gave and received the Spirit: διδοὺς μὲν ὡς Θεοῦ Λόγος, λαμβάνων δὲ ὡς ἄνθρωπος. As

but in fact Athanasius was the representative of the Egyptian Church."

[1] Erasmus (quoted in Smith's *Dict. Biogr.* art. 'Athanasius'): "habebat vere dotem illam quam Paulus in episcopo putat esse praecipuam, τὸ διδακτικόν...totus est in explicanda re."

[2] Migne, XXV. 203 sq. Canon Swainson (*N. and A. Creeds*, p. 73) doubts the Athanasian authorship of this document, though, as he reminds us, it was accepted without hesitation by the Benedictine editor, and by Dr Routh. The absence of all allusion to the Macedonian heresy seems to be sufficient proof of its early date.

[3] The formula ἐν ταῖς χερσί, κ.τ.λ seems to be borrowed from the Alexandrian Dionysius: cf. *supr.* p. 65.

[4] *Or.* I. 46 (Migne, XXVI. 108).

God, He gave the Spirit before He was made Man: πρὸ τῆς ἐνανθρωπήσεως Λόγος ὢν ἐχορήγει τοῖς ἁγίοις ὡς ἴδιον τὸ Πνεῦμα[1]. So far was He from receiving His relation to the Father from the Spirit, that the Spirit is said to receive from the Son all that He has: οὐ τὸ Πνεῦμα τὸν Λόγον συνάπτει τῷ Πατρὶ, ἀλλὰ μᾶλλον τὸ Πνεῦμα παρὰ τοῦ Λόγου λαμβάνει.... οὗτος γὰρ, ὥσπερ εἴρηται, τῷ Πνεύματι δίδωσι· καὶ ὅσα ἔχει τὸ Πνεῦμα, παρὰ τοῦ Λόγου ἔχει[2].

About the year 358 the rise of the Tropici, the Egyptian forerunners of the Pneumatomachi and Macedonians[3], compelled the great champion of the Faith to enter more directly upon the doctrine of the Holy Ghost. The *Letters to Serapion* present us with his maturer judgment upon the Procession; and their language sometimes falls very little short of that of the Western Creed which bears his name. He declares the relation of the Spirit to the Son to be the same in point of essence and rank as the relation of the Son to the Father: τοιαύτην τάξιν καὶ φύσιν ἔχοντος τοῦ Πνεύματος πρὸς τὸν Υἱὸν οἵαν ὁ Υἱὸς ἔχει πρὸς τὸν Πατέρα[4]. He proceeds to unfold the ground of this relation: as the Son is ἴδιος τῆς οὐσίας τοῦ Πατρός, inasmuch as He is ἐκ τοῦ Πατρός, so the Spirit is ἴδιον κατ' οὐσίαν τοῦ Υἱοῦ, because He also is ἐκ τοῦ Θεοῦ[5]. To

[1] *ib.* 48.

[2] *Or.* III. 24 (Migne, 376). Cf. *ib.* 44, εἰ τὸ Πνεῦμα οἶδεν πολλῷ μᾶλλον ὁ Λόγος ἢ Λόγος οἶδεν παρ' οὗ καὶ τὸ Πνεῦμα λαμβάνει.

[3] *Early history*, &c. pp. 47—49.

[4] *Ad Serap.* I. 21 (Migne, 580). Cf. *ib.* III. 1, οἵαν γὰρ ἔγνωμεν ἰδιότητα τοῦ Υἱοῦ πρὸς τὸν Πατέρα ταύτην ἔχειν τὸ Πνεῦμα πρὸς τὸν Υἱὸν εὑρήσομεν. The Spirit is thus the Image of the Son, as the Son is the Image of the Father: *ib.* 24, εἰκὼν τοῦ Υἱοῦ λέγεται καὶ ἔστι τὸ Πνεῦμα.

[5] *ib.* 25. *infr.* 31, ἡνωμένον τῷ Υἱῷ ὡς ὁ Υἱὸς ἥνωται τῷ Πατρί.

say that the Spirit proceeds out of the Father, is to say in other words that the Spirit 'shines forth' from the Son Who is of the Father: ἐκ Πατρὸς λέγεται ἐκπορεύεσθαι, ἐπειδὴ παρὰ τοῦ Λόγου τοῦ ἐκ τοῦ Πατρὸς ὁμολογουμένου ἐκλάμπει καὶ ἀποστέλλεται καὶ δίδοται[1]. It seems impossible to regard this ἔκλαμψις of the Spirit from (παρά) the Word as implying less than an essential derivation[2]. To preserve the μοναρχία S. Athanasius carefully avoids the use of ἐκ[3] and ἐκπορεύεται: yet the *Filioque* is already substantially present in his words.

Overshadowed by the grandeur of Athanasius, Didymus the blind Catechist of Alexandria is yet scarcely inferior to the Patriarch in the power with which he unfolds and defends the Faith[4]. Two of his extant treatises touch upon the doctrine of the Procession. The *De Trinitate*, of which the Greek original was happily recovered during the last century[5], is clear and strong upon the eternal procession of the Holy Ghost from the Father. S. Paul's "τὸ Πνεῦμα τὸ ἐκ τοῦ Θεοῦ" is interpreted to mean "τὸ ἐκ τοῦ Θεοῦ τῆς ὑποστάσεως ἐκπορευθέν:" and the effusion of the Spirit is represented as the out-

[1] *ib.* 20. Contrast the cautious words of the pseudo-Athanasian *Quaestiones* (Migne, XXVIII. 786): τὸ Πνεῦμα ἐκ μόνου τοῦ Πατρὸς αἰτιατὸν καὶ ἐκπορευτὸν, διὰ δὲ τοῦ Υἱοῦ ἐν τῷ κόσμῳ ἀποστελλόμενον.

[2] See the remarks of Van der Moeren, p. 82. Dean Stanley has perhaps correctly said that this is "the nearest approach to the Double Procession (*sic*) in the writings of Athanasius." (*Eastern Ch.*, p. 290.) Cf. however, *ad Serap.* iii. 1, ἐξ αὐτοῦ δίδοται πᾶσιν.

[3] Once at least he uses διά: *ad Serap.* III. 5 (Migne, XXVI. 633), οὐ γὰρ ἐκτός ἐστι τοῦ Λόγου τὸ Πνεῦμα· ἀλλὰ ἐν τῷ Λόγῳ ὂν ἐν τῷ Θεῷ δι' αὐτοῦ ἐστιν. I owe this reference to Dr Pusey's useful summary of patristic evidence on the Latin side (in the preface to Mr P. Pusey's translation of S. Cyril Alex. *Comm. on S. John*).

[4] According to Socrates (IV. 25), Didymus was in his own Church and age μέγιστος συνήγορος τῆς οἰκείας πίστεως.

[5] It was first printed in 1769 by J. A. Mingarelli.

come of this essential relation: εὖ δὲ καὶ τὸ '᾿ξέχεεν,' ἅτε ὕδωρ ἐξ αὐτοῦ ὁμοουσίως ἐκπορευθέν[1]. Both the effusion and the procession are such as to involve no separation from the Divine essence: ἔρχεται ἀνάρχως ἐκπορευθὲν παρὰ τοῦ Πατρὸς τὸ πανταχοῦ ἀεὶ παρὸν καὶ ὑπάγει πρὸς αὐτὸν, ὡς Πνεῦμα αὐτοῦ ἀχώριστον ὑπάρχον τῇ θεότητι· ἀρρήτως γὰρ προῆλθεν ἐξ αὐτοῦ φύσει καὶ ἐπέστραπται πρὸς αὐτόν[2]. In these respects the two processions from God are entirely parallel: ἐκ τοῦ ἑνὸς Πατρὸς φύσει...προῆλθον αἱ μακάριαι ὑποστάσεις αὗται. εἰς τὸν αὐτὸν ἕνα ἀνάγονται. Moreover, the two are absolutely coeternal: ἐπὶ τῶν κτισμάτων ἡγεῖται τῷ χρόνῳ ὁ πρωτότυπος· ἐπὶ δὲ τοῦ Θεοῦ οὐχ οὕτως· ἀλλὰ συνυφεστώτως καὶ συμπροεληλυθότως[3]. The Spirit, however, by virtue of the *circumincessio*, whilst eternally proceeding from the Father, eternally abides with the Son: τὸ Πνεῦμα ἐκπορεύεται παρὰ τοῦ Πατρὸς καὶ μένει παρὰ τῷ Υἱῷ θεϊκῶς[4]. If so, may He not also be said to

[1] *de Trin.* II. 2 (Migne, XXXIX. 456, 7).

[2] *ib.* (Migne, 675). Cf. II. 1, τὸ μόνον ἐκ τῆς ὑποστάσεως αὐτοῦ [*sc.* τοῦ Πατρὸς] ἀνάρχως καὶ ἀδιαιρέτως ἐκπορευθέν....μιᾶς καὶ τῆς αὐτῆς ὂν οὐσίας καὶ τῆς Πατρικῆς ἔξω γενέσθαι συνυπάρξεως μὴ δυνάμενον.

[3] *ib.* I. (Migne, 460).

[4] *de Trin.* I. 31 (Migne, 426). Cf. the Apocryphal *Acts of S. Andrew* (Tischendorf, *Acta App. Apocr.* p. 105: Migne, II. 1218): Πνεῦμα Ἅγιον τὸ ἐκ τοῦ Πατρὸς ἐκπορευόμενον καὶ ἐν τῷ Υἱῷ διαμένον ὅπως δειχθῇ ἓν Πνεῦμα Ἅγιον τὸ ἐν τῷ Πατρὶ καὶ Υἱῷ ὑπάρχον ἐν θεότητι τιμίᾳ. Didymus (*de Trin.* II. 27) cites an 'oracle,' which corresponds with this teaching:

> Πνεῦμα μὲν ἀθανάτοιο Θεοῦ Πατρὸς ἐκπροπόρευμα
> αὐτόθεν ἔνθεν ἔβη, μένον ἔμπεδον οὔτε μεριστόν·
> ἀλλὰ Θεοῖο Λόγοιο μένον ζαθέοις ὑπὸ κόλποις.
> πάντα τελεῖ ἅτε θεῖος ἃ μήδεται ἀρχέγονος φρήν.

[Even the reactionary anti-Christian poetry of the fourth century had caught the language and main idea of the Procession-dogma. The *Philopatris* of the pseudo-Lucian, which is now ascribed to the time

issue forth from the Son (παρὰ τοῦ Υἱοῦ) with Whom He dwells? Some attempt is made to answer this question in the other extant work of Didymus (*de Spiritu Sancto.*). This work, however, has reached us only in a Latin dress; the latinity is S. Jerome's, but there is reason to fear that later hands have tampered with his work. The following passages, if they truly represented the original, would seem to prove that Didymus held a doctrine of the Procession which exceeded the requirements of the present Western Creed:

§ 34. "Salvator, qui et Veritas, ait, 'non enim loquetur a semetipso;' hoc est, non sine me et sine meo et Patris arbitrio, quia inseparabilis a mea et Patris est voluntate: quia non ex se est sed ex Patre et me. hoc enim ipsum quod subsistit et loquitur a Patre et me illi est.: ego veritatem loquor; id est, inspiro quae loquitur, siquidem Spiritus veritatis est[1]." § 36. "non potest Filio loquente audire quae nescit, cum hoc ipsum sit quod profertur a Filio, id est, procedens a Veritate, consolator manans de consolatore, Deus de Deo, Spiritus veritatis procedens[2]." § 37. "neque enim quid aliud est Filius exceptis his quae ei dantur a Patre; neque alia substantia est Spiritus Sancti praeter id quod datur ei a Filio[3]."

It is probable that the weight of this testimony

of Julian, supplies a well-known instance. A Christian is asked by an enquiring Pagan,

καὶ τίν' ἐπομόσομαί γε;

He answers:

ὑψιμέδοντα Θεὸν, μέγαν, ἄμβροτον, οὐρανίωνα,
Υἱὸν Πατρὸς, Πνεῦμα ἐκ Πατρὸς ἐκπορευόμενον.]

[1] Migne, XXXIX. 1063.

[2] Migne, 1064.

[3] Migne, 1065.

would be much reduced by the recovery of the Greek treatise[1]. Yet, after making the largest allowance for interpolations, there remains wrought into the texture of these extracts enough to shew that, in the view of their author, the procession from the Father does not exclude an essential 're-ceiving from the Son:' that, in fact, he regarded these two statements as representing different as-pects of one and the same eternal truth.

Whatever doubt may remain as to the posi-tion which S. Didymus occupies in the history of this doctrine, there can be none, one would sup-pose, with regard to the views of his contemporary, S. Epiphanius. That remarkable man filled the see of Constantia in Cyprus from the year 368 down to the beginning of the fifth century. But the most im-portant of his theological works belong to the early part of this long episcopate; the *Ancoratus* was written in the year 373—4, and the *Panarium* was at least commenced within the next two years[2].

[1] In the first two passages the MSS. appear to vary considerably. Of three MSS. which I have examined one (Brit. Mus., *Burney* 281, *saec.* XI.) agrees with the printed text. The other two (Brit. Mus., *Reg.* 5. B. VII., *saec.* XII. (*b*): Gonville and Caius, 131 (*g*), written between 1438 and 1444, *i.e.* while the Co. of Florence was sitting), read as follows: "inseparabilis a mea et patris est uoluntate, hoc enim ipsum quod subsistit et loquitur ego ueritas [*so g:* ueritatem *b*] loquor." "non potest filio loquente audire quae nescit cum hoc ipsum sit quod pro-fertur a filio. denique, &c. [*omitting* id est—sp. ueritatis procedens.] A fourth MS. (Jesus Coll. Oxf. III. § 3. *saec.* XI.) agrees as to omissions with (*b*) and (*g*), though in some minor points it differs from both. [I owe this information to the kindness of Mr J. R. Thursfield, the present librarian of Jesus College, who has sent me a careful collation of the passage.] These MSS., however, contain the third extract without any substantial variation. It may be added that Ratramn, writing against the Easterns in 863, quotes the second passage in its shorter form: in the first, the printed text of his *Opposita* makes him hesitate between the shorter form and the longer (Migne, *Patr. Lat.* CXXI. 262—3). Cf. Procopowicz, p. 248.

[2] Cave, *Hist. lit.* (anno 368).

It is startling to read in any book, Greek or Latin, of this date, statements upon the doctrine of the Procession so fully developed and dogmatically precise[1] as the following:—

Ancor. 8, 9. αὐτὸς ὁ Μονογενὴς λέγει 'τὸ Πνεῦμα τοῦ Πατρός·' καὶ 'τὸ ἐκ τοῦ Πατρὸς ἐκπορευόμενον·' καὶ 'ἐκ τοῦ ἐμοῦ λήψεται·' ἵνα μὴ ἀλλότριον νομισθείη Πατρὸς μηδὲ Υἱοῦ, ἀλλὰ τῆς αὐτῆς οὐσίας, τῆς αὐτῆς θεότητος....Πνεῦμα...Θεοῦ καὶ Πνεῦμα τοῦ Πατρὸς καὶ Πνεῦμα τοῦ Υἱοῦ......ἐν μέσῳ Πατρὸς καὶ Υἱοῦ ἐκ τοῦ Πατρὸς καὶ Υἱοῦ...Θεὸς ἐκ Πατρὸς καὶ Υἱοῦ[2]: *ib.* 67, Χριστὸς ἐκ τοῦ Πατρὸς πιστεύεται Θεὸς ἐκ Θεοῦ· καὶ τὸ Πνεῦμα ἐκ τοῦ Χριστοῦ, ἢ παρ' ἀμφοτέρων: *ib.* 70, 71, τὸ δὲ Ἅγιον Πνεῦμα παρ' ἀμφοτέρων, Πνεῦμα ἐκ Πατρός....φῶς τρίτον παρὰ Πατρὸς καὶ Υἱοῦ[3]: *ib.* 73, τολμῶ λέγειν ὅτι...[οὐδεὶς ἔγνω] τὸ Πνεῦμα, εἰ μὴ ὁ Πατὴρ καὶ ὁ Υἱὸς, παρ' οὗ ἐκπορεύεται καὶ παρ' οὗ λαμβάνει· καὶ οὐδὲ τὸν Υἱὸν καὶ τὸν Πατέρα, εἰ μὴ τὸ Πνεῦμα τὸ Ἅγιον, ὃ παρὰ τοῦ Πατρὸς καὶ ἐκ τοῦ Υἱοῦ[4]. *Panar. haer.* LXII. ἀεὶ γὰρ τὸ Πνεῦμα σὺν Πατρὶ καὶ Υἱῷ, οὐ συνάδελφον Πατρὶ οὐ γεννητὸν, οὐ κτιστὸν, οὐκ

[1] Petavius (*de Trin.* VII. 3) hardly exceeds the truth when he says that the passages from Epiphanius are so clear "ut nemo clarius ac dilucidius etiam Latinorum patrum locutus sit." Attempts have been made to set aside his evidence on the plea of the expressions being ambiguous (cf. Van der Moeren, pp. 105—6) or the text corrupt (Procopowicz, p. 80, note). But allowing all due weight, especially to the latter objection, the balance of evidence seems to be greatly in favour of the view taken above. On the other hand it should be conceded that in his distinct adhesion to the doctrine expressed by the *Filioque*, Epiphanius stands alone among Greek Fathers of the fourth century.

[2] Migne, XLIII. 30.

[3] Migne, 137. This passage and the next are repeated in the *Panarium*, into which (*Haer.* LXXIV. §§ 2—11) *Ancor.* 65—74 is transcribed at length.

[4] Migne, 153.

ἀδελφὸν Υἱοῦ, οὐκ ἔγγονον Πατρός· ἐκ Πατρὸς δὲ ἐκπορευόμενον καὶ τοῦ Υἱοῦ λαμβάνον· οὐκ ἀλλότριον Πατρὸς καὶ Υἱοῦ, ἀλλ' ἐκ τῆς αὐτῆς οὐσιάς, ἐκ τῆς αὐτῆς θεότητος, ἐκ Πατρὸς καὶ Υἱοῦ, σὺν Πατρὶ καὶ Υἱῷ· Πνεῦμα Χριστοῦ, Πνεῦμα Πατρός[1].

Quotations might be multiplied[2], but these are sufficient to exhibit Epiphanius's view of the Procession. It seems clear that he regards the Son as being together with the Father, in the Unity of Their Consubstantial Life, the One Source and Origin of the Holy Ghost. His expressions cannot be limited to the temporal mission, for he speaks of the very Essence from Which the Spirit is derived. It is equally impossible to understand him as referring simply to the consubstantiality of the Persons or to the συμπεριχώρησις. The prepositions ἐκ and παρά are used as convertible forms: the Holy Spirit is ἐκ τοῦ Υἱοῦ, He is παρὰ τοῦ Πατρός: or He is ἐκ Πατρός, He is παρ' ἀμφοτέρων. In one particular only Epiphanius falls short of the theologians of Florence: he does not use, or rather he goes out of his way to avoid the use of such terms as *proceed, procession*, when speaking of the Spirit's derivation from the Son. He adheres to the very words of Christ, and teaches that the Spirit is 'from Both', inasmuch as He 'proceeds from' the Father and 'receives from' the Son.

[1] Migne XLI. 1056.

[2] See (e.g.) *haer.* LXIX. 54 (after citing Ps. XXXV. 10) ἵνα δείξῃ φῶς τὸν Πατέρα, καὶ φῶς τοῦ Πατρὸς εἶναι τὸν Υἱὸν, καὶ φῶς τὸ Πνεῦμα τὸ Ἅγιον· καὶ πηγὴν ἐκ πηγῆς, ἐκ τοῦ Πατρὸς καὶ τοῦ Μονογενοῦς τὸ Πν. τὸ Ἅ. *Ancor.* 70 (=*haer.* LXXIV. § 7), σοφία ὅλος ὁ Θεός. οὐκοῦν σοφία ὁ Υἱὸς ἐκ σοφίας...τὸ δὲ Ἅγιον Πν. παρ' ἀμφοτέρων, πνεῦμα ἐκ πνεύματος. On the other hand the Greeks cite *haer.* LXXVI. (Migne XLII. 573), Πνεῦμα ἐνηνοχέναι τὸν μόνον μόνῳ ἐπὶ Μονογενεῖ γεννήτορα, where at the most nothing is implied beyond the μοναρχία (cf. Procopowicz, 76; Neale, *H. E. Ch.* Introd. II. p. 1103).

Another remark is important. We have proof that S. Epiphanius did not include an exact definition of the Spirit's relation to the Son among the essentials of the Catholic Faith. His *Ancoratus* closes with two Creeds; a shorter form, which represents the express teaching of 'our common Mother,' the Catholic Church[1]; and a second of considerable length, which had been recently adopted by all orthodox Bishops (so Epiphanius tells us) as a fence against the thickening assaults of heresy. In the former of these documents the Holy Spirit is described simply as τὸ ἐκ τοῦ Πατρὸς ἐκπορευόμενον: in the latter it is merely added, Καὶ ἐκ τοῦ Υἱοῦ λαμβάνον (*v. l.* λαμβανόμενον). Moreover, it is a significant fact that even this scriptural προσθήκη did not succeed in establishing itself in the Creed of the Eastern Church. Whilst the shorter Epiphanian Creed received the sanction of Œcumenical Councils, the longer form remains only on the pages of the *Ancoratus*[2]. Some of the Oriental liturgies emphasize the truth that the Holy Ghost 'receives from the Son[3]'; but the Eastern Creed has steadily clung to the simple statement that He proceeds from the Father.

A less decided view of the subject was reached by the greater contemporaries of Epiphanius, S. Basil of Caesarea, his brother S. Gregory of Nyssa, and S. Gregory of Nazianzus, surnamed the Theologian.

[1] v. *supr.* p. 76, notes.

[2] See, however, Dr Hort's *Dissert.* p. 117 sq.

[3] See Renaudot, *liturg. Orient.* I. p. 199, II. pp. 354, 540; esp. his remarks in II. p. 72, "Orientales...in liturgicis aliisque precibus ubi de processione Spiritus Sancti sermo est, vulgo dicunt *qui a te procedit et a Filio accipit*...aliquando addunt *accipit ea quae ad illius essentiam pertinent.*" *Infr.* pp. 151, 152.

(*a*) By S. Basil, as by S. Athanasius, the doctrine of the Procession was regarded as one of the outworks of the greater truth of the Homoousion. To prove the essential procession of the Spirit from GOD, was to prove that the Spirit was essentially Divine. He labours, therefore, to shew that the Procession is eternal and *κατ' οὐσίαν*. The Holy Ghost is not 'of GOD' in the same sense in which the creatures are of Him: *ἐκ τοῦ Θεοῦ εἶναι λέγεται, οὐχ ὡς τὰ πάντα ἐκ τοῦ Θεοῦ· ἀλλ' ὡς ἐκ τοῦ Θεοῦ προελθόν*[1]. And a real procession from the Being of GOD must be eternal as GOD is eternal: *οὐκ ἐν χρόνῳ πρόεισι τὸ προϊὸν ἐκ Θεοῦ...ἐστὶν ἀεὶ τὸ Πνεῦμα*. The Spirit is the Breath of GOD, which proceedeth from the Father[2]: the Breath of GOD is not to be regarded as a temporary spiration, (*ἀτμὸς ἐκ τῶν ἀναπνευστικῶν μερῶν ἐξωθούμενος*); but as coeval with the Father Who breathes It forth[3]. Thus the Deity of the Spirit and His relation to the Father are determined; but what of His relation to the Son? S. Basil replies that this is similar to the relation which the Son bears to the Father: *ὡς ἔχει ὁ Υἱὸς πρὸς τὸν Πατέρα, οὕτω πρὸς τὸν Υἱὸν τὸ Πνεῦμα*[4]. If the Son is the Image of the Father, so is the Spirit the Image of the Son[5]. If the Son is the Word of the Father, the Spirit is the utterance (*ῥῆμα*) of the Son[6]. He is not indeed called the *Son*

[1] *de Sp. S.* XVIII. (Migne XXXII. 152).

[2] *hom. in Ps.* xxxii. (Migne XXIX. 334) *ὡς ὁ δημιουργικὸς Λόγος ἐστερέωσε τὸν οὐρανὸν, οὕτω τὸ Πνεῦμα τὸ ἐκ τοῦ Θεοῦ ὃ παρὰ τοῦ Πατρὸς ἐκπορεύεται (τουτέστιν ἐκ τοῦ στόματος αὐτοῦ, ἵνα μὴ τῶν ἔξωθέν τε καὶ τῶν κτισμάτων αὐτὸ κρίνῃς, ἀλλ' ὡς ἐκ Θεοῦ ἔχον τὴν ὑπόστασιν δοξάζῃς) ἁπάσας τὰς ἐν αὐτῷ δυνάμεις συνεπέφερε.*

[3] *de Sp. S.* XVI. (Migne XXXII. 136). [4] *de Sp. S.* XVII.

[5] *adv. Eunom.* v. (Migne XXIX. 723).

[6] *ad Eunom.* v. (Migne, 731).

of the Only-Begotten, because the use of such language would open the door to most serious error; *ἕτοιμον γὰρ ἦν ὑπολαβεῖν ὡς...εἴπερ Υἱὸς ἐξ Υἱοῦ γεγέννηται, καὶ ἐκ τούτου πάλιν ἕτερος ἂν εἴη γεγεννημένος, καὶ πάλιν ἄλλος καὶ ἐπὶ πλῆθος ἑξῆς*[1]. He is not Son, but He is the Spirit of the Son; and this implies two things: (1) His oneness of Essence with the Son (*ὡς ᾠκειωμένον κατὰ τὴν φύσιν αὐτῷ*)[2], and (2) His manifestation through the Son (*τὸ διὰ Υἱοῦ πεφηνέναι*)[3]. In the Life of God, the Spirit depends upon the Son as the Son upon the Father, yet so that the Father is the *αἰτία* of Both: *τὸ Ἅγιον Πνεῦμα τοῦ Υἱοῦ μὲν ἤρτηται ᾧ ἀδιαστάτως συγκαταλαμβάνεται, τῆς δὲ τοῦ Πατρὸς αἰτίας ἐξημμένον ἔχει τὸ εἶναι, ὅθεν καὶ ἐκπορεύεται.* As he who lays hold on one end of a chain draws the preceding links with it; so he who attracts to himself the Holy Ghost attracts also the Presence of the Son and of the Father: *ὥσπερ ἐξ ἁλύσεως ὁ τοῦ ἑνὸς ἄκρου ἁψάμενος καὶ τὸ ἕτερον ἄκρον συνεπεσπάσατο, οὕτως ὁ τὸ Πνεῦμα ἑλκύσας, δι' αὐτοῦ καὶ τὸν Υἱὸν καὶ τὸν Πατέρα συνεφειλκύσατο*[4]. Thus the procession of the Spirit, if *from* the Father, is *through* the Son. Our knowledge of God advances *ἀπὸ Πνεύματος διὰ Υἱοῦ ἐπὶ Πατέρα*[5]. The essential Life of God flows on in the converse order: *ἡ φυσικὴ ἀγαθότης καὶ ὁ κατὰ*

[1] *ib.* (Migne, 733), *οὐ διὰ τὸ μὴ εἶναι ἐκ Θεοῦ δι' Υἱοῦ, ἀλλ' ἵνα ὁ τριὰς μὴ νομισθῇ πλῆθος ἄπειρον.*

[2] *de Sp. S.* XVIII. (Migne XXXII. 152).

[3] *adv. Eunom.* V. (Migne XXIX. 734).

[4] *Ep.* XXXVIII. (Migne XXXII. 329 sq.). This letter is found among the works of S. Greg. Naz. under the title *ad Petrum fratrem.* But the style is Basil's, and it was cited under his name at the Council of Chalcedon. The true heading is Γρηγορίῳ (i. e. τῷ Νύσσης] ἀδελφῷ περὶ διαφορᾶς οὐσίας καὶ ὑποστάσεως.

[5] *de Sp. S.* XVIII. (Migne XXXII. 153). Cf. *Ep.* XXXVIII. ἀφ' οὗ πᾶσα ἐπὶ τὴν κτίσιν ἡ τῶν ἀγαθῶν χορηγία πηγάζει.

φύσιν ἁγιασμὸς καὶ τὸ βασιλικὸν ἀξίωμα ἐκ Πατρὸς διὰ τοῦ Μονογενοῦς ἐπὶ τὸ Πνεῦμα διήκει[1]. Eunomius indeed had erred and erred fatally in regarding the Second Person as the sole *αἰτία* of the Third[2]: yet his error does not prevent S. Basil from teaching very distinctly and repeatedly that the Spirit is *ἐκ Θεοῦ δι' Υἱοῦ.* On the contrary, the Saint regards this belief as the best safeguard of the Catholic doctrine: *οὕτω καὶ αἱ ὑποστάσεις ὁμολογοῦνται καὶ τὸ εὐσεβὲς δόγμα τῆς μοναρχίας οὐ διαπίπτει.* Yet on the other hand, he is satisfied with the simple statement of the Gospel that the Holy Ghost proceeds from the Father. Thus the confession which he offers as a test of orthodoxy to Eustathius of Sebasteia, says nothing of the δι' Υἱοῦ: *οὔτε ἀγέννητον λέγομεν τὸ Πνεῦμα τὸ Ἅγιον...οὔτε γεννητόν..τὸ δὲ Πνεῦμα τῆς ἀληθείας ἐκ τοῦ Πατρὸς ἐκπορεύεσθαι διδαχθέντες, ἐκ τοῦ Θεοῦ εἶναι ὁμολογοῦμεν ἀκτίστως*[3]. The doctrine of the relation of the Spirit to the Son may be latent in the *ἐκ τοῦ Θεοῦ* of the last clause; but it is certainly not imposed as a condition of Catholic communion.

Further, S. Basil never suffers himself to pass from the δι' Υἱοῦ into the ἐξ Υἱοῦ[4] or *παρ' ἀμφοτέρων*

[1] *de Sp. S.* XVIII. [2] *Early History*, &c., pp. 60—2.

[3] *Ep.* CXXV. (Migne XXXII. 549).

[4] Perhaps the nearest approach to this phraseology is to be found in *adv.* Eunom. III. I (Migne XXIX. 656) *ἀξιώματι μὲν γὰρ δευτερεύειν τοῦ Υἱοῦ παραδίδωσιν ἴσως ὁ τῆς εὐσεβείας λόγος...ὡς γὰρ ὁ Υἱὸς τάξει μὲν δεύτερος τοῦ Πατρὸς ὅτι ἀπ' ἐκείνου, καὶ ἀξιώματι ὅτι ἀρχὴ καὶ αἰτία...φύσει δὲ οὐκέτι δεύτερος διότι ἡ θεότης ἐν ἑκατέρῳ μία· οὕτω δηλονότι καὶ τὸ Πνεῦμα τὸ Ἅγιον εἰ καὶ ὑποβέβηκε τὸν Υἱὸν τῇ τε τάξει καὶ ἀξιώματι (ἵνα καὶ ὅλως συγχωρήσωμεν) οὐκέτ' ἂν εἰκότως ὡς ἀλλοτρίας ὑπάρχον φύσεως ἀκολουθεῖν ἐκεῖθεν δῆθεν.* I subjoin part of the foot-note of the Benedictine editor: "Locum nullum esse arbitror aut ipsius Basilii aut aliorum Sanctorum Patrum de quo acrius in concilio Florentino disputatum sit...Latini, ut patet ex sess. 20 [Mansi 31, p. 774] proferebant

of Epiphanius. He seems of set purpose to avoid expressions of this kind. Writing 'against the Anomœans' he says, Τὴν μὲν πρὸς Πατέρα οἰκειότητα [τοῦ Πνεύματος] νοῶ, ἐπειδὴ 'ἐκ Πατρὸς ἐκπορεύεται·' τὴν πρὸς Υἱὸν δὲ, ἐπειδὴ ἀκούω, 'εἴ τις Πνεῦμα Χριστοῦ οὐκ ἔχει, οὗτος οὐκ ἔστιν αὐτοῦ[1].' One can imagine that the temptation may have been strong to represent the relation of the Spirit to the Father and to the Son as resting on identical grounds—on a procession from Both. Such a representation would have supplied a readier answer to the heresies he was attacking. But S. Basil refrains.

(*b*) S. Gregory of Nyssa pursued the same train of thought, but with less caution and reserve. Thus, in a treatise against the Macedonians he illustrates the relations of the Divine Hypostases by the bold and certainly very inadequate metaphor of three torches, of which the second has been lighted from the first and the third from the second: ὡσπερανεί τις ἐν τρισὶ λαμπάσι διῃρημένον βλέπων τὴν φλόγα· αἰτίαν δὲ τοῦ τρίτου φωτὸς ὑποθώμεθα εἶναι τὴν πρώτην φλόγα ἐκ διαδόσεως διὰ τοῦ μέσου[2]. In other passages Gregory supplies the necessary correction: the Holy Ghost, he says, is posterior to the Son only in conception and with reference

codicem vetustissimum in quo sic legebatur: ἀξιώματι μὲν γὰρ δεύτερον τοῦ Υἱοῦ παρ' αὐτοῦ τὸ εἶναι ἔχον καὶ παρ' αὐτοῦ λαμβάνον καὶ ἀναγγέλλον ἡμῖν καὶ ὅλως τῆς αἰτίας ἐκείνης ἐξημμένον...Graeci vero haec verba...in suo libro vetustissimo quoque et optimo deesse affirmabant, hodieque in editis et in nostris septem MSS. desunt." On the other hand see Van der Moeren's elaborate defence of the addition (*de process.* pp. 89—94).

[1] *hom. adv. Sabell. et Anom.*

[2] *adv. Maced.* 6 (Migne XLV. 1308). Card. Mai (*nov. patr. bibl.* IV. p. 20) rightly exclaims 'en processionem a Patre per Filium!' adding, with less exactness, 'sane nihil evidentius hoc exemplo trium lucernarum est pro dogmate de processione *ab utroque*.'

to the 'Cause' (*κατὰ τὸν τῆς αἰτίας λόγον*[1]). He admits two distinctions in God: a distinction between the Cause and that which is caused (*τὴν κατὰ τὸ αἴτιον καὶ αἰτιατὸν διαφορὰν οὐκ ἀρνούμεθα*); and a distinction between two different modes of the latter (*τοῦ ἐξ αἰτίας ὄντος πάλιν ἄλλην διαφορὰν ἐννοοῦμεν*). These two modes are (1) by direct production from the *αἰτία*, (2) by indirect production through that which is produced directly. Concerning this latter distinction Gregory's own words must be given at length; they are too remarkable to be condensed. Τὸ *μὲν γὰρ προσεχῶς ἐκ τοῦ πρώτου, τὸ δὲ διὰ τοῦ προσεχῶς ἐκ τοῦ πρώτου· ὥστε καὶ τὸ μονογενὲς ἀναμφίβολον ἐπὶ τοῦ Υἱοῦ μένειν, καὶ τὸ ἐκ τοῦ Πατρὸς εἶναι τὸ Πνεῦμα μὴ ἀμφιβάλλειν· τῆς τοῦ Υἱοῦ μεσιτείας καὶ αὐτῷ τὸ μονογενὲς φυλαττούσης, καὶ τὸ Πνεῦμα τῆς φυσικῆς πρὸς τὸν Πατέρα σχέσεως μὴ ἀπειργούσης*[2]. Thus from S. Gregory's point of view the Son is the *μεσίτης* in the Divine Triad, through whom the essential life of the Father eternally flows to the Holy Ghost[3]. The Son and the Spirit have One Cause (*αἰτία*), the Father: but the Son derives His Being directly from the Father, the Spirit issues mediately through the Son.

It is disputed whether in a fragment belonging

[1] *c. Eunom.* I. (Migne XLV. 463).

[2] *Ep. ad Ablabium*, 'quod non sint tres Dii,' (Migne XLV. 133), cf. Baur, *Dreieinigkeit*, III. 163, "wie der Sohn sich zum Vater verhält, so der Geist zum Sohn, sagt Basilius; und Gregorius von Nyssa erklärte sich hierüber näher so [quoting the passage just given]. Hier ist demnach deutlich ausgesprochen dass der Geist zwar aus dem Vater ist, aber nicht unmittelbar, sondern durch die Vermittlung des Sohns."

[3] So too with regard to the Divine life in man: cf. *Ep.* 5, (Migne XLVI. 1032), ἐκ τοῦ Θεοῦ πηγάζουσα διὰ δὲ τοῦ Υἱοῦ προϊοῦσα ἐν δὲ τῷ Ἁγίῳ Πνεύματι ἐνεργουμένη.

to his third oration *On the Lord's Prayer* S. Gregory of Nyssa permits himself to express this mediate causation by the phrase ἐκ τοῦ Υἱοῦ. The words are as follows:

ἴδιον τοῦ Πατρὸς τὸ μὴ ἐξ αἰτίου εἶναι. τοῦτο οὐκ ἐστὶν ἐπὶ τοῦ Υἱοῦ καὶ τοῦ Πνεύματος· ὅ τε γὰρ Υἱὸς 'ἐκ τοῦ Πατρὸς ἐξῆλθεν'... καὶ τὸ Πνεῦμα 'ἐκ τοῦ Θεοῦ,' καὶ 'παρὰ τοῦ Πατρὸς ἐκπορεύεται'... ὁ μονογενὴς Υἱὸς 'ἐκ τοῦ Πατρὸς' παρὰ τῆς ἁγίας γραφῆς ὀνομάζεται...τὸ δὲ Ἅγιον Πνεῦμα καὶ 'ἐκ τοῦ Πατρὸς' λέγεται, καὶ †ἐκ† τοῦ Υἱοῦ εἶναι προσμαρτυρεῖται, 'εἰ γάρ τις Πνεῦμα Χριστοῦ οὐκ ἔχει, οὗτος οὐκ ἐστὶν αὐτοῦ'...οὐκοῦν τὸ μὲν Πνεῦμα τὸ ἐκ τοῦ Θεοῦ ὂν καὶ Χριστοῦ Πνεῦμά ἐστιν· ὁ δὲ Υἱὸς ἐκ τοῦ Θεοῦ ὢν οὐκέτι καὶ τοῦ Πνεύματος οὔτε ἐστὶν οὔτε λέγεται[1].

Judging from internal evidence it is difficult to believe that S. Gregory wrote the suspected preposition. Even Petavius saw and admitted that the context required its omission[2]. The writer is citing the express testimony of Scripture, and the passage which he produces goes no further than to call the Holy Spirit Πνεῦμα Χριστοῦ. Is it conceivable that upon this evidence he would have founded the statement ἐκ τοῦ Υἱοῦ εἶναι προσμαρτυρεῖται?

Cardinal Mai has recently re-asserted the claims

[1] Mai, *nov. patr. bibl.* IV. 53. Cf. J. G. Krabinger: *S. Greg. Nyss. de precatione orat.* pp. 64, 146. The entire context is wanting in Migne's reprint of Morell's edition (*Patr. Gr.* XLIV.).

[2] *de Trin.* VII. 3, "Ego vero cum illum Gregorii locum diligentius intueor in eam opinionem adducor alienam ab isto esse praepositionem ἐκ, scripsisseque Gregorium τὸ δὲ Ἅγιον Πνεῦμα καὶ ἐκ Πατρὸς λέγεται καὶ τοῦ Υἱοῦ εἶναι προσμαρτυρεῖται." Leo Allatius (*dissert. Damasc.* I. § xlvii.) adds, "subnotare quoque mihi liceat auctorem ex Scripturae variis locis argumentari in quibus Sp. S. ex Patre procedere legitur atque insuper perhibetur esse Sp. Filii; nusquam autem ex Filio esse."

of the preposition on the strength of important MS. testimony[1]. It is found in a Vatican MS. which in Mai's judgement belongs to the 7th or 8th century, and is therefore older than the time of Photius. The discovery exonerates disputants on the Latin side from the charge of interpolation, but it can hardly be regarded as having closed the question as to the genuineness of the longer form. It is perhaps safer to attribute the repetition of ἐκ to the carelessness of an early copyist than to an oversight on the part of S. Gregory himself: for more than an oversight it could scarcely have been in such a context. Even if we accept the 'ἐκ τοῦ Υἱοῦ' as Gregory's, the words must be interpreted by his own fuller formula, 'ἐκ διαδόσεως διὰ τοῦ μέσου.'

(*c*) A third member of the great Cappadocian group remains. In the history of the Church S. Gregory of Nazianzus fills a more important place than his namesake of Nyssa: and in the East he has long shared with the Apostle S. John the distinctive name of 'the Divine[2].' But it did not fall within this father's province to develope

[1] Mai found the entire passage missing in two out of eleven MSS. which he examined. Of the remaining nine, eight presented the reading καὶ τῷ Υἱῷ προσμαρτυρεῖται: but in one of these (Cod. Vat. 448 *saec.* XI.) the words τῷ Υἱῷ were written over an erasure where (in Mai's judgment) ἐκ τοῦ Υἱοῦ had formerly stood. This latter form was actually found in the ninth MS. (Cod. Vat. 2066, *saec.* VII. or VIII.), where it had been noted in the margin by some latinizing Greek of later days with a triumphant 'εὖ σοί, μέγιστε Γρηγόριε.' To the Cardinal the discovery seemed to turn the scale of victory on the Latin side: "qua visa," he confesses, "'*vicimus*' exclamavi."—[A facsimile of the MSS. is given in the frontispiece of the *nov. patr. bibl.* tom. IV.]

In a British Museum MS. which I have consulted, *Burney* 52 (*saec.* XIV.), the whole context is missing (from πᾶσα γὰρ ἡ ἐνέργεια to ἐν ἀλλήλοις ἀλλασσομένων).

[2] v. Suicer, *s. v.* θεολόγος.

the doctrine of the Procession. He was content to establish the Deity of the Holy Spirit, and for this purpose it sufficed to exhibit His relation to the Father. Circumstances also may have led Gregory to shrink from a minuter examination of the subject. The Pneumatomachi and Eunomians offered an analysis of the mystery: the Catholic Bishop refused to follow their presumptuous lead. In an oration which was perhaps his opening address to the people of Constantinople (379), he deprecates discussion in this fashion: *Ἀκούεις ὅτι τὸ Πνεῦμα προϊὸν ἐκ τοῦ Πατρός· τὸ ὅπως μὴ πολυπραγμόνει. εἰ δὲ πολυπραγμονεῖς,...κἀγώ σου πολυπραγμονῶ τὸ κρᾶμα ψυχῆς καὶ σώματος· πῶς εἶ χοῦς καὶ εἰκὼν Θεοῦ· τί τὸ κινοῦν σε, ἢ τί τὸ κινούμενον· πῶς τὸ αὐτὸ καὶ κινεῖ καὶ κινεῖται... Εἰ ταῦτα οὐ κατέλαβες,... πῶς Θεὸν ἀκριβῶς εἰδέναι ὑπολαμβάνεις*[1]; Later in the same year he sums up the Catholic doctrine in these words: *κοινὸν Πατρὶ μὲν καὶ Υἱῷ καὶ Ἁγίῳ Πνεύματι τὸ μὴ γεγονέναι καὶ ἡ θεότης. ἴδιον δὲ Πατρὸς μὲν ἡ ἀγεννησία, Υἱοῦ δὲ ἡ γέννησις, Πνεύματος δὲ ἡ ἔκπεμψις.* Again he declines to pursue the enquiry: 'to ask for further knowledge is to act as if you were content to leave nothing to be revealed in a future state, nothing to be known by God Alone[2].'

But in spite of Gregory's dissuasives the discussion continued, and in the 5th of the 'Theological Orations' (380), there is a renewed protest against the perverse ingenuity of the heterodox. 'The Holy Spirit,' they argued, 'must be either generate or ingenerate. If He is ingenerate, there

[1] *Orat.* XX. (Migne XXXV. 1077).

[2] *Orat.* XXV. (Migne XXXV. 1221), *τί καταλείψεις τοῖς μόνον γινώσκειν ἄλληλα καὶ γινώσκεσθαι ὑπ' ἀλλήλων μαρτυρουμένοις, ἢ καὶ ἡμῖν τοῖς ἐκεῖθεν ἐλλαμφθησομένοις ὕστερον;*

are Two Unoriginated Principles. If He is generate, He is so either from the Father or from the Son. If from the Father, there are two Sons in the Trinity; if from the Son, there are two Fathers.' Gregory retorts that this introduction of materialistic conceptions into the region of theology is a return to the exploded systems of gnosticism. To press the alternative of 'Generate or Ingenerate' is to raise a false issue. Why should there not be a mean between the two states? In fact, a Theologian greater than the subtlest of mere human dialecticians has revealed to us that there is a third state in GOD, viz. *τὸ ἐκπορευτόν*. That which exists by 'proceeding' from GOD is itself Divine, and yet it is neither unoriginate, nor, on the other hand, generated: *καθόσον μὲν ἐκεῖθεν ἐκπορεύεται, οὐ κτίσμα· καθόσον δὲ οὐ γεννητὸν, οὐχ Υἱός· καθόσον δὲ ἀγεννήτου καὶ γεννητοῦ μέσον, Θεός.* 'Do you still insist upon knowing what is understood by procession? On one condition only I will answer: *εἰπὲ σὺ τὴν ἀγεννησίαν τοῦ Πατρὸς κἀγὼ τὴν γέννησιν τοῦ Υἱοῦ φυσιολογήσω καὶ τὴν ἐκπόρευσιν τοῦ Πνεύματος*[1].' It will be observed that in this passage the orator abstains from following his adversary into the dilemma 'the Spirit, if generated, is either from the Father or from the Son.' He is content to shew that the Spirit was not generated at all, seeing that, according to Christ's own teach-

[1] *Orat. theol.* V. 7, 8 (Migne XXXVI. 140—1). Cf. a fine passage in the Epiphany Sermon for Jan. 6, 381 (Migne XXXV. 347), τὸ Πν. προϊὸν μὲν ἐκ τοῦ Πατρὸς οὐχ υἱϊκῶς δὲ, οὐδὲ γὰρ γεννητῶς· ἀλλ' ἐκπορευτῶς εἰ δεῖ τι καὶ καινοτομῆσαι, περὶ τὰ ὀνόματα σαφηνεέας ἕνεκεν οὔτε τοῦ Πατρὸς ἐκστάντος τῆς ἀγεννησίας...οὔτε τοῦ Υἱοῦ τῆς γεννήσεως...οὔτε τοῦ Πνεύματος ἢ εἰς τὸν Πατέρα μεταπίπτοντος ἢ εἰς Υἱὸν· ὅτι ἐκπεπόρευται καὶ ὅτι θεός...ἡ γὰρ ἰδιότης ἀκίνητος. See also *Orat. theol.* IV. (Migne XXXVI. 127), ταῦτα μὲν οὖν ἐστὶ κοινὰ θεότητος τὰ ὀνόματα ἴδιον δὲ, κ.τ.λ.

ing, He proceeds from the Father. The question of His relation to the Son is alien to S. Gregory Nazianzen's purpose: nor does it seem to have been once raised in the great battle between Arianism and Catholicity which was fought out at Constantinople during Gregory's episcopate.

The poems of S. Gregory are, like his orations, explicit as to the procession from the Father, but silent as to any derivation either from or through the Son. In the following lines he seems almost willing to exclude the thought of such a derivation, in his anxiety to refute the heretical *ex Filio:*

* * * * ἐκ μὲν ἀνάρχου
Πατρὸς Υἱός... ἐκ δ' ἄρα Παιδὸς
οὐκέτι παῖς ἀγαπητὸς ὁμοίϊον εὖχος ἐφέλκων·
ὥς κεν ὁ μὲν μίμνῃ γενέτης ὅλος, αὖταρ ὅ γ' Υἱὸς
οἶον καὶ μούνοιο μονώτατος· εἰς ἓν ἰόντε
Πνεύματι σὺν μεγάλῳ, τό ῥα Πατρόθεν εἶσιν ὁμοῖον[1].

In a dogmatical poem on the Holy Spirit, Gregory ventures so far as to illustrate the relations of the Holy Trinity by those of Adam, Eve, and Seth:

ἐξ ἑνὸς ἀρχεγόνοιο δάμαρ καὶ Σὴθ ἐγένοντο.
* * * * * * * *
οὐ τεκτὴ τεκτός τε, βροτοί γε μὴν ἔσκον ὁμοίως[2].

Here Eve is plainly the type of the ἐκπορευτόν, Seth of the γεννητόν, whilst Adam represents the common ἀρχή. The comparison must not be pressed, but it is scarcely consistent with any belief in a procession from the Son.

[1] *Carm. moral.* I. (Migne XXXVII. 524). Cf. *carm. hist.* II. I (Migne, 630).

[2] *carm. dogmat.* III. (Migne XXXVII, 408). The comparison seems to have been traditional: cf. *supr.* p. 68.

On the whole, the mind of the Eastern Church at this period is perhaps more faithfully reflected by the reticence of S. Gregory the Theologian than by the more speculative tone of S. Basil and S. Gregory of Nyssa, or the dogmatic precision of S. Epiphanius. The procession of the Holy Ghost through the Son was undoubtedly maintained by a majority of the great Church teachers who flourished in the East during the Fourth Century: by one of them, perhaps by two, the Father and the Son were regarded as the joint Source from which the Spirit issues forth. But the Church, as represented by her Councils and Creeds, was content to assert that He 'proceedeth from the Father;' or if any attempt was made to supplement the words of Christ, this was done by appending to them other words bearing the same Divine sanction—'And which receiveth of the Son.'

CHAPTER V.

THE WEST, FROM A.D. 325 TO A.D. 431.

"Patre et Filio auctoribus confitendus est."
S. HILAR. *de Trin.* II. 29.

"Fatendum est Patrem et Filium principium esse Spiritus Sancti."
S. AUG. *de Trin.* V. 15.

IN summoning the Bishops to Nicaea, Constantine hoped to secure the attendance of representatives from the West as well as from the East[1]. How far he succeeded with regard to the West is uncertain. The extant list of subscribing Bishops contains few Western names, but it is explained that "the names of the Westerns (i.e., of the less illustrious among them) were not written[2]." Of those who undoubtedly were members of the Council several occupied positions of the widest influence. The Spanish Church sent Hosius of Cordova, the African Church was represented by Caecilian of Carthage: Eustorgius came from Milan, Nicasius from Gaul, Protogenes from Sardica: two Roman presbyters sat in the place of the aged Bishop of the capital[3].

[1] Cowper's *Analecta Nicaena*, p. 21. [2] *ib.* p. 27.

[3] Cf. Dean Stanley's graphic account of the Westerns, *Eastern Church*, pp. 127—130.

These deputies from the West upon their return to their several dioceses could scarcely have failed to infuse into the Latin Churches somewhat of that zeal for the Faith which was manifested at Nicaea. The case of S. Hilary, who had been a Bishop for some time before he heard the Nicene Creed[1], may be regarded as exceptional: it proves nothing more than the isolation of Western Gaul during the quarter of a century which followed the Council of Nicaea. Long before 350 the war cries of the Catholic and Arian camps must have been familiar to the less secluded dioceses of the West: if little was known or remembered of the doings at Nicaea, the visits of S. Athanasius to Treves and to Rome [336—343] afforded Western Catholics ample opportunities of becoming acquainted with the intricacies of Eastern controversy. After the death of Constans, the West became, almost more than the East, the battle-field of Arianism and orthodox Christianity. Under these circumstances it is not strange that the Western Church, hitherto so reticent on strictly theological subjects, about the middle of the fourth century begins to take its full share in the history of Trinitarian doctrine. In the West, as in the East, the Procession of the Holy Ghost occupied at this period a secondary place in Christian thought: yet from the first it was seen to be an element in the wider question of the Homoousion which neither side could safely disregard.

First among the Westerns who touched upon

[1] Hil. *de Syn.* (Migne x. 545), "regeneratus pridem et in episcopatu aliquantisper manens fidem Nicaenam numquam nisi exsulaturus audivi, sed mihi homousii et homoeusii intelligentiam evangelia et apostoli intimaverunt."

this point was the Bishop of Poitiers who had lived so long in happy ignorance of the Arian innovations. During his exile in Phrygia[1] S. Hilary had opportunities of studying Arianism in its latest developements, and though the Macedonian heresy had not yet come to the birth, he was able to foretell its approach. A denial of the proper Deity of the Son was fast leading the various schools of Arian misbelief to reject the Deity of the Holy Ghost: "quid mirum ut de Spiritu Sancto diversa sentiant qui in largitore eius creando et demutando et abolendo tam temerarii sint auctores atque ita dissolvant perfecti huius sacramenti veritatem...... Spiritum Sancto negando dum et usum et auctorem eius ignorant[2]?" It is not clear from these words in what sense Hilary regards the Son as the *auctor* of the Spirit; but presently he proceeds, although with evident reluctance, to unfold his view—heresy demands the formal expression of a truth which otherwise it might have sufficed to leave to the field of the Christian consciousness: "de Spiritu autem Sancto nec tacere oportet nec loqui necesse est. Sed sileri a nobis eorum causa qui nesciunt non potest; loqui autem de Eo non necesse est qui Patre et Filio auctoribus confitendus est[3]." To the question "per quem sit" Hilary answers still more specifically, "Per quem omnia et ex quo omnia"—words which must be interpreted by another passage in the same book, "Unus est Deus Pater, ex quo omnia, et unus Unigenitus Dominus noster Jesus Christus per quem omnia[4]." According to this

[1] *de Trin.* X. 4 (Migne X. 346), loquimur enim exsules per hos libros.

[2] *de Trin.* II. 4 (Migne, 53).

[3] *de Trin.* II. 29 (Migne, 69).

[4] *de Trin.* II. I.

teaching the Holy Spirit has His Being from the Father and through the Son. Both are His *auctores:* the Father ultimately, the Son as holding the middle order in the eternal course of the Divine life.

In the 8th book of the *de Trinitate* Hilary returns to this topic[1]. He is treating of the essential unity of the Father and the Son; and he finds a proof of this unity in the fact that the Son sends the Spirit Who proceeds from the Father. The question whether the Spirit is "from the Son" is then raised and briefly dismissed in the following manner: "Neque in hoc nunc calumnior libertati intelligentiae utrum ex Patre an ex Filio Spiritum Paracletum putent esse. Non enim in incerto Dominus reliquit [S. John xvi. 12 sq.].......A Filio igitur accipit qui et ab eo mittitur et a Patre procedit. Et interrogo utrum id ipsum sit a Filio accipere quod a Patre procedere. Quod si differre[2] credetur inter accipere a Filio et a Patre procedere, certe id ipsum atque unum esse existimabitur a Filio accipere quod sit accipere a Patre.... Hoc quod accipiet, sive potestas est sive virtus sive doctrina est, Filius a se accipiendum esse dixit; et rursum hoc ipsum significat accipiendum esse de Patre.... A Patre procedit Spiritus veritatis, sed a Filio a Patre mittitur. Omnia quae Patris sunt Filii sunt, et idcirco quidquid accipiet, a Filio accipiet."

It is interesting to observe how in this passage S. Hilary seems to stand upon the very edge of the *Filioque* controversy, to foresee the issue which

[1] *de Trin.* VIII. 19. 20 (Migne, 250 sq.).

[2] The Benedictine Editor annotates, "In vulgatis *nihil differre.* Rectius abest *nihil* a MSS. Conceditur adversariis quidquid voluerint ut invincibiliter revincantur." The 'concession' is surely an act of simple justice.

must arise, and yet deliberately to retire without committing himself to the support of either side. If any one chooses to say that the Holy Spirit is from the Son, the Bishop of Poitiers will not stop to censure the boldness of the phrase. He considers it a question fairly open to discussion whether 'receiving' is the same as 'procession.' His own mind evidently inclines to the affirmative. But he is not prepared, or he does not care to answer: it was enough to establish the consubstantiality of the Father and the Son by shewing that the same Holy Ghost receives of Both, is alike the Spirit of God and the Spirit of Christ. Here he makes his final stand: "non permittenda itaque ad impiae intelligentiae libertatem haeretica perversitas est ut dictum hoc Domini...non ad unitatem confiteatur referendum esse naturae."

In a word, if Hilary would not have been staggered by the *Filioque*, explained as the West has explained it, yet he does not go out of his way to anticipate it: his own belief is sufficiently expressed by the *per Filium* which was current in the orthodox teaching of his age[1]. The *de Trinitate* ends with the prayer, "Sanctum Spiritum tuum Qui ex Te per Unigenitum tuum est promerear[2]." It is a summary of what Hilary regarded as ascertained truth upon the procession of the Holy Ghost.

[1] See the remarks of Mr Ffoulkes, *Divisions of Christendom*, ii. p. 426. It is scarcely correct to say (p. 470) that "the East...came suddenly by intuition in the 8th century to tolerate the doctrine of procession through the Son." In the 4th century that doctrine was held by Basil as distinctly as by Hilary: v. *supr.* p. 100.

[2] *de Trin.* XII. 57 (Migne X. 472). Cf. c. 53, "huius ego nominis [creaturae] consortium ne in Sancto quidem Spiritu tuo patiar ex te profecto et per eum misso;" c. 56, "ex te per eum Sanctus Spiritus tuus est."

To these passages from the *de Trinitate* must be added another which claims S. Hilary as its author. The fragmentary *Opus Historicum* thus contrasts the Arian with the Catholic Trinity: "ubi a diversis substantiis Filium a Patre impio et maledico ore disciderint, et in separatis duobus adsistat auctoritas, tertia dinumeratur in Spiritu; ut cum sit Pater in Filio et Filius in Patre, et Spiritus Sanctus accipiat ex Utroque, in eo quod Spiritus exprimitur sanctae huius inviolabilis unitas [Trinitatis], haeretica parte parturiat Trinitas pronuntiata dissidium[1]." This was probably written after the *de Trinitate*, and seems to shew that Hilary's view of the relation in which the Spirit stands to the Son was gathering strength in his last years. There is but a step between the 'accipit ex Utroque' of this passage, and the 'ex Utroque procedit' which ultimately received the sanction of the Latin Church[2].

With S. Hilary may be connected the name of another Western Catholic of the same age, who speaks from the somewhat different platform of the cultivated lay mind. Marius Victorinus, an African by birth, taught rhetoric at Rome about the middle of the 4th century, with such general applause that

[1] *Fragm.* II. 31 (Migne X. 656). I give the passage as the Benedictine editor proposes to restore it. Cf. a hymn attributed to S. Hilary (Daniel, *thes. hymnol.* I. p. 2): "Deus Pater ingenite | et Fili unigenite | Quos Trinitatis unitas | Sancto connectit Spiritu."

[2] A Greek fragment in Mai's *Spic. Rom.* VI. p. XXXV., represents S. Hilary as having worked out the doctrine so far as to foresee and guard against a misinterpretation of the Western view. "S. Hilary in his Commentary on the Apostolic Epistles, treating of the doctrine of the Father and the Son, says, *Μηδεμίαν ἐν τῷ Ἁγίῳ Πνεύματι διπλόην νοεῖσθαι διὰ τὸ τὸν Πατέρα καὶ τὸν Υἱὸν τὸ εἶναι παρέχειν αὐτῷ· ὅθεν ἄμφω μία ἀρχὴ τοῦ Ἁγίου Πνεύματος χρηματίζουσιν.*" Mai justly exclaims, "En miram atque perspicuam...doctrinam de Spiritus Sancti processione a Patre Filioque tanquam unico principio!" To many it will seem too striking and clear to be S. Hilary's.

he was honoured by a statue in the Forum[1]. In old age, but while his fame as a rhetorician was still unabated, he embraced the Faith of Christ, and became its warm defender against Arian misrepresentations. His treatise *Against Arius* was probably written in or about the year 365[2]. It enters at considerable length into the doctrine of the Holy Spirit, and the following extracts, however far from being authoritative or even dogmatically exact[3], are of some historical value as shewing the tendency at this time of Christian thought in Western Europe." "Paracletus (Victorinus writes) a Deo et a Christo ... Duo ergo et isti; ex alio alius. Ex Filio Spiritus Sanctus sicuti ex Deo Filius conrationaliter; et Spiritus Sanctus a Patre ... Pater ... vox in silentio, Filius jam vox, Paracletus vox vocis ... Spiritus a Christo accipit, ipse Christus a Patre, et idcirco et Spiritus a Patre[4]." "Confitemur ergo et Spiritum Sanctum ex Deo Patre omnia habentem, τῷ Λόγῳ (hoc est, Jesu Christo) tradente illi omnia quae Christus habet a Patre[5]." "Jam vero Spiritum Sanctum alio quodam modo ipsum esse Jesum Christum occultum, interiorem, cum animis fabulantem ... et a Patre per Christum genitum ... multis nos libris exposuimus ... Patre cum Spiritu Sancto per Christum juncto, singulis quidem existentibus unum[6]." The language is untheological, and there is a touch of Origen in the last few sentences: but the main idea is the same as S. Hilary's. The Spirit receives of the Father in receiving of the Son. As the Son is 'ex Deo,' so is the Spirit 'ex

[1] S. August. *Confess.* VIII. 2.
[2] Migne VIII. 998.
[3] Cf. S. Hieron. *de vir. illustr.* 101. Migne XXIII. 701.
[4] *Adv. Arium*, I. 13, 14 (Migne VIII. 1048).
[5] *ib.* 47 (Migne, 1077).
[6] *ib.* 55 (Migne, 1082).

Filio.' With this view of the Procession Victorinus, like Hilary, combines the idea of the Holy Spirit being the bond of union in the Trinity. His '*Hymn on the Trinity*' contains the following singular address to the Third Person of the GODHEAD: "Tu, Spiritus Sancte, connexio es . . . primo connectis duo, esque ipsa tertia complexio duorum atque ipsa complexio nihil distans uno unum cum facis duo [1]."

S. Phoebadius of Agen in Aquitania, a contemporary and a fellow-countryman of S. Hilary, has left an important treatise in refutation of Arianism. He was alive in A. D. 392, when S. Jerome wrote the *De viris illustribus*. But his *Contra Arianos* was composed more than 40 years before that date, probably before the rise of Macedonianism. He has little to say in this book about the Holy Spirit, and contents himself with asserting that the Spirit is "de Deo", and personally distinct from the Father and the Son (alius a Filio sicut a Patre Filius) [2]. But if the *De fide orthodoxa* be due to Phoebadius, he must have held a doctrine of the procession in advance of S. Hilary's, as the following remarkable passage will shew. "Ascendit in caelos...misit nobis Spiritum Sanctum de propria sua et ipsa una substantia sua...'De meo', inquit, 'accipiet', ex eo utique quod est Filius; quia et Filius de eo quod Pater est [3]."

[1] Migne, 1146.

[2] Migne XX. 30.

[3] Migne XX. 49. To another contemporaneous Bishop of Gaul, S. Eusebius of Vercellae († 371), is attributed a confession which, if it really belonged to this period, would shew that individuals in the West had already begun to assert the procession from the Son *totidem verbis*. The words are: "S. Spiritum...credimus ab utroque procedentem amborum esse Spiritum...nec enim de Patre procedit in Filium vel de Filio procedit ad sanctificandam creaturam, sed simul ab utroque processisse monstratur, quia caritas sive sanctitas amborum esse

More than one profession of faith bears the name of Pope Damasus[1], whose episcopate, reaching from 366 to 384, covered the most important period of the final struggle between Arianism and the Church. His synodical letter to Paulinus of Antioch, which is admitted to be genuine, deals with the question of the Procession, but contents itself with asserting the essential derivation from the Father, and denying the heretical *per Filium*, both the assertion and the denial being now, however, for the first time fenced by an anathema: "si quis non dixerit Spiritum Sanctum de Patre esse vere ac proprie sicut Filius de divina substantia . . . . si quis dixerit Spiritum Sanctum facturam aut per Filium factum, anathema sit[2]." It is instructive to notice how at this period the two great sees of Rome and Constantinople seem to have been agreed in abstaining from a minuter definition of the Procession. Both in East and West the relations of the Spirit to the Son were being examined by individual theologians; but S. Gregory and S. Damasus[3] appear to have alike refrained from entering upon a question which did not touch the essentials of the Faith.

agnoscitur" (Migne XII. 961). Few will believe that this passage was written before Augustine's 99th Tract on S. John. In the MS. the document is anonymous.

[1] These documents are collected in Walch's *Bibl. Symb.* p. 179 sq.; cf. Swainson's *N. and A. Creeds*, pp. 92, 256. A form which Dr Swainson prints (*App.* III. p. 273—4) professes simply "Spiritum Sanctum Deum non ingenitum neque genitum, non creatum nec factum, sed *Patris et Filii, semper in Patre et Filio* coaeternum." One MS. copy of this Creed which I have examined (Gonville and Caius, 265), inserts before *Patris et Filii* the words "de Patre procedentem et Filio." The scribe appropriately assigns the authorship to the Bp. of Hippo: "incipit simbolum dictatum a beato Augustino."

[2] Migne XIII. 558, *ib.* LVI. 636. Cf. Theodoret *H. E.* V. 11.

[3] This is the more remarkable because Damasus was of Spanish birth.

In the year 374 the voice of a child[1] gave to the Western Episcopate one of its brightest ornaments in the person of the Prefect of Milan. Suddenly and in middle life converted from a Catechumen into a Bishop of the Church, S. Ambrose at once applied himself to theological study[2], and with such success that within three years of his baptism and consecration he was able, at the request of Gratian, to compose an elaborate defence of the Nicene Faith as it regards the Person of Christ[3]. This was followed (probably in 381) by the three books *de Spiritu Sancto,* which constitute the first separate treatise in the Latin tongue upon the Person of the Holy Ghost[4].

To establish the Deity of the Spirit is the primary object of this work. The subject of the procession, however, comes into sight early in Book i. S. Ambrose meets the objection that the Holy

[1] *Vit. Ambros. auct. Paulino.* § 6, (Migne XIV. 31), subito vox fertur infantis in populo sonuisse 'Ambrosium episcopum.' Cf. Socr. IV. 30, Θεοῦ ἔργον τὸ γενόμενον.

[2] *Vit. Ambros. ex ejus scriptis coll.* § 16, (Migne XIV. 79).

[3] *De fide ad Gratianum Aug. libr.* V.

[4] The *De Spiritu Sancto* can hardly lay claim to originality; the ex-Prefect wisely availed himself of the labours of Didymus, S. Basil, and other Greek writers of his own and of the previous generation, a circumstance which certainly diminishes the interest of his work as a specimen of Western Theology. But S. Jerome's taunt is unjust, if it is aimed at this book: "ex Graecis bonis Latina non bona." With regard to S. Jerome himself it may be presumed that he coincided in opinion with S. Didymus. His own writings are nearly silent on the subject, unless we admit the genuineness of a more than doubtful fragment assigned to him in a Greek MS. which Card. Mai discovered in the Vatican (*Spic. Rom.* VI. praef. XXXV.). I quote the passage as the Cardinal prints it: Ἱερώνυμος ὁ ἅγιος ἐν τῷ περὶ Τριάδος λόγῳ φησί. Τὸ Πνεῦμα τὸ Ἅγιον παρὰ τοῦ Πατρὸς καὶ τοῦ Υἱοῦ ἐκπορευόμενον κατὰ πάντα τῷ Πατρὶ καὶ τῷ Υἱῷ ὁμότιμον καὶ συναΐδιον ὑπάρχει. On Isa. lvii. 16, S. Jerome only comments, "de Patre egreditur, et propter societatem naturae a Filio mittitur." (Migne XXIV. 558.)

Spirit is sent, just as the created Seraphim are said to have been sent. The mission of the Spirit, he replies, involves no change of place, no separation from Him from Whom He comes. "Si de loco procedit Spiritus et ad locum transit, et ipse Pater in loco invenietur et Filius....non ergo quasi ex loco mittitur Spiritus aut quasi ex loco procedit quando procedit ex Filio...cum procedit a Patre et Filio non separatur a Patre, non separatur a Filio[1]". It is urged with reason that this passage refers to the temporal rather than to the eternal procession[2]; yet the latter seems certainly to be implied: for if the Spirit proceeds from the Son (ex Filio) in any other sense than that of motion from place to place, it can only be by some essential derivation from Him; and an essential relation within the GODHEAD must be timeless, without beginning or end. Moreover, as we read on, this view of S. Ambrose's teaching is confirmed. "As the Father is the Fountain of Life, so (he argues) is the Son: does not the Psalmist sing '*With Thee*,' Almighty GOD, '*is*' Thy Son *the Fountain of Life*'? i.e. the Fountain of the Holy Spirit, for the Holy Spirit is Life[3]." S. Basil's teaching[4] is thus reproduced: "ex uno Spiritu per unum Fi-

[1] *de Sp. S.* I. 11, (Migne XVI. 762).

[2] The Benedictine editor admits this: "Ambrosius hic...ut missionem temporalem Spiritus significet adhibet verbum *procedere*." The same remark perhaps holds good of the passage in the Commentary on Psalm lxi. "et Filius a Patre procedit et Spiritus ab ipso procedit:" yet the procession there intended is one which presupposes an essential unity, for it is added, "de unitate ergo divinitatis ambiguum nihil." (Migne XIV. 1227).

[3] *de Sp. S.* I. 15, (Migne XVI. 769). "Apud te, inquit, Deus omnipotens, Filius tuus fons vitae...hoc est fons Spiritus Sancti quia Spiritus vita." For S. Ambrose's interpretation of Apoc. XXII. 1, v. *supr.* p. 8, note.

[4] v. *supr.* p. 100 sq.

lium in unum Patrem cognitio nostra procedit; et ex uno Patre per unum Filium in unum Spiritum Sanctum bonitas et sanctificatio et imperiale jus aeternae traditur potestatis[1]." The Spirit's receiving from the Son is treated as at least analogous to His procession from the Father: "Secundum divinitatem non super Christum est Spiritus sed in Christo...manet enim in Deo qui ex Deo est...et manet in Christo qui a Christo accipit[2]." The Spirit receives from the Son His Divine attributes: "accepit per unitatem substantiae, sicut accepit a Patre Filius... quae habet Pater Filii sunt; quae habet Filius accepit et Spiritus[3]." Nay, He receives from the Son His very essence: "quod ex aliquo est aut ex substantia est aut ex potestate ejus. Ex substantia...sicut Spiritus qui a Patre procedit, de quo dicit Filius, 'ille me clarificabit quia de meo accipiet[4].'" This is put still more explicitly in the later *Commentary on S. Luke:* where S. Ambrose, arguing that our Lord's οὐδεὶς ἀγαθὸς εἰ μὴ εἷς ὁ Θεός could not have been meant to exclude Himself, asks, "quomodo non bonus, cum bonitatis substantia assumpta ex Patre non degenerarit in Filio quae non degeneravit in Spiritu? quod si 'bonus' Spiritus [Ps. cxlii. 10] qui accepit ex Filio, bonus utique et ille qui tradidit[5]."

Nevertheless it can hardly be said that in the genuine works of S. Ambrose the phrase *procedere ex* [*a*] *Filio* is used with direct reference to an eternal

[1] *de Sp. S.* II. 12. (Migne XVI. 802).

[2] *de Sp. S.* III. I. Migne, 810.

[3] *de Sp. S.* II. 11. (Migne, 800, cf. *infr.* 803, "quae accepit ipse per unitatem naturae, ex ipso per eandem unitatem accepit et Spiritus."

[4] ib. 5. (Migne, 783).

[5] *expos. in Luc.* VIII. (Migne XV. 1876).

ἐκπόρευσις. The Benedictine editors have, rightly no doubt, relegated to the Appendix a Sermon in which some zealous controversialist of a much later age preaches on Whitsun Day under the name of the great Bishop of Milan, "Magna est, fratres carissimi, hodierna festivitas in qua sicut audivistis acceperunt apostoli Spiritum Sanctum...Qui non ex tempore sed ab aeterno a Patre Filioque inseparabiliter procedit[1]."

But S. Ambrose's place in the history of the Procession-dogma is not to be fixed altogether by a reference to his books. To Ambrose, under GOD, the Church owes Augustine: and it was from the Bishop of Hippo more than from any other individual teacher that the Western doctrine of the Procession received both form and authority[2]. The Church of North Africa in the person of Tertullian laid the foundation of that doctrine early in the third century: by a singular coincidence the same Church, after an interval of two centuries, completed in the person of S. Augustine the work which it had begun.

The baptized life of S. Augustine extends from A. D. 387 to A. D. 430, thus nearly bridging over the interval between the Councils of Constantinople and Ephesus. He was raised to the priesthood in 391; to the episcopal office in 395. The four treatises from which his doctrine of the Procession is chiefly

[1] *Serm.* XXXVI. in append. (Migne XVII. 693). Of the phrase 'procedit a Patre et Filio,' apart from the 'ab aeterno', S. Ambrose seems to have been the originator: cf. Langen, *die Trinitarische Lehrdifferenz*, p. 47.

[2] The later Greeks regarded him as the inventor of the doctrine: e. g. Gregor. Scholar. (*de proc. Sp. S.* I. 3), who views the Latin dogma as a protest on S. Augustine's part against Nestorianism. Cf. Le Quien, *dissert. Damasc.* I. § VIII. Hergenröther, *Photius*, I. 685.

to be gathered were written between 393 and 428, and the date of each can be approximately ascertained. We are thus in a position to trace with some degree of accuracy the growth of the conception in Augustine's mind.

The earliest of these treatises is a book *de fide et Symbolo*, which contains the substance of a discourse delivered by Augustine, while yet a simple Presbyter, before a Council of North African Bishops held at Hippo in the year 393[1]. The 9th chapter of this book treats of 'faith in the Holy Ghost.' The extraordinary difficulty of the subject is at once acknowledged, and also the want of any full or thorough discussion of it by the great teachers of the Church: "de Spiritu Sancto autem nondum tam copiose ac diligenter disputatum est a doctis et magnis divinarum Scripturarum tractatoribus, ut intelligi facile possit et ejus proprium[2]." Certain points, however, might be regarded as already ascertained; as that the Holy Ghost is consubstantial with the Father and the Son, yet personally distinct: that He is not derived by generation either from the Father or from the Son: that, notwithstanding, He is not ἄναρχος, but owes His personal Life to the Father, "of Whom are all things[3]." Drawing nearer to this question of the Spirit's relation to the Father and the Son, Augustine repro-

[1] *Retract.* I. 17. "Per idem tempus coram episcopis hoc mihi jubentibus qui plurimum totius Africae concilium Hippone Regio habebant de Fide et Symbolo presbyter disputavi."

[2] *de F. et S.* 9. (Migne XL. 191, sq.).

[3] *ib.* "Servant tamen ut non genitum Spiritum Sanctum tamquam Filium de Patre praedicent ... neque de Filio tamquam nepotem summi Patris: nec tamen id quod est nulli debere, sed Patri ex quo omnia, ne duo constituamus principia sine principio; quod falsissimum est et absurdissimum et non catholicae fidei."

duces with certain changes and additions, and not without an apology for their inadequacy[1], the illustrations first employed by Tertullian: the Holy Spirit is the Water of Life "de fonte *vel* de fluvio:" the branches of the Tree are not identical, although they are substantially one, with its trunk or its root. To these imperfect figures he adds a mystical view which he evidently prefers, but refuses as yet to adopt or to discuss: "ausi sunt quidam ipsam communionem Patris et Filii, atque ut ita dicam, *deitatem* (quam Graeci θεότητα appellant), Spiritum Sanctum credere...quam etiam dilectionem in se invicem amborum caritatemque volunt intelligi." One objection to this hypothesis is stated, and at once set aside: 'the communion and mutual love of two Persons can have no personal existence[2].' Doubtless, Augustine replies, this is true in reference to material substances: "copulatio non est corpus:" the union of two bodies does not constitute a third. But when we speak of GOD, we are in the presence of a Nature where the distinction vanishes between the essential and the accidental: "quidquid ibi intelligi potest, substantia est."

[1] *de F. et S.* 9. "Haec non propter illius divinae naturae similitudinem, sed propter visibilium etiam unitatem corporalia exempla data sunt, ut intelligeretur fieri posse ut aliqua tria non tantum singillatim, sed etiam simul unum singulare nomen obtineret:" i. e. they are more useful as illustrations of the Unity, than as helping men to understand the mysteries of Generation and Procession. Augustine adds the image of three cups filled from one spring, "quamvis nullus hic transitus fiat sicut de fonte in fluvium dicebamus."

[2] *ib.* "Huic sententiae contradicunt qui arbitrantur istam communionem quam sive deitatem sive dilectionem sive veritatem appellamus non esse substantiam...Sed hi tales cor mundum faciant quantum possunt ut videre valeant in Dei substantia non esse aliquid tale, quasi aliud ibi sit substantia, aliud quod accidat substantiae." Cf. *de Trin.* XV. 27, communio quaedam consubstantialis Patris et Filii.

S. Augustine's greatest dogmatic work—the *de Trinitate*—occupied his spare time during some twenty years of his episcopate. He writes to Aurelius of this work, "Libros juvenis inchoavi, senex edidi[1]." His friends and disciples were less patient, and a portion of the MS. was stolen from the author's *scrinia*, and published in an imperfect form about the year 415. At that period the 12th book was not yet complete, and the earlier books needed revision. Under these circumstances S. Augustine felt himself obliged to hasten on the publication of the entire work, and at some time previous to the year 428 appeared the author's complete edition of the fifteen books, revised and perfected, "non ut volui (he says) sed ut potui." Thus we may expect to find in the *de Trinitate*, so far as our present text is trustworthy, a faithful reflection of the workings of S. Augustine's mind upon this question, corrected throughout by his maturer judgement.

In the 4th and 5th Books the writer already displays a remarkable advance upon the cautious language of the *de Fide et Symbolo*. Distinguishing between *mission* and *procession*, he asserts a true procession of the Spirit from the Son: "nec possumus dicere quod Spiritus Sanctus et a Filio non procedat . . . Flatus ille corporeus [S. John XX. 22.] . . fuit . . demonstratio per congruam significationem non tantum a Patre sed et Filio procedere Spiritum Sanctum[2]." "Fatendum est Patrem et Filium principium esse Spiritus Sancti: non duo principia; sed sicut Pater et Filius unus Deus . . . sic

[1] *Ep.* CLXXIV. (Migne XXXIII. 758); cf. *Retract.* II. 15 (Migne XXXIII. 635).

[2] *de Trin.* IV. 29. (Migne XLII. 908).

relative ad Spiritum Sanctum unum principium[1]." In these few words we at length have the statement to which Western, and to a considerable extent Eastern thought had been tending for two centuries. Tertullian's *a Patre per Filium*, Hilary's *Patre et Filio auctoribus*, the παρ' ἀμφοτέρων of S. Epiphanius, the διὰ τοῦ μέσου of S. Gregory of Nyssa, find at last their logical outcome and expression in the *Pater et Filius unum principium* of the greater Bishop of Hippo[2].

Between this passage and the 15th book of the *de Trinitate* must be placed the teaching of the *Tractatus in S. Joannem*[3]. These are sermons on the Fourth Gospel preached during the Donatist and Pelagian troubles, probably in the winter and spring of 415—6. In Tract. xcix. (on S. John xvi. 13) the question of the Spirit's procession from the Son is formally raised: "hic aliquis forsitan quaerat utrum et a Filio procedat Spiritus Sanctus. Filius enim solius Patris est Filius, et Pater solius Filii est Pater; Spiritus autem Sanctus non est

[1] *de Trin.* V. 14 (Migne, 921). Augustine proceeds to meet the question (*c.* 15), "utrum erat [Spiritus S.] antequam daretur." The alternative is "an semper procedit Spiritus Sanctus et non ex tempore sed ab aeternitate procedit"?

[2] On Augustine's position in reference to the doctrine see Neander, *Ch. H.* IV. p. 88 (Bohn). Mr Ffoulkes (*Christendom's Divisions*, I. p. 69 sq.) thinks that the anthropological tone of Western Christianity led to the stronger statements of Augustine and the Latin Church upon the subject of the Procession. His reasoning is not very convincing. The practical tone of Latin theology explains more: if the Spirit were of the Son, as in some sense all allowed that He was, and if He moreover proceeded from the Father, as the Scripture declared, why not express both truths under the common formula, 'De utroque procedit'?

[3] *Tract.* XCIX. is referred to in *de Trin.* XV. 27, "de hac re in sermone quodam proferendo ad aures populi Christiani diximus, dictumque conscripsimus."

minus eorum Spiritus, sed amborum...Cur ergo non credamus quod etiam de Filio procedat Spiritus Sanctus, cum Fili quoque ipse sit Spiritus?...Quid aliud significavit illa insufflatio [S. John xx. 22], nisi quod procedat Spiritus Sanctus de ipso[1]?" Then, boldly facing the obvious objection that 'the Son Himself speaks only of a procession from the Father', the preacher replies, "Cur putas, nisi quemadmodum ad eum [*sc.* Patrem] solet referre et quod ipsius est, de quo et ipse est?" *E.g.* in S. John vii. 16 our Lord says 'My doctrine is not mine.' It was not His, it was the Father's, inasmuch as He Himself is of the Father. Yet it was His nevertheless, since He and the Father are One. "Quanto magis illic intelligendum est et de ipso procedere Spiritus Sanctus, ubi sic ait 'de Patre procedit' ut non diceret, 'de me non procedit.' From Augustine's point of view, the παρὰ τοῦ Πατρός is not exclusive: it asserts the μοναρχία, but does not lose sight of the ὁμοούσιον; does not shut out the Consubstantial Son from being with the Father, though subordinately to Him, the One Principle of the Holy Ghost. "A quo autem habet Filius ut sit Deus (est enim de Deo Deus), ab illo habet utique ut etiam de illo procedat Spiritus Sanctus; ac per hoc Spiritus Sanctus ut etiam de Filio procedat sicut procedat de Patre, ab ipso habet Patre[2]." The procession from the Son must not, however, be regarded as posterior in time to the procession from the Father, or as distinct from it in fact: "Spiritus Sanctus non de Patre procedit in Filium et de Filio procedit ad sanctificandam creaturam, sed simul de utroque procedit[3]."

[1] *Tract.* XCIX. § 6, 7 (Migne XXXV. 1888 sq.). [2] *ib.* § 8.

[3] *ib.* § 9. Thus there is no parallel between the Procession of the

The whole of this context is repeated in the 15th book of the *de Trinitate*[1]. The later work, however, prefaces the teaching of the earlier with a new and important illustration of the mystery, derived from the constitution of man[2]. 'In man himself there is a kind of trinity; the memory, the understanding, the will, are three, and yet one. In man, indeed, these three are impersonal; they do not together constitute the *ego:* "ego.....memini, ego intelligo, ego diligo, qui nec memoria sum nec intelligentia nec dilectio, sed haec habeo." It is otherwise in the Life of God: "in illius vero summae simplicitate Naturae quae Deus est, quamvis unum sit Deus, tres tamen personae sunt." As far, then, as comparison is possible, the Holy Spirit in God corresponds to Will or Love in man: "de Spiritu Sancto nihil in hoc aenigmate quod ei simile videretur ostendi, nisi voluntatem nostram, vel amorem, quae valentior est voluntas...Amor hominis de scientia procedens et memoriam intelligentiamque conjungens, tamquam parenti prolique communis, unde nec parens intelligitur esse nec proles, habet in

Spirit from the Father and the Son, and the generation of man: "quia nec filius hominem simul et ex patre et ex matre procedit, sed cum in matrem procedit ex patre, non tunc procedit ex matre, et cum in hanc lucem procedit ex matre, non tunc procedit ex patre."

[1] *de Trin.* XV. *c.* 27 (Migne XLII. 1095): with the caution, "fidelibus non infidelibus loquens."

[2] *ib.* c. 20 (Migne, 1088 sq.), "si possent cernerent trinitatem Deum in nostra memoria, intelligentia, voluntate." Cf. *de Trin.* XIII. 11. "Vellem ut haec tria cogitarent homines in seipsis. Longe aliud sunt ista tria quam illa Trinitas, sed dico ubi se exerceant et sibi probent et sentiant quam longe sunt. Dico autem haec tria, esse, nosse, velle. Sum enim et novi et volo: sum sciens et volens et scio esse me et velle et volo esse et scire...In his igitur tribus quam sit inseparabilis vita...quam denique inseparabilis distinctio et tamen distinctio videat qui potest."

hac imagine aliquam licet valde imparem similitudinem Spiritus Sancti."

There is another correction which must be applied to this comparison: in the human mind, the will precedes the thought, aids in its production, and when it is produced, finds rest in it, and in the form of love, embraces it and works from it. In the Life of God, nothing precedes, nothing follows: "nulla sunt tempora." "Quapropter qui potest intelligere sine tempore generationem Filii de Patre, intelligat sine tempore processionem Spiritus Sancti de utroque...intelligat sicut habet Pater in semetipso ut de illo procedat idem Spiritus Sanctus, sic dedisse Filio ut de illo procedat idem Spiritus Sanctus, et uterque sine tempore... Si enim quidquid habet de Patre habet Filius, de Patre habet utique ut et de illo procedat Spiritus Sanctus...Filius autem de Patre natus est, et Spiritus Sanctus de Patre principaliter et ipso sine ullo temporis intervallo dante communiter de utroque procedit[1]."

There remains another and yet later work of S. Augustine which bears upon this subject. The *libri contra Maximinum* appear to have been written in the year 427—8. The 2nd Book contains the Bishop of Hippo's detailed reply to the arguments of the Arian Bishop, who urged that if the Son and the Spirit were alike of the essence of the Father,

[1] *c.* 47. Cf. *supr.* c. 29. "Ideo autem addidi 'principaliter,' quia et de Filio Spiritus Sanctus procedere reperitur; sed hoc quoque illi Pater gignendo dedit." On *principaliter* Baur writes (*Dreieinigkeit*, II. 166), "Nur konnte auch Augustinus jenes andere Moment nicht ganz aus dem Auge verlieren, weswegen er auch wieder sagt, dass der Geist *principaliter* vom Vater ausgehe, und ausdrücklich bemerkt, dass auch das Ausgehen des Geistes vom Sohn dem Sohn vom Vater mitgetheilt sey."

the Spirit Himself might be called Son of God[1]. Augustine replies by distinguishing between 'proceeding' and 'begotten': the terms are not always convertible: "non omne quod procedit nascitur, quamvis omne procedat quod nascitur." "Ideo ille Filius est Patris de quo est genitus; iste autem Spiritus utriusque, quoniam de utroque procedit. Sed ideo cum de illo Filius loqueretur ait, 'de Patre procedit,' quoniam Pater processionis ejus est auctor qui talem Filium genuit et gignendo ei dedit ut etiam de ipso procederet Spiritus Sanctus." At this point Augustine stops short. He seems conscious that in his hands the doctrine of the Procession has reached its extreme limit of developement[2]; and he leaves the subject with the salutary caution, "Satis sit ergo nobis quia... non est a seipso Spiritus Sanctus, sed ab illo de quo procedit; et quia de utroque procedit...unde et Spiritus Patris dictus est...et Spiritus Filii...non enim duo sunt Spiritus Sancti tanquam singuli singulorum, unus Patris, alter Filii; sed unus potius Patris et Filii."

It would be easy to multiply quotations from S. Augustine, as will appear from a glance at the copious index attached to the Benedictine edition of his works. But his relation to the doctrine of the Procession and to the *Filioque* controversy has been made sufficiently clear. It is simply impossible either to reject as interpolated[3], or to set

[1] *c. Maximin.* II. c. 14. (Migne XLII. 770).

[2] "Haec scio: distinguere autem inter illam generationem et hanc processionem nescio, non valeo, non sufficio....sicut propheta de Filio...ita de Spiritu Sancto verissime dicitur, 'processionem ejus quis enarrabit.'"

[3] As Dr Neale has attempted to do: *H. E. Ch.* Introd. ii. pp. 1125—8. His suspicions do not seem to have been based on an

aside as ambiguous, the long passages in the *De Trinitate* and the *Tractatus in S. Joannem* which affirm the Western view of the Procession. Whether their author would have approved the insertion of the *Filioque* in a Catholic Creed is another question. To the idea which it expresses he would probably have applied the opening words of the *De Trinitate*, "Quisquis haec legit ubi pariter certus est pergat mecum: ubi pariter haesitat, quaerat mecum." Ultimately S. Augustine himself entertained no doubt upon the subject: but he never asserts his view in the spirit of a controversialist. If he lays stress upon the procession of the Holy Ghost from both the Father and the Son, if he enforces this opinion with a plainness and explicitness of language hitherto without a precedent, his purpose is neither to encourage speculation nor to provoke discussion, but rather to add completeness and stability to the Catholic Doctrine of the Holy Trinity. He is conscious

examination of the MSS. Photius expressed similarly vague misgivings, *Mystagog.* 71 (Migne CII. 352), εἶπεν Αὐγουστῖνος καὶ Ἱερώνυμος [in his version of Didymus *de Sp. S.*?] τὸ Πνεῦμα ἐκ τοῦ Υἱοῦ ἐκπορεύεσθαι. καὶ πόθεν ἐστι λαβεῖν ἢ δοῦναι πίστιν τοσούτου χρόνου ὅτι μὴ αὐτῶν κεκακούργηται τὰ συντάγματα; In the case of Augustine, the frequency and length of the passages seem to preclude the thought of falsification. Moreover, the text of S. Augustine's dogmatic works must have been to a great extent protected against Western interpolations by the process of translation into Greek, which had begun within the life-time of Possidonius, Augustine's biographer and friend (*vit. Aug. c.* xi.). Card. Mai has printed (*Patr. nov. bibl.* I. 428) specimens of a Greek version of the *De Trinitate* made in the 14th century by Maximus Planudes, a strong opponent of the Latin doctrine, but an exact and faithful translator (cf. Cave, *hist. lit.* App. p. 38). The following extracts will show that Planudes at least had no suspicions as to the purity of the Latin text. *De Trin.* IV. 29 (cf. *supr.* p. 125), οὐ μέντοι δυνάμεθα λέγειν ὅτι τὸ Πνεῦμα τὸ Ἅγιον οὐχὶ καὶ ἐκ τοῦ Υἱοῦ ἐκπορεύεται. *ib.* XV. 47 [= *Tract in S. Joann.* xcix. § 9: cf. *supr.* p. 127] τὸ δὲ Πν. τὸ Ἅ. οὔκουν ἐκ τοῦ Πατρὸς πρόεισιν εἰς τὸν Υἱὸν κἀκ τοῦ Υἱοῦ πρόεισιν ἐπὶ τὸ ἁγιάζειν, τὴν κτίσιν ἀλλὰ ὁμοῦ ἐξ ἑκατέρου πρόεισιν.

of no conflict of opinion within the Church: his quarrel is only with Arian and the Macedonian: the *Filioque* is part of his answer to those who denied the Deity of the Son and of the Holy Ghost.

Two Christian poets of the age may have helped to familiarize the mind of the Latin Church with the language which theologians, like S. Augustine, were beginning to employ in reference to the procession of the Holy Ghost. S. Paulinus of Nola, who was the friend as well as the contemporary of the Bishop of Hippo (353—431), speaks at one time of a procession from the Father:—

> * * * * "Filius ex Patre natus
> Spiritus ex Patre procedens" * * *[1]

at another, of a procession from Both; as where he says that Our Lord, being exalted to the Right Hand of God,

> * * * "inde suis caelestia dona profudit,
> Spiritum ab Unigena Sanctum et Patre procedentem."[2]

S. Prudentius, a Spaniard by birth, who died while Augustine was still engaged upon his *De Trinitate* (circ. 410), thus ends the fifth Hymn of his *Liber Cathemerinon*:—

> "Lumen! quod famulans offero suscipe,
> Tinctum pacifici chrismatis unguine,
> Per Christum Genitum, Summe Pater, tuum
> In quo visibilis stat tibi gloria:

[1] *poem.* XIX. 138—9 (Migne LXI. 321).
[2] *poem.* XXVII. 92—3 (Migne 650).

Qui noster dominus, qui tuus unicus
Spirat de Patris corde Paraclitum[1]."

The next hymn begins :—

"O Trinitatis hujus Vis una, Lumen unum,
Deus ex Deo perennis, Deus ex utroque missus[2]."

It is easy to see how much the poetical use of such words as these would smooth the way to the recitation of the *Filioque* in the Catholic Creed. But we must turn once more to the East, before our attention is directed to this final stage in the history of the Western belief.

[1] *Cathem.* v. 155 sq. (Migne LIX 830).

[2] *Cathem.* vi. 5—8 (Migne, 831). Cf. Daniel, *thes. hymnol.* i. 134: "locus memoratu dignissimus quo demonstratur jam illo tempore hanc loquendi formulam, 'Christus spirat Spiritum Sanctum', orthodoxis hominibus fuisse usitatam. Verbum spirare est verbum apud poetas quoque solemne de actione Patris et Filii, qua ab utroque procedit Spiritus S.; unde saepissime spiramen dicitur."

CHAPTER VI.

"SAECULUM NESTORIANUM."

Ἐξαπέστειλεν ὁ Θεὸς τὸ Πνεῦμα τοῦ Υἱοῦ αὐτοῦ. S. Paul, *Galat.* IV. 6.

DR DORNER has pointed out that two distinct and in some respects opposite schools of Christian thought developed themselves at an early period in the Churches of Eastern and Western Syria[1]. The Mesopotamian or Assyrian Church was distinguished by its ascetic piety, and by a tendency to mysticism which was combined with a firm adherence to the traditional Faith. In the fourth century this school is represented by Aphraates, and S. Ephraem of Edessa; in the fifth, by S. James of Sarug, S. Isaac of Seleucia, S. Maruthas of Tagrit. Among these East-Syrian divines the doctrine of the Procession appears to have been worked out in the same manner as by the Catholics of the West. In S. Ephraem's writings we meet the old illustration of the sun, its light and its heat[2]. The Generation and the Procession are both, he teaches, from the Essence of God; both are alike eternal: Πνεῦμα Ἅγιον ἐκ τῆς οὐσίας αὐτοῦ συνέστησεν· οὐ πρὸ τοῦ Λόγου τὸ Πνεῦμα προήγαγεν...Πνεύματος γὰρ

[1] Dorner, *Doctr. of the Person of Christ*, II. i. 25 sq.

[2] Hymn 73. (Assemani, *bibl. oriental.* I. 114.)

καὶ Λόγου εἷς ὁ χρόνος. ἐν λόγῳ καὶ ἡμεῖς τὸ πνεῦμα προάγομεν. οὔτε οὖν ὁ Πατὴρ χρειώδης χρόνου γέγονε προαγαγεῖν τὸν Λόγον· οὐδ᾽ ἐν χρόνῳ ὕστερον τοῦ Λόγου τὸ Ἅγιον Πνεῦμα προήγαγε, διόπερ καὶ συναΐδιος ἡ Θεότης ἐστὶ τῆς ἁγίας Τριάδος[1]. Aphraates preaches that the Holy Spirit belongs to the Son: "if we make light of His Pledge, He will withdraw It from us and take back to Himself That which is His own[2]." S. James of Sarug writes to Samuel, Abbat of Gabala, "There is one Holy Father, one Holy Son, one Holy Ghost; the Father ingenerate, the Son begotten, the Spirit proceeding from the Father *and receiving from the Son*" (ܪܘܚܐ ܕܗܘ ܢܦܩ ܡܢ ܐܒܐ ܘܢܣܒ ܡܢ ܒܪܐ)[3]. Lastly, in the year 410 the Council of Seleucia, of which S. Isaac and S. Maruthas were joint presidents, seems to have made use in a Synodical ἔκθεσις of language which almost anticipates the *Filioque*: "we confess the Living and Holy Spirit, the Living Paraclete, Who is *from the Father and the Son*" (ܕܡܢ ܐܒܐ ܘܒܪܐ).[4]

[1] S. Ephr. Syr. *Gr.* I. p. 127. On Gen. i. 2, S. Ephraem comments "That is, the Holy Spirit of God the Father, from Whom He proceeds timelessly, and with Whom and with His only begotten Son He is equal in essence and power" (Assemani *bibl. orient.* I. 65).

[2] From the Armeno-latin in Galland. *bibl. patr.* v. p. xlviii (ascribed there to S. James of Nisibis). Cf. Wright, Syriac Homilies of Aphraates, p. 119.

[3] Assemani *b. o.*, I. 302. Ass. annotates, "Quae communis est secundum Evangelii verba Orientalium theologia;" quoting (*e.g.*) the liturgies of Xystus and Ignatius.

[4] Assemani, *ib.* 194. Mansi, III. 1166. Renaudot, II. 272. Cf. Van der Moeren, p. 133, note. Bickell (*Conspect. rei Syr. liter.* p. 22), "S. Maruthas...una cum Isaac archiepiscopo Seleuciae canonis condidit in Synodo a. 410 ibidem coacta. Quos canones...nuper Lamy syriace e codice saec. VIII. edidit: eos genuinos esse testatur Simon Betharsamensis, nec refelli debet propter mentionem processionis S. Spiritus a Patre Filioque, quia *probari potest antiquam Syrorum ecclesiam orthodoxam de hac quaestione sententiam tenuisse.*" In sup-

In Western Syria theology took a different course. After the Council of Nicaea the Church of Antioch was invaded by a succession of Arian prelates: the great majority of its presbyters became infected with heresy, and the Catholics of the West Syrian metropolis were reduced to the numbers of an insignificant sect. The minority was led by two faithful laymen, Flavian and Diodore, of whom the former afterwards became Bishop of Antioch, the latter was promoted to the see of Tarsus[1]. Diodore in particular signalized himself by extraordinary devotion to the Catholic cause when it was at its lowest ebb in Antioch[2]. He has acquired a more lasting reputation as an expositor of Holy Scripture. Of his own exegetical writings fragments only are extant[3]: but his system of hermeneutics has survived in the pages of his greater disciples, S. John the Golden-mouthed and Theodore the Interpreter.

About the year 370, in the heat of the Arian controversy, the younger Apollinaris, Bishop of the Syrian Laodicea, was tempted to deny the existence in Christ of a human intellect[4]. To hold that Our Lord possessed the rational soul of a man was in his judgement the same thing as to distinguish two Persons in the Incarnate Word, the Son of Mary and

port of this statement Bickell quotes *inter alia* the Acts of Sarbelius (Cureton, *Ancient Syriac documents*, p. 43).

[1] Neale, *Antioch*, p. 137.

[2] Theodoret. *H. E.* IV. 22 (Migne LXXXII. 1184).

[3] Migne *P. Gr.* XXXIII. 1546—1628. Cramer's *Catenae*, passim. Diodore was raised to the Episcopate in 378, and died in or about 392. Amongst his works was one on the Holy Spirit, of which nothing is left: but Photius had read it, and seems to have been dissatisfied with its teaching: *Bibl.* Cod. CII. Διοδώρου Ταρσοῦ περὶ τοῦ Ἁγίου Πνεύματος διάφορα ἐγχειρήματα.

[4] Cf. Dr Newman's Essay, *The Heresy of Apollinaris* (Theol. Tracts, pp. 257—281).

the Son of God[1]. It was to introduce a fourth Person into the Godhead—to place a human being before the Holy Ghost. Apollinaris is further charged by S. Gregory of Nazianzus with having represented the Spirit as inferior to the Logos, and thus denying what in words he affirmed, the proper Deity of the Holy Ghost[2]. This charge does not seem to be supported; and it may be that S. Gregory was misled by Apollinaris's strong way of affirming the dependence of the Third Person upon the Second. The following paraphrase of S. John xvi. 15 will shew how decidedly he held the procession from the Son: εἰς ἐμὴν ἔσται δόξαν ἡ τοῦ Πνεύματος ἐνέργεια καὶ διδασκαλία, ὅτι καὶ παρ' ἐμοῦ ὁρμᾶται· τὸ δὲ 'παρ' ἐμοῦ' λέγων δηλῶ καὶ τὸ 'παρὰ Πατρός'· ἐμὰ γάρ ἐστι τὰ Πατρῷα. The words "He shall receive of mine &c." (Apollinaris adds) cannot refer to an accession of knowledge derived from the Son for the fulfilment of the temporal mission; they must be understood of an essential procession: ἀντὶ τοῦ λέγειν ὅλον παρ' ἑαυτοῦ τὸ Πνεῦμα ὁρμᾶσθαι εἴρηκε τὸ 'ἐκ τοῦ ἐμοῦ λήψεται'[3].

The historico-grammatical expository school of Antioch at once took up a position of strong antagonism to the teaching of Apollinaris. While fully acknowledging the proper Deity of the Son, it desired to give equal prominence to the Sacred

[1] Athan. *c. Apollin.* I. 21. ὑμεῖς συκοφαντοῦντες λέγετε ἡμᾶς δύο λέγειν Υἱούς, καὶ ἀνθρωπολάτρας ἡμᾶς ὀνομάζετε.

[2] *Ep.* CI. (*ad Cledon.*) Migne XXXVII. 191. Ἀπολινάριος μὲν τό τῆς θεότητος ὄνομα τῷ Ἁγίῳ Πνεύματι δοὺς τὴν δύναμιν τῆς θεότητος οὐκ ἐφύλαξε. τὸ μὲν γὰρ ἐκ μεγάλου καὶ μείζονος καὶ μεγίστου συνιστᾶν τὴν Τριάδα ὥσπερ ἐξ αὐγῆς καὶ ἀκτῖνος καὶ ἡλίου τοῦ Πνεύματος καὶ τοῦ Υἱοῦ καὶ τοῦ Πατρός—ὅπερ σαφῶς ἐν τοῖς ἐκείνου γέγραπται λόγοις—κλίμαξ ἐστὶ θεότητος οὐκ εἰς οὐρανὸν ἄγουσα ἀλλ' ἐξ οὐρανοῦ κατάγουσα. Theodoret repeats the accusation (*haeret. fab.* IV. 8).

[3] Corderii *Catena*, p. 396. Cf. Mai *Spicil. Rom.* X. 148.

Humanity. The historical Christ of the Gospels and of the ancient Creeds was as perfectly Man as He was perfectly God; the Apollinarian theory was a denial of the reality of this Christ of history. In their recoil from one error the Antiochenes unhappily fell into another, or at least approached dangerously near to such a fall. Both Diodore[1] and Theodore allowed themselves to use language which anticipated the heresy of Nestorius[2]. Theodore seems to have regarded the Incarnation as a union—effected indeed at the moment of the Conception—between the Virgin's Child and the Eternal Word[3]. The Man thus assumed by the Divine Logos was filled in a manner altogether unique by the Grace of the Holy Ghost: *ἠξιώθη γοῦν καὶ τῆς τοῦ Πνεύματος ἐνοικήσεως πρῶτος παρὰ τοὺς λοιποὺς ἀνθρώπους καὶ ἠξιώθη ταύτης οὐχ ὁμοίως τοῖς λοιποῖς. οὗτος μὲν γὰρ ὅλην τὴν χάριν τοῦ Πνεύματος ἐν ἑαυτῷ ἐδέξατο· ἑτέροις δὲ μερικὴν παρεῖχεν τοῦ παντὸς Πνεύματος τὴν μετουσίαν*[4]. Of this indwelling of the Spirit in the Sacred Manhood and the consequent participation of the baptized in the Gift, Theodore's writings are full: of any relation of the Spirit to the Eternal Word, he has little or nothing to say. Perhaps the latter was

[1] In a fragment of his treatise *κατὰ τῶν Συνουσιαστῶν* we read, *χάριτι υἱὸς ὁ ἐκ Μαρίας ἄνθρωπος φύσει δὲ ὁ Θεὸς Λόγος...καὶ περὶ τῶν κατὰ φύσιν γεννήσεων ὅταν ᾖ λόγος μὴ τῆς Μαρίας υἱὸς ὁ Θεὸς Λόγος ὑποπτευέσθω...δύο γεννήσεις ὁ Θεὸς Λόγος οὐχ ὑπέμενε, τὴν μὲν πρὸ αἰώνων, τὴν δὲ ἐν ὑστέροις χρόνοις.* (Migne XXXIII. 1560—1.)

[2] Cf. Anastas. Sinait. *ap.* Fabric. VIII. 352. *ταύτης δὲ τῆς διαιρέσεως ἀρχηγοὶ γεγόνασι Θεόδωρος ὁ Ἀντιοχείας καὶ Διόδωρος ὁ Ταρσοῦ.*

[3] Migne LXVI. 980. *ἥνωτο μὲν γὰρ ἐξ ἀρχῆς τῷ Θεῷ ὁ ληφθεὶς κατὰ πρόγνωσιν, ἐν αὐτῇ τῇ διαπλάσει τῆς μήτρας τὴν καταρχὴν τῆς ἑνώσεως δεξάμενος.* In this way Theodore escaped from the charge of actually dividing the One Person: *ib.* 981, *οὐκέτι εἰσὶ δύο πρόσωπα ἀλλ' ἕν...ὅταν ἐπὶ τὴν συνάφειαν ἀπίδωμεν ἓν πρόσωπον τότε φαμέν.*

[4] Migne, 980. See *Church Quarterly Review*, I. p. 129, *sq.*

thrown into the shade by the prominence which he gave to the nearer and less mystical truth: perhaps the strong assertion of the *a Filio* by Apollinaris may have led Theodore to regard it with suspicion and dislike: perhaps he deemed it dishonouring to the Blessed Spirit that He should be thought to owe His origin to any but to the Father only. Whatever may have been the cause, it is certain that whilst asserting in the clearest terms the essential and eternal procession of the Holy Spirit from the Father, the Bishop of Mopsuestia is silent as to His derivation from or through the Son, or expresses a view antagonistic to that which S. Augustine was working out in the West. The following *e.g.* is his exposition of S. John xv. 26: ἐπιμαρτυρεῖ τὸ Πνεῦμα τοῖς λεγομένοις ὃ ἐξ αὐτῆς τοῦ Πατρὸς τῆς οὐσίας ἔχει τὴν ὕπαρξιν. εἰ γὰρ μὴ φυσικὴν ἐκεῖθεν πρόοδον ἔλεγε διὰ τοῦ 'ἐκπορεύεται', ἀλλὰ τὴν ἀποστολὴν ἔξωθεν γενομένην, ἄπορον περὶ τίνος λέγει· πολλῶν ὄντων κοινῶς τῶν κατὰ διακονίαν ἀποστελλομένων πνευμάτων...ἐνταῦθα δὲ ἰδικόν τί φησι, καὶ ὡς ἂν ἐκεῖνο γνωρίσαι ἱκανὸν ὃ μόνον ἐκ τοῦ Πατρὸς ἐκπορεύεται[1]. The comment on chap. xvi. 11, 12, is unfortunately lost[2]; but on c. xx. 22, Theodore opposes the idea that the Holy Spirit was given by our Lord's insufflation; "receive ye the Holy Ghost" meant only 'ye shall receive Him after My ascension[3].' On Rom. viii. 11, he remarks,

[1] Corderii *Catena*, p. 388. Cramer, II. 359 (Migne LXVI. 780).

[2] S. Chrysostom, Theodore's fellow-disciple, explains the ἐκ τοῦ ἐμοῦ λήμψεται to mean, ἐξ ὧν ἐγὼ οἶδα, ἐκ τῆς ἐμῆς γνώσεως· συνῳδὰ τοῖς ἐμοῖς ῥήμασιν (Corderii *Caten.* pp. 394—5).

[3] This fragment is extant only in a Latin version: Migne LXVI. 783. "hoc quod dictum est 'accipite' pro 'accipietis' dicit. Si enim cum insufflasset Spiritum dedisset discipulis quod valde quidam stulte existimaverunt superfluum erat dicere postea his...expectare promissionem Spiritus," &c. Contrast with this the comment of the Alexandrian Ammonius (Corder. *Caten.* p. 461): δι' ὧν ἐμφυσήσας ἔδωκε τὸ

Προειπὼν Πνεῦμα Χριστοῦ πάλιν φησὶ 'τὸ Πνεῦμα τοῦ ἐγείραντος Χριστόν'...ἐπαναγαγὼν ἀπὸ τοῦ Χριστοῦ ἐπὶ τὸν Πατέρα, οὐδὲν ἕτερον ἀλλ' ἢ σαφῶς διδάσκων ὅτι τοῦ Υἱοῦ καὶ τὸ Πνεῦμα οὐκ ἀλλότριον τῆς Πατρικῆς θεότητος[1]. The ἔκθεσις which bears the name of Theodore and is probably a genuine work, contains an explicit denial of the essential derivation through the Son: καὶ [πιστεύομεν] εἰς τὸ Πνεῦμα δὲ τὸ Ἅγιον ἐκ τῆς Θεοῦ τυγχάνον οὐσίας, οὐχ Υἱὸν, Θεὸν δὲ ὄντα τῇ οὐσίᾳ, ὡς ἐκείνης ὂν τῆς οὐσίας ἧσπερ ἐστιν ὁ Θεὸς καὶ Πατὴρ, ἐξ οὗπερ κατ' οὐσίαν ἐστιν...καὶ οὔτε Υἱὸν νομίζομεν οὔτε διὰ Υἱοῦ τὴν ὕπαρξιν εἰληφός[2].

The Bishop of Mopsuestia had scarcely passed away when both his Christology and his doctrine of the Procession were called into question[3]. Theodore died in the year 428—9; and on Nov. 22, 429[4], a sermon preached at Constantinople by one of the Antiochene clergy who had followed Nestorius to the capital fired the train unconsciously laid by the Syrian theologians. It is not within the scope of this essay to enter upon the history of the Nestorian controversy as it related to the Person of Christ; and it does not appear that Nestorius expressed himself distinctly upon the Procession of

Πνεῦμα ἔδειξεν ὅτι ὁμοούσιον αὐτοῦ ἐστι, καὶ οὐκ ἀλλότριον καὶ δι' αὐτοῦ προϊὸν ἐκ Πατρός.

[1] Migne, 821. Cramer gives (IV. 129) ὅτι ἐκ τοῦ Υἱοῦ καὶ τὸ Πνεῦμα. The preposition was removed by Fritzsche, as indeed the context imperatively required. Van der Moeren, following Cardinal Mai, retains ἐκ, and on the strength of it cites Theodore as a supporter of the *Filioque*. (p. 115.)

[2] Hahn, *Bibliothek der Symbole*, pp. 203—4. On its genuineness, see Fritzsche, *de Theod. vita et scriptis* p. 119 *sq.*: on the theological aspect of the οὔτε δι' Υἱοῦ, cf. Neander, *C. H.* IV. 89.

[3] Toe Water *de Theod. Antioch.* p. 6. "vix anno 429 ultimis in terra fatis functus erat; ecce, plures prodierunt haeresis notam ei inurere studentes."

[4] Neale, *Alexandria*, I. p. 235.

the Holy Ghost. But circumstances brought this collateral point into view at an early period in the dispute, which was in fact a battle all along the line between the rival schools of Antiochene and Alexandrian theology.

Nestorius, preaching at Constantinople during the winter of 428-9, had described in language novel and strange to the ears of Catholics, the office which God the Holy Ghost sustained toward the Humanity of our Lord. The Spirit, he said, had given to the Sacred Manhood the glory which distinguished it: the Spirit had formed the Flesh of Christ in the Virgin's womb; had endowed Him with the power of working miracles; had made His Body the Temple of God; had exalted it to Heaven (τὴν τοῦ ἀναληφθέντος τὸ Πνεῦμα κατελθὸν συνεκρότησε δόξαν...τὸ τὴν ἀνθρωπότητα αὐτοῦ διαπλάσαν...τὸ δαίμοσι φοβερὸν ἐργασάμενον. . .τὸ τὴν αὐτοῦ σάρκα πεποιημένον ναόν ...τὸ τὴν ἀνάληψιν αὐτῷ χαρισάμενον[1]). This teaching at once attracted the notice of the West, where in the summer of 430 it was examined at length by John Cassian, in his treatise on the Incarnation[2], written at the request of Leo, then Archdeacon of Rome. S. Cyril of Alexandria, to whom the Roman Patriarch committed the more responsible office of grappling with the heresiarch himself, attacked the new doctrine in a synodical letter which he addressed to Nestorius in the name of the Egyptian Church. The Holy Spirit, he argues, is not alien in essence from the Incarnate Son: Πνεῦμα γὰρ ἀληθείας ὠνόμασται, καὶ ἔστι Χριστὸς ἡ ἀλήθεια· καὶ προ-

[1] S. Cyrill. Alex. *c. Nestor.* IV. (Migne LXXVI. 170—181). Cf. *Sermones Nestorii* ap. Mar. Mercat. (Migne *P. L.* XLVIII. 767 sq.).

[2] Cassian. *de Incarn.* VII. 17—23. Migne *P. L.* L. 235 sq. Cf. Neale, *Alexandria*, pp. 249 sq.

χεῖται παρ' αὐτοῦ καθάπερ ἀμέλει καὶ ἐκ τοῦ Θεοῦ καὶ Πατρός[1]. This strongly Alexandrian statement is clenched by the following 'anathematism', which Nestorius is required to subscribe: *Εἴ τις φησὶ τὸν ἕνα Κύριον Ἰησοῦν Χριστὸν δοξάζεσθαι παρὰ τοῦ Πνεύματος, ὡς ἀλλοτρίᾳ δυνάμει τῇ ἰδίᾳ αὐτοῦ χρώμενον, καὶ παρ' αὐτοῦ λαβόντα τὸ ἐνεργεῖν δύνασθαι κατὰ πνευμάτων ἀκαθάρτων καὶ τὸ πληροῦν εἰς ἀνθρώπους τὰς θεοσημείας· καὶ οὐχὶ δὴ μᾶλλον ἴδιον αὐτοῦ τὸ Πνεῦμά φησι δι' οὗ καὶ ἐνήργησε τὰς θεοσημείας, ἀνάθεμα ἔστω.*

The Alexandrian manifesto reached Constantinople in December, 430; before it arrived the Emperor had issued orders for the assembling of an Œcumenical Synod at Ephesus the following Whitsuntide[2]. Meanwhile the literature of the subject continued to accumulate, and the 9th anathema in particular provoked considerable comment[3]. Nestorius contented himself with a counter-anathema against any who should pronounce the Spirit to be consubstantial with the "form of a servant[4]." But from two of his brother-Orientals to whom he applied for help through John of Antioch, there came a more definite reply to Cyril's challenge. Theodoret, Bishop of Cyrrhus in the patriarchate of Antioch[5], whose theological opinions had been

[1] S. Cyrilli *Ep.* XVII. (Migne LXXVII. 117 sq.) The *παρ' αὐτοῦ* refers to an essential derivation, for it is added, *Ἐπειδὴ τῆς τοῦ Πατρὸς δυνάμεως καὶ σοφίας, τουτέστι τοῦ Υἱοῦ Πνεῦμά ἐστιν, αὐτόχρημά ἐστι σοφία καὶ δύναμις.*

[2] Neale, *Alexandria*, p. 254.

[3] Mar. Mercat. *Nestor. Capit.* XII. (Migne *P. L.* XLVIII. 918).

[4] By the Antiochenes the *Capitula* were regarded as sheer Apollinarianism: cf. Theodoret. Ep. CXII. *γέγραφεν Ἰωάννης...Ἀπολιναρίου διδασκαλίαν τὰ κεφάλαια ταῦτα καλέσας.*

[5] See Dr Newman's account of Theodoret, *Historical Sketches*, III. p. 307 sq.

formed by Theodore of Mopsuestia, fastened at once upon the statement that the Spirit is ἴδιον τοῦ Υἱοῦ, and was led into a direct denial of this teaching *so far as it involved the idea of derivation* from the Son: ἴδιον δὲ τὸ Πνεῦμα τοῦ Υἱοῦ εἰ μὲν ὡς ὁμοφυὲς καὶ ἐκ Πατρὸς ἐκπορευόμενον ἔφη, συνωμολογήσομεν καὶ ὡς εὐσεβῆ δεξόμεθα τὴν φωνήν· εἰ δὲ ὡς ἐξ Υἱοῦ ἢ δι' Υἱοῦ τὴν ὕπαρξιν ἔχον, ὡς βλάσφημον τοῦτο καὶ ὡς δυσσεβὲς ἀπορρίψομεν. πιστεύομεν γὰρ τῷ Κυρίῳ λέγοντι, 'τὸ Πνεῦμα ὃ ἐκ τοῦ Πατρὸς ἐκπορεύεται·' καὶ τῷ θειοτάτῳ δὲ Παύλῳ ὁμοίως φάσκοντι, 'ἡμεῖς δὲ οὐ τὸ πνεῦμα τοῦ κόσμου ἐλάβομεν ἀλλὰ τὸ Πνεῦμα τὸ ἐκ τοῦ Θεοῦ.' In his reply to Theodoret S. Cyril is evidently unwilling to be drawn off from his main topic to this collateral point; but he clearly implies that there is a sense in which the Spirit may be said to be ἐξ Υἱοῦ without blasphemy or impiety: ἦν γὰρ καὶ ἔστιν αὐτοῦ τὸ Πνεῦμα καθάπερ ἀμέλει καὶ τοῦ Πατρός... ἐκπορεύεται μὲν γὰρ ὡς ἐκ τοῦ Θεοῦ καὶ Πατρὸς τὸ Πνεῦμα τὸ Ἅγιον...ἀλλ' οὐκ ἀλλότριον ἐστὶ τοῦ Υἱοῦ· πάντα γὰρ ἔχει μετὰ τοῦ Πατρός· καὶ τοῦτο αὐτὸς ἐδίδαξεν εἰπὼν περὶ τοῦ Ἁγίου Πνεύματος, 'Πάντα ὅσα ἔχει ὁ Πατὴρ ἐμά ἐστιν· διὰ τοῦτο εἶπον ὑμῖν ὅτι ἐκ τοῦ ἐμοῦ λήψεται καὶ ἀναγγελεῖ ὑμῖν[2].'

The other Eastern answer to S. Cyril's *capitula* was the work of Andrew of Samosata, but possessed a quasi-synodical character, having received the sanction of the Bishops then sitting in council at Antioch. Its language is more cautious than that of Theodoret's reply: the miracles of Christ had been wrought, the Orientals say, both by His own

[1] *repreh.* XII. *cap. Anath.* 9 (Migne *P. G.* LXXVI. 432).
[2] *ib.* (Migne, 433).

power and by the energy of the Spirit[1]: the same acts are attributed sometimes to the Father, sometimes to the Son, sometimes to the Holy Ghost: *οὕτω γὰρ καὶ μιᾶς τινὸς οὐσίας θείας ἠρτῆσθαι πάντα νοοῦμεν. ὡς γὰρ ἐνούσιος καὶ ἐνυπόστατος ὁ Μονογενὴς ἐξ αὐτῆς [v. l. αὐτοῦ] ἀπαθῶς ἐγεννήθη, καὶ τὸ Πνεῦμα δὲ καὶ αὐτὸ ἐξ αὐτῆς [v. l. αὐτοῦ] ἐκπορευόμενον ἐν ἰδίᾳ ὑποστάσει τυγχάνει.* Cyril again refuses to enter upon the question of derivation, simply adhering to his original point: *οὐκοῦν οὐχ ὡς ἀλλοτρίᾳ δυνάμει τῇ διὰ Πνεύματος ἐνηργῆσθαί φαμεν τὸν Ἐμμανουήλ· ἀποκεχρῆσθαι δὲ μᾶλλον αὐτῇ θεικῶς καὶ ἰδίαν ἔχειν τὴν τοῦ ὁμοουσίου Πνεύματος δύναμιν*[2].

The Œcumenical Council met June 22, 431. The third letter of S. Cyril to Nestorius, which contains the anathemas, was read and tacitly approved, no remark being elicited by the statement as to the Holy Ghost. This is the more noticeable, because the *capitula* were accompanied by an explanation (ἐπίλυσις) in which the language of the 9th anathema is considerably strengthened. The Word (S. Cyril now affirms) is all that the Father is, excepting the being Father (*πάντα ὑπάρχων ὅσα καὶ ὁ Πατὴρ δίχα μόνον τοῦ εἶναι Πατήρ*). Hence His relation to the Holy Spirit is the same as that which the Father bears to the Third Person: *ἴδιον ἔχων τὸ ἐξ αὐτοῦ καὶ οὐσιωδῶς ἐμπεφυκὸς αὐτῷ Πνεῦμα Ἅγιον εἰργάζετο τὰς δυνάμεις· ὥστε ἰδίᾳ δυνάμει τῇ διὰ τοῦ Πνεύματος ἐπλήρου τὰ θαύματα*[3].

But if the Council suffered this direct statement

[1] Migne, 356: ἀλλ' ἡμεῖς τὸν Κύριον ἡμῶν Ἰησοῦν Χριστὸν καὶ τῇ οἰκείᾳ δυνάμει καὶ τῇ τοῦ Πνεύματος ἐνεργείᾳ ἐπιτελέσαι τὰ σημεῖα ὁμολογοῦμεν.

[2] Migne, 360.

[3] *explic.* XII. *cap.* Anath. 9. (Migne LXXVI. 307.)

of the *Filioque* to pass without censure, it seems to have been equally unprepared to condemn the opposite view by any direct judgment of the Church. The opportunity for doing so presented itself, and was allowed to slip by. It so happened that in the sixth Session of the Council Nestorius was accused by Charisius, a Philadelphian Priest, of having employed agents to circulate his opinions in Lydia. These persons had offered to certain illiterate Quartodecimans who wished to return to the Catholic Church an exposition or rather a negation of the Faith (πίστεως ἔκθεσις μᾶλλον δὲ ἀπιστίας)[1], which they required the latter to subscribe. The ἔκθεσις was that which has been already noticed as the work of Theodore of Mopsuestia. In asking for a synodical condemnation of this document, Charisius seems to have proved his own orthodoxy by reciting a Creed which is now supposed to have been the symbol of the Philadelphian Church[2]. We have already quoted the words in which the Theodorean Creed sets forth the doctrine of the Holy Ghost: the Creed of Charisius does not touch upon the Procession, but professes faith εἰς τὸ Πνεῦμα τῆς ἀληθείας τὸ παράκλητον, ὁμοούσιον Πατρὶ καὶ Υἱῷ.

The Council replied to this communication by a double decree. (1) It forbade any member of the Church, priest or layman, to hold or teach the Nestorian doctrine of the Incarnation which was expressed in the Creed of Theodore (τὰ ἐν τῇ προσκομισθείσῃ ἐκθέσει ... περὶ τῆς ἐνανθρωπήσεως τοῦ

[1] Mansi 4 p. 1347. In the Acts of the Council it is styled Ἡ ἔκθεσις τοῦ παραπλασθέντος συμβόλου.

[2] See Dr Hort's *Dissertations*, p. 135. Dr H. points out that "in two respects the article on the Holy Spirit is unique: it omits ἅγιον and inserts ὁμοούσιον."

Μονογενοῦς Υἱοῦ τοῦ Θεοῦ, ἤγουν τὰ μιαρὰ καὶ διεστραμμένα Νεστορίου δόγματα, ἃ καὶ ὑποτέτακται). (2) It prohibited for the future the composition or use of any Creed differing from that of the Nicene Fathers (ἑτέραν πίστιν μηδενὶ ἐξεῖναι προσφέρειν ἤγουν συγγράφειν ἢ συντιθέναι παρὰ τὴν ὁρισθεῖσαν παρὰ τῶν ἁγίων πατέρων τῶν ἐν τῇ Νικαέων συνελθόντων σὺν Ἁγίῳ Πνεύματι)[1]. Both decisions have an indirect but important bearing on the history of the *Filioque* controversy. The first, by condemning only those portions of the Theodorean Creed which related to the doctrine of the Incarnation[2], practically postponed the Procession-question, leaving the door open for the interminable disputes of later times[3]. The second, by seeming to restrict the Church to the Creed of Nicaea, furnished Eastern controversialists of generations to come with one of their strongest arguments against the Latin προσθήκη[4]. The added *Filioque*, it was urged, had changed the character of the ancient Creed: the Latin Symbol was virtually "another Faith": it fell under the ban of the Ephesian decree. Thus the Council of

[1] Mansi 4 p. 1362—3. This Canon was re-enacted at Chalcedon and at the second and third Councils of Constantinople.

[2] Natal. Alex. *Diss.* XVIII. "Respondeo, Synodi Ephesinae patres non omnes Nestorii errores examinasse aut damnasse, sed eos tantum quos in mysterium Incarnationis evomuerat....Verba porro symboli quod a Charisio presbytero lectum est sensum Catholicum patiebantur, sc., Spiritum S. non fuisse factum nec creatum a Deo per Filium."

[3] It is difficult to repress speculation as to the course which the history and theology of the Church might have taken had the Ephesian Fathers judged this question ripe for a solution. Possibly the *ex solo Patre* of the East might in that case have been confined to the Nestorian Communion; whilst Catholics of East and West might have agreed to expound the Procession-clause of the Creed on the basis of S. Cyril's view, or by the insertion of words drawn, like the original clause, from the Gospel of S. John—'τὸ ἐκ τοῦ Υἱοῦ λαμβάνον.'

[4] Cf. Le Quien, *dissert. Damasc.* I. 34 (Migne *P. G.* XCIV. 230).

Ephesus, whilst it adjourned the battle of the *Filioque* to a later age, unconsciously prepared a weapon for the use of the future combatants.

After the Third Council the Antiochian view of the Procession fell into the shade, partly because it failed to attract any particular notice from the opposite party, partly in consequence of the absorbing interest which belonged to the Christological controversies of the fifth century. But the later works of Theodoret shew that his judgment in this particular underwent no real change; if he does not continue to meet S. Cyril's doctrine with a flat denial, he still lays exclusive emphasis on the procession from the Father. Thus in the *Compendium haereticarum fabularum*, written in the year 453, he sums up the doctrine of the Holy Ghost as follows: τὸ Πνεῦμα τὸ Ἅγιον ἐκ τοῦ Θεοῦ καὶ Πατρὸς ἔχειν τὴν ὕπαρξιν μεμαθήκαμεν· [S. John xvi. 7, xv. 26 are here cited] τῷ δὲ εἰπεῖν 'ἐκ τοῦ Πατρὸς ἐκπορεύεται' ἔδειξε πηγὴν ὄντα τοῦ Πνεύματος τὸν Πατέρα. καὶ οὐκ εἶπεν 'ἐκπορεύσεται' ἀλλὰ 'ἐκπορεύεται,' δεικνὺς καὶ τῆς φύσεως τὴν ταυτότητα καὶ τῆς οὐσίας τὸ ἄτμητον ...τὸ γὰρ ἐκπορευόμενον ἀχώριστον ἐξ οὗ ἐκπορεύεται[1]. A believer in the *Filioque* might have written thus, but he could scarcely have stopped at the point where Theodoret stops. The latter has exhausted his doctrine of the relation of the Spirit to the Son when he has mentioned the two points of *consubstantiality* and *mission*. Τὸ πανάγιον Πνεῦμα (he writes again, on Rom. viii. 9) καὶ Θεοῦ προσηγόρευσεν [ὁ ἀπόστολος] καὶ Χριστοῦ· οὐκ ἐπειδὴ κατὰ τοὺς δυσωνύμους αἱρετικοὺς ἐκ τοῦ Θεοῦ διὰ τοῦ Υἱοῦ δεδημιούργηται[2], ἀλλ' ἐπειδὴ ὁμοούσιόν ἐστι Πατρὸς

[1] *Haer. fab.* v. 3 (Migne LXXXIII. 454).

[2] One chief cause of the inveterate opposition which Theodoret

καὶ Υἱοῦ, καὶ ἐκ Πατρὸς μὲν ἐκπορεύεται κατὰ τὴν τῶν εὐαγγελίων διδασκαλίαν· ἡ δὲ τούτου χάρις τοῖς ἀξίοις διὰ τοῦ Χριστοῦ χορηγεῖται[1]. There is no room in this Pneumatology for an eternal procession either from or through the Son[2].

Theodoret's antagonist, S. Cyril, was taken to his rest A.D. 444, after an episcopate of more than 30 years. During this long official life his literary industry was equal to his energy in action, as the long list of his extant commentaries, letters, and dogmatic treatises attests. These remains afford ample opportunities of studying his view of the Procession. S. Cyril starts from the stand-point of his great predecessor, S. Athanasius, of whose

and his school manifested to the Western view of the Procession comes into sight here. It was confounded with the Macedonian doctrine of the Holy Spirit's creation by the Son. Cf. Neander, *Ch. H.* IV. 89, "On the part of the Oriental Church it was not the Western Church doctrine, but the doctrine of the creation of the Spirit which constituted the matter of dispute." See Le Quien, *diss. Damasc.* I. 3. But this was scarcely all; cf. Baur, *Dreieinigkeit* II. p. 165: "Es ist aus diesem Gegensatz deutlich zu ersehen, dass man, wie man auf der einen Seite das Interesse hatte, um dem Sohn nichts zu entziehen und ihn in seiner Einheit mit dem Vater aufzufassen, den Geist in der engsten Beziehung zum Sohn zu betrachten, so auf der andern Seite um dem absoluten Wesen des Vaters nichts zu vergeben, den Geist ausschliesslich dem Vater vindiciren zu müssen glaubte, wenigstens sofern er das Princip seines Daseyns nur im Vater haben sollte."

[1] Migne LXXXII. 132.

[2] Among the spurious works attributed to S. Justin is an ἔκθεσις τῆς ὀρθῆς ὁμολογίας which appears to be due to a Nestorian writer of the fifth century. In this treatise we notice the same tendency to lay stress upon the procession *from the Father*: ἐκ τῆς οἰκείας οὐσίας ὁ Πατὴρ τὸν Υἱὸν ἀπεγέννησεν, ἐκ δὲ τῆς αὐτῆς τὸ Πνεῦμα προήγαγεν.... ὥσπερ ὁ Υἱὸς ἐκ τοῦ Πατρὸς, οὕτω καὶ τὸ Πνεῦμα· πλήν γε δὴ τῷ τρόπῳ τῆς ὑπάρξεως διοίσει. ὁ μὲν γὰρ φῶς ἐκ φωτὸς ἐξέλαμψε· τὸ δὲ φῶς μὲν ἐκ φωτὸς καὶ αὐτό· οὐ μὴν γεννητῶς ἀλλ' ἐκπορευτῶς προῆλθεν. That the Holy Spirit is called 'Spirit of Christ,' 'Spirit of the Son,' is owing to the συνάφεια (Migne VI. 1209 sq.). On the date of this ἔκθεσις see Neale, *H. E. Ch.* Intr. ii. p. 1098.

writings he was a diligent student[1]. With Cyril as with Athanasius, the relation of the Spirit to the Son is a direct consequence of the Homoousion; but Cyril carries the inference further: ᾗ μὲν γάρ ἐστι Θεὸς καὶ ἐκ Θεοῦ ὁ Υἱὸς...ἴδιον αὐτοῦ καὶ ἐν αὐτῷ τε καὶ ἐξ αὐτοῦ τὸ Πνεῦμα, καθάπερ ἀμέλει καὶ ἐπ' αὐτοῦ νοεῖται τοῦ Θεοῦ καὶ Πατρός[2]. This passage well exhibits the points of S. Cyril's doctrine, and the order in which it was probably developed. (1) He saw that if the Son is True God, the Spirit of God must be His very own: οὐκ ὀθνεῖον...ἀλλὰ τὸ τῆς οὐσίας αὐτοῦ καὶ τῆς τοῦ Πατρὸς αὐτοῦ ἴδιον Πνεῦμα[3]. (2) Next, this relation of the Spirit to Christ involves an immanence in the Son, and a dependence upon the Person of the Son, with which the procession from the Father does not interfere. Thus, in the commentary on S. Luke xi. 20 we read, Ὥσπερ ὁ δάκτυλος ἀπήρτηται τῆς χειρὸς, οὐκ ἀλλότριος ὢν αὐτῆς ἀλλ' ἐν αὐτῇ φυσικῶς· οὕτω καὶ τὸ Πνεῦμα τὸ Ἅγιον τῷ τῆς ὁμοουσιότητος λόγῳ συνῆπται πρὸς ἕνωσιν τῷ Υἱῷ, κἂν ἐκ τοῦ Θεοῦ καὶ Πατρὸς ἐκπορεύηται[4]. (3) Further, from the essential relation of the Son to the Father and of the Spirit to Both, it follows that the Spirit in proceeding from the Father, goes forth (*a*) through, (*b*) from, and (*c*) out of the Son. The following are instances of S. Cyril's teaching on these points: (*a*) ὥσπερ γὰρ πρόεισιν ἐκ τοῦ Πατρὸς τὸ Πνεῦμα τὸ Ἅγιον αὐτοῦ κατὰ φύσιν ὑπάρχον, καὶ κατὰ τὸν ἴσον τούτῳ τρόπον καὶ δι' αὐτοῦ τοῦ Υἱοῦ, φυσικῶς ὂν αὐτοῦ

[1] Neale, *Alexandria*, p. 226.

[2] *In Joel.* ii. 28, 29 (Migne LXXI. 378). [In quoting from S. Cyril I have made free use of Mr Philip Pusey's Preface to his English translation of S. Cyril on S. John (pp. IX—XXI)].

[3] *De SS. Trin. dial.* vii. (Migne LXXV. 1094).

[4] *In S. Luc.* xi. 20 (Migne LXXII. 704).

καὶ ὁμοούσιον αὐτῷ[1]. (*b*) τὸ ἴδιον αὐτοῦ καὶ παρ' αὐτοῦ κατὰ φύσιν προχεόμενον Πνεῦμα[2]. (*c*) ὁ δέ γε Κύριος ἡμῶν Ἰησοῦς Χριστὸς ἐξ ἰδίου πληρώματος προιεὶς τὸ Πνεῦμα, καθὰ καὶ αὐτὸς ὁ Πατὴρ, οὐχ ὡς ἐκ μέτρου δίδωσιν αὐτὸ τοῖς ἀξίοις ἐλεῖν[3]. Again: ἐξ αὐτοῦ κατὰ φύσιν ὑπάρχον καὶ ἐπὶ τὴν κτίσιν παρ' αὐτοῦ πεμπόμενον τὸν ἀνακαινισμὸν ἐργάζεται[4]. The last passage seems specially important as clearly distinguishing the essential derivation from the temporal mission, and basing the latter upon the former. (4) Lastly, S. Cyril does not hesitate to include the procession from the Father, and the 'going forth out of' the Son, under the common formula "from the Father and the Son" or "from Both": (*a*) ὅτε τοίνυν τὸ Πνεῦμα τὸ Ἅγιον ἐν ἡμῖν γενόμενον συμμόρφους ἡμᾶς ἀποδεικνύει Θεοῦ, πρόεισι δὲ ἐκ Πατρὸς καὶ Υἱοῦ· πρόδηλον ὅτι τῆς θείας ἐστὶν οὐσίας, οὐσιωδῶς ἐν αὐτῇ ὂν καὶ ἐξ αὐτῆς προϊόν[5]. (*b*) εἴπερ ἐστὶ τοῦ Θεοῦ καὶ Πατρὸς καὶ μὴν καὶ τοῦ Υἱοῦ τὸ οὐσιωδῶς ἐξ ἀμφοῖν ἤγουν ἐκ Πατρὸς δι' Υἱοῦ προχεόμενον Πνεῦμα[6]. From (*b*) it appears that in S. Cyril's Pneumatology δι' Υἱοῦ and ἐξ Υἱοῦ are of identical meaning; and that by both expressions he intended to convey the idea of an essential derivation from the Son, as being One in Essence with the Father from Whom the Holy Ghost proceeds.

[1] *Adv. Nestor.* IV. 3 (Migne LXXVI. 184). Cf. *supr.* αὐτοῦ δηλονότι τὸ Πνεῦμά ἐστιν ὡς δι' αὐτῆς προϊὸν τῆς ἀπορρήτου φύσεως αὐτοῦ.

[2] In S. Joann. i. 33 (Migne LXXIII. 212).

[3] *Adv. Nestor.* IV. I (Migne LXXVI. 173).

[4] *Thesaurus*, (Migne LXXV. 608)—a passage "likewise extant in a Syriac translation in the MS. in the Brit. Mus. Additional 14556, assigned by Dr Wright to the 6th or 7th century." (Mr P. Pusey, *Preface to Comm. on S. John*, p. xii. : see his remarks on the corroborative evidence supplied by the Syriac MSS. of S. Cyril, *infr.* p. xx).

[5] *Thesaur.* (Migne LXXV. 585).

[6] *De adorat.* I. (Migne LXVIII. 147).

We have seen how some sixteen hundred miles further to the West S. Augustine had recently proclaimed in the Latin tongue the Procession of the Holy Ghost from the Father and the Son. S. Cyril, following the tradition of his own Church, and working under the guidance of the earlier Greek theologians, reached substantially the same result; and his teaching received at least the tacit consent of contemporary Eastern Catholics. In one point only the Latin West was now in advance of the Greek East. The great North African Bishop had used *procedere* of the Father and the Son, without distinction: the great Alexandrian Patriarch had kept ἐκπορεύεσθαι, as Scripture keeps it, to express the derivation of the Third Person from the First. The difference might have seemed to be unimportant, lying in the use of words, rather than in the truth of things: yet in it there lay the germ of a long and yet unfinished strife between the Churches of Eastern and Western Christendom[1].

[1] Of the dispute as to the Procession between Alexandria and the Syrian School we hear nothing more: but it seems possible to trace indications of a lasting although unconscious difference upon this point in the liturgical forms of the Eastern sects who owe their origin to the Nestorian and Eutychian controversies. In the recitation of the Creed, indeed, all the Oriental sects agree to reject the *Filioque*. Renaudot (*L. O.* II. 198, sq.) states that no interpolated MS. copy of any authority, whether ancient or modern, exists amongst either Nestorians or Monophysites. The Maronite office-books contain the Latin addition; but they have confessedly been revised by Latin hands: and even in some of the Maronite MS. liturgies, written since the submission to Rome, the *Filioque* is missing. In Oriental expositions of the Creed the προσθήκη is often made the ground of an accusation against the "Franks," *i.e.* Latin Christians.

But in the prayers of the Liturgy a distinction is visible. The Nestorian Liturgies lay a marked emphasis on the Procession from the Father; e. g. *Lit. of the Apostles*, "the Holy Ghost of Thine own glorious Essence [i. e. the Father's]:" *Lit. of Theodore*, "the Spirit of Truth Who, O Father, is from Thee:" *Lit. of Nestorius*,

"Who proceedeth forth from Thee, O Father, and Who is of the hidden Essence of Thy Godhead." (*Syriac Liturgies*, transl. by Dr Badger for East. Ch. Assoc., Rivingtons, 1875; cf. Renaudot, II. pp. 601, 621, 614.) On the other hand the Jacobite and Melchite Liturgies repeatedly refer to the Holy Spirit's "receiving from the Son," and bring this phrase close up to the Latin view by adding "the things which pertain to the Son's Essence" (Renaudot, I. 198, II. 136, 263, 348, 529); whilst in one Jacobite office, the *Liturgy of S. Clement*, we even find the words "Send down to us Thy Holy Spirit...Who proceedeth from Thee eternally through Thy Only Begotten Son" (Renaudot, II. 191, 200). It does not appear, however, that the Oriental sects were conscious of any practical difference in the teaching of their office-books. The Nestorians never converted the simple statement of the Constantinopolitan Faith into the *ex solo Patre:* nor did their opponents pass from their *ex Filio accipit essentialiter* into the *ex Patre Filioque procedit* of the West (Assemani, *Bibl. Orient.* III. § *de Syris Nestor.*, pp. CCXXXII—V. Ib. *de Syris Monoph.* p. 16). Their descendants in Syria and South India appear on the whole to follow in this respect in their fathers' steps (Badger, *Nestorians*, p. 78 sq.: Howard, *Christians of S. Thomas*, pp. 294, 316). The Armenian Church, indeed, although regarded as Jacobite, seems now to teach *ex solo Patre* (Malan, *S. Gregory the Illuminator*, p. 49). Yet Mr Malan himself quotes the following from the Armenian acts of S. Thaddeus: "Call him not a deceiver who gave me to know my Lord the Maker of heaven and earth, and the Only Son of God, with the Holy Ghost, *Who comes from Them.*" For further evidence that a view approaching the *Filioque* was held in the ancient Armenian Church, see Van der Moeren, p. 139 sq.

CHAPTER VII.

THE WEST, FROM THE DEATH OF S. AUGUSTINE TO THE ACCEPTANCE OF THE *Filioque* BY THE CHURCH OF SPAIN.

"Symbolo Catholicae fidei nova nolite inserere."
Alcuin, *Ep.* LXIX.

AFTER the death of S. Augustine Western Europe appears to have generally adopted the Augustinian view of the Procession, almost without being conscious of the change thus made in its theology. At Aquileia[1], indeed, after the middle of the fifth century, S. Nicetas taught the Procession from the Father with an emphasis which seems to prove either that the *Filioque* was unknown in his Church, or that it was regarded there as being an unnecessary refinement upon the simple faith: "sufficit fidelibus hoc scire quia Filius quidem genitus est, Spiritus autem de Patre procedens est...credimus ergo Spiritum Sanctum Paraclitum de Patre procedere; esse autem non Filium, neque Filium Filii ...sed Spiritum veritatis, cujus processio aut qualis aut quanta sit nulli conceditur scire[2]." But it was

[1] On the position of Aquileia as a border town, and the seat of an independent Patriarchate, see the remarks of Mr Ffoulkes, *Ath. Creed*, p. 14 sq. The fact may account for the absence in the teaching of Nicetas of all trace of the growing Western belief.

[2] Migne LII. 854. Cf. the *expl. Symb.* p. 870. "Credis et in Spiritum S. Hic Spiritus S. unus est, sanctificans omnia; qui de Patre procedit solus scrutans mysteria et profunda Dei." Again not a word of His relation to the Son.

otherwise in Gaul, in Africa, and at Rome, where, during this century and the next, the fuller doctrine of the Procession seems to have gradually established itself as an authorized gloss upon the Catholic doctrine of the Holy Ghost.

Thus, from Gaul between the years 430 and 530 we receive the following chain of testimony to the belief in a Procession from the Son. S. Eucherius, Bishop of Lyons, who died A. D. 454, writes, "Spiritus Sanctus nec genitus nec ingenitus...sed potius qui ex Patre et Filio procedat, velut quaedam Patris Filiique concordia[1]." Faustus, Bishop of Riez (*ob.* 485), notwithstanding his Semi-Pelagian sympathies, is said to have preached as follows: "Quia Spiritus S. de utroque procedit, ideo dicitur 'qui autem Spiritum Christi non habet hic non est ejus'; et alio loco, 'insufflavit et dixit Accipite Spiritum Sanctum[2].'" Gennadius, a priest of Marseilles (*ob.* 495), in his book *On the Doctrines of the Church*, thus expounds the faith as it regards the Person of the Holy Ghost: "Credimus unum esse Deum, Patrem et Filium et Spiritum Sanctum... Spiritus Sanctus eo quod sit ex Patre et Filio procedens Patri et Filio coaeternus. Pater ergo principium Deitatis...a quo Spiritus Sanctus, non natus, quia non est Filius; neque ingenitus, quia non est Pater; neque factus, quia non est ex nihilo, sed ex Deo Patre et Deo Filio Deus procedens[3]." Julianus Pomerius, a priest of Arles (*ob.* 498), writing *On the Contemplative Life*, reckons

[1] Migne L. 774.

[2] Mai, *Spic. Rom.* V. 93. Another passage, cited by Card. Mai as from Faustus (*nov. Patr. bibl.* IV. 45), had been printed in t. I. p. 293 of the same work as part of a sermon of S. Augustine. Cf. Van der Moeren, pp. 55, 60.

[3] Migne LVIII. 980.

the *Filioque* among points of doctrine which ought to be taught to all the faithful: "cum...fideles qui nobis divinitus instituendi commissi sunt instruere debeamus de Patre...de Filio...de Spiritu Sancto, quomodo ex Patre et Filio procedens nec ingenitus possit dici, nec genitus[1]." Lastly, Avitus, Archbishop of Vienne (*ob.* 523), in his defence of the Deity of the Spirit against the Arian Gothic king, Gundobad, seems to have openly professed, "Nos vero Spiritum Sanctum dicimus a Filio et Patre procedere." Another fragment of the same book even claims for this view the support of the Catholic Faith; "sicut est proprium Spiritui Sancto a Patre Filioque procedere, istud catholica fides etiamsi renuentibus non persuaserit in suae tamen disciplinae regula non excedit[2]." Unless we regard the word *Filioque* in this passage as interpolated, or dispute the genuineness of the passage, it would appear as if the Western doctrine had already found place in a Creed used in the South of France at the beginning of the sixth century.

About the same time S. Fulgentius, Bishop of Ruspe (*ob.* 533), thus teaches what we may presume to have been the current belief of the African Church: "Firmissime tene et nullatenus dubites eundem Spiritum Sanctum, qui Patris et Filii unus Spiritus est, de Patre et Filio procedere...De Filio quoque procedere Spiritum Sanctum, prophetica atque apostolica nobis doctrina commendat[3]." To

[1] Migne LIX. 432.

[2] Migne LIX. 385—6.

[3] *De fide* 11 (Migne LXV. 696). The words suggest, however, that the Augustinian view was not undisputed even in the Church where it had been first distinctly taught. The profession addressed in 484 to the Arian king Huneric by Eugenius of Carthage, with the concurrence of the Catholic bishops of Africa, Mauritania, Sardinia and Corsica, is silent

Ferrandus he writes, "Non potuit Spiritum Sanctum divinitas Filii accipere, cum ipse Spiritus Sanctus sic procedat a Filio sicut procedit a Patre et sic detur a Filio sicut datur a Patre; nec illa natura unde Spiritus Sanctus habet originem [*sc.* natura Filii] potuit ejus vel exspectare vel accipere largitatem. Spiritus ille totus est Patris, totus est Filii, quia unus naturaliter est Spiritus Patris et Filii. Proinde totus de Patre procedit et Filio, totus in Patre manet ac Filio; quia sic manet ut procedat, sic procedit ut maneat[1]." A fragment of his work *On the equality and unity of the Holy Spirit with the Father and the Son* exhibits the ground on which this clear exposition of the *Filioque* is based: "de natura Patris natus est Filius, et exinde procedit Spiritus Sanctus...de Patre et Filio Spiritus Sanctus audit, quia de Patre et Filio divinitatis aequalitate procedit[2]." In other words, Fulgentius, like his master Augustine, teaches that the Holy Ghost proceeds *principaliter de Patre;* and that He proceeds from the Son by virtue of the *Homoousion* and of the Father's gift, without detriment to the μοναρχία or to the personal unity of Him Who thus proceeds from Both.

At Rome during this period S. Augustine's view of the Procession appears to have received occasional sanction even from the Popes. S. Leo the Great, who was a younger contemporary of the Bishop of Hippo, preaches in his first sermon on the

as to the *Filioque:* "accipimus...ingenitum Patrem et de Patre genitum Filium et de Patre procedentem Spiritum Sanctum." (Migne LVIII. 219: "de Patre *et Filio*" is printed in the text, but a foot-note points out that the MSS. are not unanimous. Cf. *infr.* 231, "de Patre procedit," where there is no variant.)

[1] *Ep.* XIV. 28 (Migne, 373).

[2] *c. Fabian. fragm.* XXVIII. (Migne LXV. 732).

Feast of Pentecost, "Spiritus Sanctus Patris Filiique...Spiritus non sicut quaecumque creatura quae et Patris et Filii est, sed sicut cum utroque vivens et potens, et sempiterne ex eo quod est Pater Filiusque subsistens[1]." In the second sermon he thus expounds our Lord's *de meo accipiet:* "quod accipit Spiritus Sanctus, Patre dante, dat Filius[2]." Pope Hormisdas (*ob.* 523), if the printed text of his epistles is to be trusted, wrote to the Greek Emperor Justin as follows: "Proprium Spiritus Sancti ut de Patre et Filio procederet sub una substantia Deitatis[3]." On the other hand, in the confession of faith sent by Pope Pelagius (*ob.* 559) to the Frank king Childebert, we read only, "Credo in...Spiritum Sanctum omnipotentem utrique consempiternum atque consubstantialem, qui ex Patre intemporaliter procedens Patris est Filiique Spiritus[4]." Forty years later the writings of S. Gregory the Great give no uncertain sound. The Spirit is said to be sent by the Father and the Son, because He proceeds from Their Essence: "mitti etiam juxta naturam divinitatis possit intelligi...ejus [*sc.* Spiritus Sancti] missio ipsa processio est qua de Patre procedit et Filio[5]." "The Redeemer imparted to the hearts of His disciples the Spirit who proceeds from Himself (qui a se [*v. l.* ex se] procedit)[6]." The

[1] *Serm.* LXXVI. (Migne LIV. 402).

[2] *Serm.* LXXVI. (Migne, 404). For the still more explicit statement in his letter to Turibius, see below, p. 165.

[3] *Ep.* LXXIX. (Migne LXXIII. 514, note: "In eodem cod. primigenia manus ita hunc textum ferebat: *notum etiam quod sit proprium Spiritus Sancti, proprium autem Filii Dei ut &c.*, quam lectionem ita reformat manus antiqua et fere aequalis," [as in text]. So that the passage cannot be regarded as certain.)

[4] *Ep.* XV. (Migne LXIX. 409).

[5] *Hom. in Evang.* ii. 26 (Migne LXXVI. 1193).

[6] *Moral.* I. 22 (Migne, 541).

promise, "I will shew you plainly of the Father," is thus interpreted: "per patefactam tunc majestatis suae speciem et quoniam ipse Genitori non impar oriatur, et quomodo utrorumque Spiritus utrique coaeternus procedat ostendet; aperte namque tunc videbitur quomodo... is qui per processionem producitur a proferentibus non praeitur[1]."

Paschasius, a deacon of the Roman Church, who died A.D. 512, has left a treatise *On the Holy Spirit* which teaches the *Filioque* distinctly enough: "mitti a Patre et Filio dicitur et de ipsorum substantia procedere...si requiras quid inter nascentem et procedentem distet evidenter hoc interest, quod iste ex uno nascitur, ille ex utroque procedit[2]." About the middle of the same century (549) Rusticus, another Roman Deacon, expresses doubt upon the subject. His words suggest that a difference of opinion upon the Procession was already making itself felt, and that the sentiments of Theodore and Theodoret were being appealed to by those who hesitated to receive the Augustinian doctrine[3]: "quidam vero antiquorum et hoc proprietatibus adjecerunt quia sicut Spiritus cum Patre Filium sempiterne non

[1] *Moral.* XXX. 4 (Migne LXXVI. 534). Still more decisive is the passage in *Dialog.* ii. 38 (Migne LXVI. 204). "Cum enim constet quia Paracletus Spiritus a Patre semper procedat et Filio, cur se Filius recessurum dicit ut ille veniat quia a Filio nunquam recedit?" But the Greek version of Pope Zacharias gives 'ἐκ τοῦ Πατρὸς προέρχεται καὶ ἐν τῷ Υἱῷ διαμένει,' and this suits the context: see Le Quien, *diss. Damasc.* I. § xxii. On the other hand, cf. Van der Moeren, p. 63.

[2] *De Sp. S.* I. 12 (Migne LXII. 23).

[3] See next chapter, p. 180. Rusticus had just written, "Nos enim tres esse subsistentias ob hoc confitemur, quod non in eo quod quid est secundum naturam, sed in eo quod qualiter sit unumquodque, proprietatibus distinguatur. Nam Pater quidem generat et genitus non est; et ex aliquo alio non est, sicut ex eo sunt alii: Filius vero genitus est et nihil consempiternum generat; et Spiritus S. a Patre procedit vel genitus est ab eo."

genuit, sic nec procedit Spiritus a Filio sicut a Patre; ego vero quia Spiritus quidem Filium non genuerit sempiterne confiteor (nec enim duos dicimus Patres); utrum vero a Filio eodem modo quo a Patre procedat, nondum perfecte satisfactum habeo[1]." But though the writer suspends his judgment, it is obvious that he regards the denial of the *Filioque*, rather than its assertion, as an innovation upon the original Faith. His own doubt appears to have reference to the exact meaning of the *Filioque:* is the procession from the Son precisely analogous to the procession from the Father; or does the Spirit proceed from the Father alone as the Fountain of His Divine life? from the Son mediately and by the Father's gift? But unfortunately we are left to conjecture the nature of his difficulty, for he at once dismisses this subject as irrelevant to the matter which he had in hand; "quoniam vero ad id quod nunc quaeritur nihil attinet, signandum quidem est, sed transeundum[2]."

Lastly, before leaving the Roman Church for the present, two of its greatest laymen must be heard, both in favour of the now popular view. "Ita cogitemus," writes the philosopher Boetius in his book *On the Trinity*, "processisse quidem ex Deo Patre Filium Deum, et ex utrisque Spiritum Sanctum[3]." To Cassiodorus, a few years later, the doctrine of the Procession from the Son came with all the authority of the Catholic Church: "O vere sancta,

[1] *c. Acephalos* (Migne LXVII. 1237).

[2] To this the heretical interlocutor is made to assent: "Et ego nunc interim de his ipsis loqui non arbitror utile." The remark is instructive, as shewing how the Procession controversy was shelved, generation after generation, owing to the pressure of more important questions.

[3] *de Trin.* 5 (Migne LXIV. 1254).

o immaculata, o perfecta mater ecclesia," he exclaims, "cujus piae confessioni nihil addi, nihil minui potest.... Patrem..docens ingenitum, Filium genitum, Spiritum Sanctum de Patre et Filio procedentem...unum Deum.... Dominumque Christum.. unam confiteri esse personam[1]." The great Senator was doubtless wrong: the Church Catholic had not proclaimed the *Filioque;* she has not proclaimed it yet. Even Rome at this period had not learned to regard the Procession from the Son as *de fide.* Nevertheless the time was close at hand when the words which express it were to receive synodical approval and admission into the Creed from one of the principal branches of the Western Church.

Spain, which probably received the Gospel from S. Paul himself[2], had won an honourable place in the annals of early Christianity. S. Irenaeus bears witness to the soundness of her faith[3]: Tertullian, to the progress of her Church, even then conterminous with the peninsula[4]. Spanish martyrs are among the Saints: S. Fructuosus of Tarragona, who suffered under Valerian; S. Vincentius of Saragossa, who confessed Christ in the persecutions of Diocletian[5]. One of the earliest of Western Synods

[1] *In psalt. praef.* 17 (Migne LXX. 23). Cf. *Expos. in Ps.* 4 (Migne, 367). "Proprium est Filio quod naturaliter a Patre generatus est: proprium est Spiritui Sancto quod a Patre et Filio procedit."

[2] Rom. xv. 24, 28, *ὡς ἂν πορεύωμαι εἰς τὴν Σπανίαν...ἀπελεύσομαι δι' ὑμῶν εἰς Σπανίαν*: S. Clem. *ad Cor.* I. 5, *ὁ Παῦλος...ἐπὶ τὸ τέρμα τῆς δύσεως ἐλθών* (cf. Dr Lightfoot's note): *Muratorian Canon* (Westcott *on the Canon*, p. 479), "profectionem Pauli ab urbe ad Spaniam proficiscentis." Cf. Florez, *España Sagrada*, III. 144 sq.

[3] Iren. I. x. 2, *ἡ δύναμις τῆς παραδόσεως μία καὶ ἡ αὐτή· καὶ οὔτε αἱ ἐν Γερμανίαις ἱδρυμέναι ἐκκλησίαι ἄλλως πεπιστεύκασιν...οὔτε ἐν ταῖς Ἰβηρίαις.*

[4] Tertull. *adv. Judaeos*, 7, 8, "Hispaniarum omnes termini" [crediderunt Christo].

[5] Baronius, *a.* 262. Fleury VIII. § xlviii. Florez, *Esp. Sagr.* VI. 347 sq.

was held in Spain[1]; and at the first Œcumenical Council a Spanish Bishop was the acknowledged leader of the orthodox West[2], subscribing the Canons before the representatives of the See of Rome. The fall of Hosius in extreme old age, and under physical pressure, can hardly be regarded as a blot upon the fair fame of the early Spanish Church. A darker cloud gathered over the Catholic cause in Spain during the last five and twenty years of the fourth century. In the very year which saw the defeat of Macedonianism and Apollinarianism in the East, a Council of Spanish Bishops was less successfully contending with the rising heresy of Priscillian[3]. The new doctrine appears to have been a *farrago* of earlier and exploded errors, combining Gnostic and Manichean fancies with a Sabellian confusion of the Persons in the Holy Trinity[4]. Priscillian was executed by the civil power, but his sect continued to spread; and in 415 the Spanish priest Orosius was sent into Africa to ask the aid of the already renowned Bishop of Hippo[5]. A tract by the latter (*Contra Priscillianistas*) remains as the result of this mission. But even the authority of

[1] The Council of Elvira, which Mr Ffoulkes (*Dict. of Christian Antiq.* I. 606) places between 313 and 324 A. D.

[2] Cf. Stanley, *Eastern Church*, p. 129.

[3] At Caesaraugusta (Saragossa) 380—1. (Baronius, *a.* 381.)

[4] S. Aug. *de Haer.* 70, "Maxime Gnosticorum et Manichaeorum dogmata sectantur; quamvis et ex aliis haeresibus in eas sordes tamquam in sentinam quamdam horribili confusione confluxerint." *Contr. Priscill.* 4, "Priscillianus Sabellianum antiquum dogma restituit, ubi ipse Pater qui Filius, qui et Spiritus Sanctus perhibetur." Cf. Orosii *Comment. ad Aug.* 2, "Trinitatem autem solis verbis loquebatur; nam unionem absque ulla existentia aut proprietate asserens, sublato et Patre, Filium et Spiritum Sanctum hunc esse unum Christum dicebat." The last words, if the reading is correct, seem specially deserving of notice in connexion with the present subject.

[5] Fleury, XXIII. § xvi.

Augustine failed to extirpate the heresy; at a Council of Braga held in the year 563, it was still necessary to anathematize the Priscillianist doctrines, and foremost among them the revived Sabellianism which taught "unam tantum ac solitariam...esse personam, ita ut sit Pater qui Filius, ipse etiam sit Paracletus Spiritus [1]."

It was while the Church of Spain was battling with this formidable enemy, that the peninsula was deluged by a succession of Arian invaders who for more than a century and a half resisted the Faith which they could not destroy. In 409 the Vandals, Suevi and Alani swept across the Pyrenees into Spain: in 416 the Visigoths followed. The West Goths had received at their conversion an Arian form of Christianity: the Suevi, originally Catholic, yielded to the stronger race[2]. It was not till past the middle of the sixth century that the province of Gallaecia returned to the Faith; the conversion of the Visigoths was delayed nearly thirty years more. In no part of Europe, Lombardy alone excepted, did Arianism so long retain the upper hand. The Church of Spain doubtless required all the discipline which she underwent; the purity of her morals was not equal to the orthodoxy of her creed. "Gothos ac Wandalos haeretici nominis exprobatione despicimus"—is Salvian's honest confession—"cum ipsi haeretica pravitate vivamus[3]." It seems also to be a well

[1] Mansi, *Conc.* 9, 774 sq. Cf. Neander, *Ch. H.* IV. pp. 497 (note), 502.

[2] Cf. Cennius, *de antiq. Eccl. Hispan.* I. pp. 186, 218.

[3] *de gubern. Dei*, VII. 11 (Migne LIII. 135). The writer is speaking primarily of Gaul; but Spain, he implies, was, if anything, worse: *infr.* 7: "Hispanias nonne vel eadem vel majora forsitan vitia perdiderunt?......dupliciter in illa Hispanorum captivitate ostendere Deus voluit quantum et odisset carnis libidinem et diligeret castitatem, cum et Wandalos ob solam maxime pudicitiam superponeret, et Hispanos

ascertained fact that the Arian masters of Spain did not generally abuse their power to the direct persecution of their Catholic subjects. Gibbon is perhaps not quite impartial when he states that "the Catholics of Spain enjoyed under the reign of the Arians the free and peaceful exercise of their religion;" and he subsequently admits that to one of the Visigothic kings "the guilt of persecution may be imputed[1]." Still it does not appear that during the greater part of this period the public functions of the Church were suspended. Councils were occasionally held; bishoprics were for the most part filled up when vacancies occurred; communications were maintained with other Churches and with the see of Rome. Nevertheless the fact remains that from the beginning of the fifth century to the last quarter of the sixth, Catholicism in Spain had to maintain its ground in the face of a dominant Arianism—an Arianism which included the errors of Macedonius and Eunomius and represented God the Holy Ghost as the creature of a created Son[2].

ob solam vel maxime impudicitiam subjugaret." See Dr Neale's Essay on the Mozarabic Liturgy (*Essays on Liturgiology*, p. 125 sq.). I extract the following: "In Spain all seems out of joint...there are however two key-notes which unhappily characterize the whole history of the Peninsular Church—laxity of morals, and violence in the propagation of the faith...How it was that Spain and Aquitaine were plunged into such an excess of licentiousness at the time of the Visigothic invasion is one of those mysteries of ecclesiastical history that cannot be solved...Doubtless the Arian domination purified the lives of the Catholics...But it is even more curious to trace from the very earliest times that headstrong violence which is the great characteristic of the Spanish Church." Dr Neale then instances the punishment of Priscillian, and the unauthorised introduction of single affusion into the ritual, and of the *Filioque* into the Creed.

[1] *Decline and Fall*, ch. XXXVII. Euric, Gibbon's persecutor, reigned A.D. 467—485.

[2] Roderic. Tolet. *de reb. Hisp.* II. I: "talia juxta eundem Arium de ipsa divinitate documenta sumpsere ut crederent...Spiritum S. nec

It is not surprising that, between Priscillianism on the one hand and Arianism on the other, the Spanish Church was forced into a controversial and dogmatic attitude unique in the West[1]. Nowhere else in Western Christendom was the Catholic doctrine of the Holy Trinity so strenuously affirmed or so minutely defined by ecclesiastical authority. At Spanish Councils it became usual, even when the subject of their deliberations was of a purely practical character, to open the proceedings by reciting the Nicene or the Constantinopolitan Creed, or both, followed by an exposition of the faith in language adopted or approved by the particular Synod. It is easy to see that such a practice, although not without its uses in a disturbed condition of ecclesiastical affairs, had its elements of danger also; in the eagerness of men to defend the Faith against local adversaries, the wise reticence of Catholic tradition upon certain mysterious points of doctrines would not improbably be broken through and the unity of Catholic doctrine impaired.

The *Concilia* contain the acts of a Council held at Toledo in 398 or 400[2], to which is attached a document headed "Regulae fidei catholicae contra omnes haereses et quam maxime contra Priscillianos, quas

Dominum esse, nec ex substantia Patris existere, sed per Filium creatum esse."

[1] There is probably a good deal of truth in Dr Neale's explanation of the appearance of the *Filioque* in the Spanish Creed. "No European Church had suffered so much from the Arians as the Spanish, and by none therefore was it so likely that every possible effort should be made to state Our Lord's divinity as strongly as possible.......This wish made the Spanish Church to dislike the idea that the Father should have an attribute (namely, of producing the Holy Ghost) which the Son had not, and therefore to make the addition to the Constantinopolitan Creed." (*H. E. Ch.* Intr. Vol. II. p. 1153.)

[2] Or possibly in 396: see Loaisa, *Conc. Hisp.* p. 45.

episcopi Tarraconenses Carthaginenses Lusitani et Baetici fecerunt, et cum praecepto papae urbis [Romae] Leonis ad...episcopum Gallaeciae transmiserunt." The collector has added, "Ipsi etiam et supra scripta viginti canonum capitula statuerunt in Concilio Toletano[1]." If he refers to the Council known as the 1st of Toledo, his statement is refuted by the preceding words; for the mention of Pope Leo serves to connect these *Regulae* with a second Council, which is ascribed to the year 447. In that year S. Turibius, Bishop of Astorga, in Gallaecia, wrote to S. Leo an account of his proceedings against the Priscillianists, asking at the same time for his sanction and advice[2]. The answer of Leo is preserved[3], and contains, if the text is trustworthy, a remarkable testimony to the Pope's individual acceptance of the *Filioque.* Leo recapitulates the sixteen heads under which Turibius had disposed of the new heresy: first among these is the Priscillianist doctrine of the Trinity: "primo itaque capitulo demonstratur quam impie sentiant de Trinitate divina, qui et Patris et Filii et Spiritus Sancti unam atque eandem asserunt esse personam, tamquam idem Deus nunc Pater nunc Filius nunc Spiritus Sanctus nominetur; nec alius sit qui genuit, alius qui genitus est, alius qui de utroque processit[4]." There is no important variation in the reading of the last clause[5],

[1] *Coll. canon. S. Isidoro ascr.* (Migne LXXXIV. 333): or Mansi, 3. 1002: Aguirre, *Conc. Hisp.* II. 13.

[2] Fleury, XXVII. 9—10.

[3] S. Leonis M. *Ep.* XV. (Migne LIV. 678 sq.).

[4] Migne, 680.

[5] The only variants mentioned are *aut qui, procedit:* "de utroque" appears to be well established. Dr Neale rejects it on purely internal grounds: *H. E. Ch.* Intr. II. p. 1129. On the other hand see Le Quien, *Diss. Damasc.* I. § viii. Le Q. reminds the Greeks that on

and considering the evidence already given of Leo's belief upon this point, it seems not unlikely that he wrote *de utroque*, as it stands; merely endorsing, it may be, the words of the Spanish Bishop[1]. The Pope's letter ends by giving instructions for the assembling of a national council of the Spanish Church (*concilium synodi generalis*), or failing that, of a Council of the Bishops of Gallaecia[2]. To the synod or synods held in consequence of this papal recommendation the *Regulae fidei*, already mentioned as appended to the records of the Council of A.D. 400, may very possibly be due, as the first paragraph of the heading certainly suggests. This document consists of a confession of faith in the Holy Trinity and the mystery of the Incarnation, to which are appended eighteen anathemas, pronounced against the doctrines of Priscillian. The confession runs: "Credimus in unum verum Deum Patrem et Filium et Spiritum Sanctum...Patrem autem non esse ipsum Filium...Filium non esse Patrem, sed Filium Dei de Patris esse natura; Spiritum quoque Paraclitum esse qui nec Pater sit ipse nec Filius, sed a Pătre Filioque procedens. Est ergo ingenitus Pater, genitus Filius, non genitus Paraclitus, sed a Patre Filio-

Orthodoxy Sunday they yearly anathematize all who reject the teaching of S. Leo.

[1] See last page: "demonstratur" *sc.* a Turibio. S. Leo may therefore be simply borrowing, but of course at the same time reaffirming with the weight of his own authority, the words of the Spanish Bishop. Further on in the letter Leo is content to assert the procession from God: "quod de ipso est id [idem?] est quod ipse: neque id aliud est quam Filius et Spiritus Sanctus."

[2] Migne LIV. 691. The chief object of the Council was to depose Bishops, if there should be any such, who taught the doctrines of Priscillian, and thus to reaffirm the teaching of the Catholic Creed: "nulla enim ratione tolerandum est ut qui praedicandae fidei suscepit officium, is contra evangelium Christi, contra Apostolicam doctrinam, contra *universalis ecclesiae symbolum* audeat disputare."

que procedens[1]." It is remarkable that the *Filioque* does not find place in the anathemas; it had not been directly attacked by the Priscillianists, nor was it yet regarded as a controverted point by Catholics, who had unconsciously drifted into the use of the words[2].

For more than a century after this synodical utterance the Church of Spain is silent upon dogma. Her traditional spirit of orthodoxy seems to have been revived by the return to Catholicism first of the Suevi in Gallaecia, and then of the Visigoths throughout the peninsula. At Braga in 560 or 563 a provincial Council was held[3], at which the foregoing *Regulae* with the annexed *capitula* were read, and a fresh set of anathemas was levelled against the expiring but not extinct sect of Priscillian. The Metropolitan opened this synod with the significant words, "Prius si placet de statutis fidei Catholicae perquiramus." Yet the Council of Braga does not seem to have put together any exposition of its own; and the new *capitula* contain no allusion to the procession of the Holy Ghost. It was at the general Council which followed the conversion of the whole nation to Catholicism, that the Augustinian doctrine was to receive final recognition and expression in the Creed of the Spanish Church.

[1] The *Filioque* is characteristically omitted in the copy of this document which is found in the *Codex Ecclesiae Romanae*. Some MSS. omit the entire clause *est ergo—procedens:* Hahn, p. 132.

[2] In the records of another Spanish Council of the fifth century as given in the *Concilia* (1st Co. of Braga, A.D. 411), a very distinct assertion of the *Filioque* is found: Pancratianus, Bp. of Braga, is represented as offering the Council a confession of his faith, in which he says "Credo in Spiritum Sanctum procedentem a Patre et Verbo unicum in Deitate cum ipsis, &c." The Bishops reply, "Credimus." It has been doubted however whether the whole account of this Council is not a forgery: see Pagi, *in Ann. Baronii*, a. 411, § xix. It is defended by Cardinal de Aguirre, *Conc. Hisp.* II. p. 191 sq.

[3] *Conc. Bracarense* II. (? I.), (Mansi 9, 774 sq.). See p. 162 (*supr.*).

In Spanish ecclesiastical history the most important event of the sixth century is the Council held at Toledo in the year 589[1]. On this occasion the Visigoths of Spain, led by their king Reccared, renounced Arianism and threw themselves at the feet of the Catholic Church. Whatever were the motives which influenced Reccared, he appears to have carried his whole people with him; a nation was born in a day; and the homily which S. Leander delivered at the close of the Council bears witness to the joyful surprise with which the Church welcomed her returning sons[2]. The Archbishop's address contains no doctrinal statement: it would in fact have been superfluous after the explicit enunciation of Catholic dogma which had been offered by the King and accepted by the Council. In his opening speech Reccared had acknowledged the dogmatic decisions of the first four Œcumenical Councils, and had recited the Creeds of Nicaea and Constantinople and part of the Definition of Chalcedon. His zeal prompted him to add a personal profession of faith, in which the Procession of the Holy Ghost from the Father and the Son occupies a prominent place: "Spiritus aeque Sanctus (he says) confitendus a nobis et praedicandus est a Patre et a Filio procedere et cum Patre et Filio unius esse substantiae[3]." That the words *et a Filio*

[1] Mansi 9, p. 978 sq.

[2] "Pro qua re et nos majoribus gaudiis elevamur quia repente novos Ecclesiam parturisse populos intuemur." On the part which Leander took in the conversion of the Goths see Florez, *España Sagrada*, V. 463 and VI. 467.

[3] Mansi, *l. c.* Roderic of Toledo was struck by this feature of Reccared's address: "praedicans trium Personarum unitatem...Spiritum S. inseparabiliter a Patre et Filio procedentem et esse amborum unum Spiritum, unde et unum sunt." (*Hist. Hisp.* II. 20.)

were not casually introduced appears from their repetition in the anathemas which the Council proceeded to level against the opponents of the Catholic Faith; third among these comes the following, "Quicunque Spiritum Sanctum non credit aut non crediderit a Patre et Filio procedere eumque non dixerit coaeternum esse Patre et Filio et coaequalem, anathema sit." So positive an assertion of the *Filioque* as *de fide* would be difficult to explain did we not possess a key to the mystery in the version of the Constantinopolitan Creed which was recited by Reccared and the Bishops. It contained the words "Et in Spiritum Sanctum Dominum et Vivificatorem, ex Patre ET FILIO procedentem." It is incredible that the addition was made either by the newly converted King or by the Bishops assembled at Toledo. Neither King nor Bishops displayed the slightest consciousness that their Creed varied from the Greek original, or that their doctrine exceeded the teaching of the Catholic Church. On the contrary, Reccared subscribes the Creeds and his own profession in the form, "Ego Reccaredus rex fidem hanc sanctam et veram confessionem quam unam per totum orbem Catholica confitetur Ecclesia ...subscripsi." The Bishops add "Haec est vera fides quam omnis ecclesia Dei per totum mundum tenet." In their second Canon they describe the Latin Creed then in use among them as being "secundum formam Orientalium ecclesiarum Concilii Constantinopolitani." In the face of these declarations it is scarcely just without direct evidence to charge the Toletan fathers with a wilful corruption of the Catholic Symbol. It is more probable that the new words *et Filio* as well as the restored *Deum ex Deo*

—another peculiarity of this Spanish version[1]—had crept in during the long years of the Arian persecution[2]. Originating very possibly in a gloss upon the *ex Patre*, and put forth under circumstances which might seem to require or to justify a local expansion of the Creed, the interpolation had made its way from Church to Church, and before the conversion of the Visigoths had established so firm a footing in the Latin Creed that no suspicion of its genuineness was entertained by Reccared or by his Catholic instructors. Both the King and his Bishops believed them to be a true part of the original Faith, just as they believed the Creed itself to have been drawn up by the fathers of Constantinople. In proclaiming the *Filioque* as *de fide*, in anathematizing its rejection, in reciting it as part and parcel of the "Eastern" symbol, Reccared and the Council may be assumed to represent the honest conviction of the Spanish Church. It is clear that nothing was further from the thoughts of the newly converted people than a departure, whether by addition or the contrary, from the teaching of the Catholic Church, or of its Eastern branch.

The Council of 589 was not content with subscribing that which it believed to be the true Creed of Constantinople: it provided for the perpetuity of

[1] See the remarks of Mr Ffoulkes, *Christendom's Divisions*, II. 358.

[2] See Dr Swainson's *N. and A. Creeds*, ch. XII. (p. 144 sq.). He suspects that the words *et Filio* were "added intentionally," not "merely by mistake." Is it necessary to adopt either of these alternatives? Why should not the Council have simply accepted the Creed as they found it? The "local or independent rendering from the Greek" of the Nicene Creed may have been inherited from Hosius: does it follow that the Spanish Church would have equally ready access to the original of the Constantinopolitan form?

the newly established Faith by ordering the Creed to be used at every celebration of the Holy Eucharist. The second Canon runs, "Pro reverentia sanctissimae fidei et propter corroborandas hominum invalidas mentes...sancta constituit synodus ut per omnes ecclesias Hispaniae vel Gallaeciae...CL. episcoporum symbolum fidei recitetur, ut prius quam Dominica dicatur oratio voce clara a populo decantetur, quo et fides vera manifestum testimonium habeat et ad Christi Corpus et Sanguinem praelibandum pectora populorum fide purificata accedant." This rule was not without precedent: the East had already begun to use the Constantinopolitan symbol in the Liturgy[1]. The custom is said to have been introduced at Antioch "about the year 471[2]," at Constantinople in 511[3]. It had been enforced and made general by an edict issued by the Emperor Justin some twenty years before the date of the Toletan Council. Justin's decree contemplated the recitation taking place before the Lord's Prayer, and the Spanish canon adopted precisely the same order. But in Spain a practice was founded upon this general rule which seems to have been peculiar to the Mozarabic liturgy. In the Spanish rite, probably from the days of the Visigothic conversion, the Symbol was said

[1] Walafrid Strabo (*de reb. Eccl.* XXII: Migne CXIV. 947) regards the Western use of the Creed at Mass as borrowed from the East: "nos ad imitationem eorum [sc. Graecorum] intra missas assumimus."

[2] Bingham, *Antiquities*, XV. § iii. Theodorus Lector, II. 48 (Migne LXXXVI. 209), *Πέτρον φησὶ τὸν κναφέα ἐπινοῆσαι...ἐν πάσῃ συνάξει τὸ σύμβολον λέγεσθαι.*

[3] By the Patriarch Timothy: Theodorus Lector, II. 32 (Migne, 201), *Τιμόθεος τὸ τῶν τριακοσίων δέκα καὶ ὀκτὼ πατέρων τὸ ἅγιον σύμβολον καθ' ἑκάστην σύναξιν λέγεσθαι παρεσκεύασεν ἐπὶ διαβολῇ δῆθεν Μακεδονίου*—the last words shewing that the Constantinopolitan Creed is intended.

after the act of Consecration and while the Priest held in his hand the Body of the Lord. At that solemn moment he turned to the People with the words, "Fidem quam corde credimus ore autem dicamus." The Creed was then recited by Priest and Choir, and the communion of Clergy and People shortly followed[1]. It is difficult to conceive of any more effectual method of securing the veneration of the faithful for the *ipsissima verba* of the Symbol; and among these consecrated words the *Filioque* would, after the Council of Toledo, be heard in most of the churches of Spain[2].

From that time forth the faith of the Spanish Church upon this point was fixed unalterably. Spanish writers, Spanish liturgies and service-books, above all Spanish Councils, with conscious or unconscious zeal, propagated the new clause with which the Creed of Constantinople had been enriched by the great National Synod of Toledo. (1) S. Leander has left us no dogmatic remains; but his younger and more famous brother, S. Isidore, who in the year 600 succeeded to the Archbishopric of Seville, taught the Procession from the Son in no doubtful terms. Thus in the *Etymologiae*, when he comes to treat of the Holy Ghost, Isidore at once begins, "Spiritus Sanctus ideo praedicatur Deus quia ex Patre Filioque procedit et substantiam eorum habet." "Hoc autem interest (he continues)

[1] Mabillon, *de liturg. Gallic.* p. 2, "quo in genere [*sc.* rituum singularium] praeclarum est in missa Mozarabica institutum ut recitato canone sacerdos Hostiam consecratam super calicem tenens symbolum CP. praecinat ex decreto Concilii tertii Toletani, subsequente cleri et populi concentu." Cf. *Lit. Mozarab.*, Migne LXXXV. 117.

[2] At the 8th Council of Toledo (653) the Creed was recited "as it is said at mass:" and the *Filioque* again appears. So at the 12th Toletan Council (681). Cf. however, Isidor. *de Eccl. Off.* I. 16.

inter nascentem Filium et procedentem Spiritum Sanctum, quod Filius ex uno nascitur, Spiritus Sanctus ex utroque procedit[1]." In the *Sententiae* the Procession from Both is so absolutely assumed as to be used in an argument for the essential unity of the Father and the Son; "non enim res una et duorum consubstantialis potuit simul ab eis procedere et simul inesse, nisi unum fuerit a quibus procedit." The Holy Ghost, it is added, is the Agent of this unity, "per quem Pater et Filius unum essentialiter sunt[2]." Lastly in S. Isidore's treatise *On Church Offices* the following is delivered as part of the traditional rule of faith; "Patrem confiteri ingenitum, Filium genitum; Spiritum autem Sanctum nec genitum nec ingenitum, sed ex Patre et Filio procedentem[3]." (2) The Spanish rite, besides its adoption of the interpolated Creed, contained the *Filioque* in more than one of its Collects. At the first vespers of the Pentecost, the following *oratio* is prescribed by the Gothic Breviary: "O Sancte Spiritus, qui a Patre Filioque procedis, doce nos facere veritatem; ut qui de Patre Filioque accepisti processionem, nos his a quibus tam ineffabiliter procedis adsocias caritate[4]." And at matins on the festival itself: "Spiritus Sancte qui ex Patre Filioque procedis, locupleta nos dono tuae benedictionis." Similarly, on the vigil, the Mozarabic

[1] *Etymol.* VII. 3 (Migne LXXXII. 268). Cf. S. Hildefons. *de cogn. bapt.* LIX. (Migne XCVI. 135). See also *Etymol.* VII. 4, "Spiritus Sanctus solus de Patre et Filio procedit: ideo solus amborum nuncupatur Spiritus."

[2] *Sentent.* I. 15 (Migne LXXX. 568).

[3] *De Eccles. Officiis*, II. 23 (Migne, 817). The chapter *de regula fidei* begins, "Haec est autem post symbolum apostolorum certissima fides quam doctores nostri tradiderunt."

[4] *Brev. Goth.* in sanct. Pentecosten. (Migne LXXXVI. 691, cf. LXXXV. 612).

Liturgy offers the prayer, "Spiritus Sancte qui a Patre et Filio procedis, his propitius inlabere holocaustis[1]." (3) In the course of the seventh century the *Filioque* was reasserted by as many as eleven Spanish Councils, mostly national in character. The Constantinopolitan Creed was solemnly recited at Toledo in the years 653, 681, 683, 688, 694[2]: also at Merida in 666[3], and at Braga in 675[4]; on each occasion the interpolation appears as matter of course. Five of the Toletan Councils during this period offer expositions of the Faith, in which the procession of the Holy Ghost from the Son is deliberately affirmed. The 4th Council of Toledo (A.D. 633) declares: "Spiritum Sanctum nec creatum nec genitum sed procedentem ex Patre et Filio profitemur[5]." This language is repeated by the 6th Council (638) with the addition, "Per hoc substantialiter unum sunt [Pater et Filius] quia et unus ab utroque procedit[6]." The 11th Council (675) appears to have been only a provincial gathering of some seventeen or nineteen Bishops; but it has left an elaborate confession of its faith which is peculiarly full upon the doctrine of the Holy Spirit. The Bishops say, "Spiritum quoque Sanctum, qui est tertia in Trinitate persona, unum atque aequalem cum Deo

[1] *Lit. Mozarab.* in vig. Pentecost. (Migne LXXXV. 612). Mai (*Patr. nov. coll.* IV. 51) cites a similar form from a liturgical MS. which he says was written in Spain during the seventh century.

[2] By the 8th, 12th, 13th, 14th, and 17th Councils of Toledo (Mansi 10, p. 1206: 11, p. 1027 sq.: 12, p. 93).

[3] Mansi 11, p. 77.

[4] By the 4th Co. of Braga (Mansi 11, p. 151), with the noteworthy comment, "fidei regulam ipsis verbis atque sententiis... quibus eam declaratam esse scimus in conventu Nicaeni Concilii."

[5] Mansi 10, p. 613. Cf. Mr Ffoulkes *On the Athanasian Creed*, p. 220 and Append. pp. 153, 4.

[6] Mansi 10, p. 659.

Patre et Filio credimus esse Deum, unius substantiae, unius quoque esse naturae: non tamen genitum vel creatum, sed ab utrisque procedentem, amborum esse Spiritum... Nec Patris tantum sed simul Patris et Filii dicitur; nec enim de Patre procedit in Filium, vel de Filio procedit ad sanctificandum creaturam; sed simul ab utrisque processisse monstratur, quia caritas sive sanctitas amborum agnoscitur... Nullum fuisse credimus temporis intervallum quo... procedens Spiritus Patre vel Filio posterior appareret[1]." The 15th Council (688) adopts more of this Augustinian phraseology: "Mens si in persona Patris ponatur, Verbum jam ex mente prodiens Filius intelligitur; et Voluntas procedens ex Mente et Verbo, Spiritus significatur[2]." The 16th Council (693), after professing "credimus... Spiritum Sanctum ex Patre Filioque atque aliquo initio procedentem," builds upon this Eternal Procession the doctrine of the Temporal Mission: "Spiritus Sanctus ex Patris Filiique unione procedit... In sancta praenoscitur Trinitate tertia esse persona, pro eo quod a Patre Filioque cum quibus unius essentiae per omnia creditur, fidelibus condonetur[3]."

The long series of Toletan Councils closes in the year 694; and the Saracenic invasion and fall of the Visigothic kingdom (711) checked for a while the energies of the Spanish Church. But a century of distinctive dogmatic teaching had left its mark upon Spanish[4] and even upon European Christianity. Before the year 700 there was at least one part of Western Christendom where the *Filioque* had taken such firm root that its excision from the Creed would

[1] Mansi 11, p. 131 sq.

[2] Mansi 12, p. 10 sq.

[3] Mansi 12, p. 64 sq.

[4] See Dorner, II. i. 249.

have seemed nothing less than an abandonment of the Faith itself. This example could hardly fail to be followed in due course by the other Churches of the West, where the doctrine was known as a well-accredited opinion of the theologians, and had long been growing in popular esteem. There was one power which might have checked this result by the weight of its authority. But Rome had hitherto regarded the growth of the new phraseology, and even the interpolation of the Creed, with an indifference which fell little short of tacit consent[1].

[1] No reference has been made in this chapter to the influence of the Athanasian Creed upon the growth of the *Filioque*-dogma, because in the present state of our knowledge it is unsafe to assume that the *Quicunque* existed as a whole before the time of Charlemagne. Gieseler was disposed to ascribe its composition to Spain: see however Dr Swainson's remarks, *A. and N. Creeds*, chh. XIX. and XXVI. But if the Toletan Councils of the seventh century did not borrow from the *Quicunque*, they may be regarded as having supplied the nucleus of that portion which contains the *Filioque*. The paragraph, "Pater a nullo est factus nec creatus: Filius a Patre solo est, non factus nec creatus sed genitus: Spiritus S. a Patre et Filio, non factus nec creatus, sed procedens"—occurs with verbal variations in the Toletan confessions of 633, 638, 675, and a part of it in the confession of 693 (Swainson, pp. 244—5, 444). So carefully balanced a formula, it may well be believed, impressed itself readily upon the Spanish mind, travelled from Spain into other countries (*v. infr.* p. 191), and went far to popularize the doctrine which it enshrined.

CHAPTER VIII.

THE EAST AND ITS INTERCOURSE WITH THE WEST FROM A.D. 451 TO A.D. 681.

"Scilicet et nos et Graecos edocet [S. Maximus] secundum quiddam procedere et secundum quiddam non procedere Spiritum Sanctum ex Filio."

Anastas. Biblioth. *ad Joann. Diaconum.*

In the fifth session of the Council of Chalcedon the Constantinopolitan Creed was formally accepted, with its additional clauses upon the Doctrine of the Holy Spirit[1]. It is not pretended that the copy which received synodical sanction contained the *Filioque;* yet the Council in its *Definition* asserted the completeness of the Creed as a summary of the Church's faith in the Holy Trinity: περί τε τοῦ Πατρὸς καὶ τοῦ Υἱοῦ καὶ τοῦ Ἁγίου Πνεύματος ἐκδιδάσκει τὸ

[1] Mansi, 7, p. 112. Routh, *Opusc.* II. p. 75 sq. The following are the words in which the Fathers of Chalcedon confirm the clauses supposed to have been added at Constantinople: *καὶ διὰ τοὺς τῷ Πνεύματι τῷ Ἁγίῳ μαχομένους τὴν χρόνοις ὕστερον παρὰ τῶν ἐπὶ τῆς βασιλευούσης πόλεως συνελθόντων ἑκατὸν πεντήκοντα ἁγίων πατέρων περὶ τῆς τοῦ Πνεύματος οὐσίας παραδοθεῖσαν διδασκαλίαν κυροῖ· ἣν ἐκεῖνοι τοῖς πᾶσιν ἐγνώρισαν, οὐχ ὥς τι λεῖπον τοῖς προλαβοῦσιν ἐπάγοντες, ἀλλὰ τὴν περὶ τοῦ Ἁγίου Πνεύματος αὐτῶν ἔννοιαν κατὰ τῶν τὴν αὐτοῦ δεσποτείαν ἀθετεῖν πειρωμένων γραφικαῖς μαρτυρίαις τρανώσαντες.* It may of course be argued that the procession from the Son was included in the '*ἐκ Πατρός*', as the latter had been included in the simple '*καὶ εἰς τὸ Ἅγιον Πνεῦμα*' of the Nicene Creed. But the absence of all attempt to expand the *ἐκ Πατρός*, either at Chalcedon, or at subsequent Œcumenical Councils, shews that the *Filioque* had not yet won for itself the attention which seems to have been accorded only to controverted points of doctrine.

τέλειον[1]. The West was represented at Chalcedon by Pope Leo's legates, and by two Bishops from Africa; but no one challenged the statement, or claimed for S. Augustine's fuller view of the Procession a place in the Catholic Symbol.

After the Council of Chalcedon no disposition was shewn by Catholics or Monophysites to push to any greater length the language which S. Cyril had held upon the Procession, or even, with some exceptions, to maintain the doctrine as fully as he had taught it. At the end of the fifth century we find Gelasius of Cyzicus putting into the mouths of the Nicene fathers the following sentiments, which are doubtless meant to represent the most perfect orthodoxy of his own age: *τῆς αὐτῆς θεότητος καὶ οὐσίας καὶ τοῦ αὐτοῦ κρίματος* [?] *τὸ Πνεῦμα τὸ Ἅγιον οὗπερ ὁ Πατὴρ καὶ ὁ Υἱὸς, καὶ συνυπάρχον ἀεὶ τῷ Πατρὶ καὶ τῷ Υἱῷ, ἀχώριστον ἀεὶ ἐστὶν τοῦ Πατρὸς καὶ τοῦ Υἱοῦ, καθὰ καὶ ὁ Υἱὸς τοῦ Πατρὸς καὶ ὁ Πατὴρ τοῦ Υἱοῦ*[2]. The relation between the Persons is then illustrated by the well-known analogies of fire and water: the Father, the Son and the Spirit are respectively compared to the *πῦρ*, *ἀπαύγασμα*, *φῶς* of the one element, and to the *πηγή*, *ποταμός*, *ὕδωρ*, under which the other presents itself. With the help of these illustrations the doctrine of the Procession is thus formally explained: *λέγει οὖν περὶ τοῦ Υἱοῦ ἡ θεία γραφὴ 'Κλίνω, φησὶν, ἐπ' αὐτοὺς ὡς ποταμὸς εἰρήνης·' ἐκπορευόμενος δηλονότι ἐκ τῆς ἀληθοῦς πηγῆς τῆς ζωῆς τῆς τοῦ Πατρὸς θεότητος . . . καὶ τὸ Πνεῦμα δὲ τὸ Ἅγιον ...ἐξ αὐτοῦ λαμβάνομεν ἅπαντες οἱ πιστοὶ, τῆς αὐτῆς ὂν οὐσίας ἧς ὁ Πατὴρ καὶ Υἱὸς, ἐκπορευόμενον μὲν ἐκ τοῦ*

[1] See above, p. 1, note.

[2] *Hist. Conc. Nicaen.* II. 20 (Migne, LXXXV. 1285 sq., or Mansi, 2, 860).

Πατρὸς ἴδιον δὲ ὂν τοῦ Υἱοῦ......φῶς καὶ ὁ Υἱὸς, ἐκ φωτὸς τοῦ Πατρὸς· φῶς καὶ τὸ Πνεῦμα τὸ Ἅγιον ἐξ αὐτοῦ τοῦ φωτός. This is on the whole a retreat from Cyril's position; and the same tendency is more decidedly manifested in the teaching of the Pseudo-Areopagite, whose writings are thought to have emanated from the monasteries of Egypt about the same period[1]. In the second chapter of the *De divinis nominibus* the μοναρχία is taught in such terms as almost to exclude an essential derivation of the Spirit from or through the Son: *μόνη δὲ πηγὴ τῆς ὑπερουσίου θεότητος ὁ Πατὴρ, οὐκ ὄντος Υἱοῦ τοῦ Πατρὸς οὐδὲ Πατρὸς τοῦ Υἱοῦ...ὅτι μὲν ἔστι πηγαία θεότης ὁ Πατήρ· ὁ δὲ Ἰησοῦς [v. l. Υἱὸς] καὶ τὸ Πνεῦμα τῆς θεογόνου θεότητος—εἰ οὕτω χρὴ φάναι—βλαστοὶ θεόφυτοι καὶ οἷον ἄνθη καὶ ὑπερούσια φῶτα πρὸς τῶν ἱερῶν λογίων παρειλήφαμεν*[2]. A contemporary metrical paraphrase of S. John's Gospel by Nonnus of Panopolis in the Thebaid thus interprets S. John xv. 26:

Πνεῦμα Θεοῦ νοεροῖο διορνύμενον Γενετῆρος,
Πνεῦμα τόπερ παρὰ Πατρὸς ἐς ὑμέας αὐτὸς ἰάλλω·

whilst ch. xvi. 14 appears in the following form:

Οὗτος ἰὼν παρὰ Πατρὸς ἀνυψώσει με γεραίρων,
ὅττι κεν ἡμετέροιο δεδεγμένος ἐκ Γενετῆρος
ὑμῖν συμμιγεέσσι προώρια θέσφατα φαίνει
ὅσσαπερ ἔσσεται ὔμμι· καὶ ἀρχεγόνῳ τινὶ θεσμῷ
κλῆρος ἐμὸς πέλε πάντα Πατὴρ ἐμὸς ὅσσα κομίζει.
οὗ χάριν ὔμμιν ἔειπον ὅτι ζαθέοιο Τοκῆος
δέγμενος ἡμετέροιο προαγγέλλει τέλος ἔργων[3].

It would not have been strange if the breaking off of communion between Rome and Constantinople

[1] Gieseler, II. p. 88. Dorner, II. i. pp. 422—3.
[2] *De Divin. Nom.* c. II. §§ 5, 7.
[3] *Paraphr. in Joann.* (Migne, XLIII. 877, 881).

in 484, and the resistance of the West to the condemnation of the 'Three Chapters', had led the East to pass adverse comments on the view of the Procession which had become prevalent in Western Europe. The letter of Rusticus already noticed[1] may point to something of this sort: but in the absence of other evidence it is unsafe to infer that the matter was actually discussed at the time. A fifth Œcumenical Council was held at Constantinople in 553, only four years after the date of the letter, but no allusion was then made to any controversy relating to the Procession, although the condemnation of Theodore and Theodoret might have been expected to bring the point into notice. One of the canons of the Council does in fact approach very near to the subject; Theodore is condemned for having said *ὅτι μετὰ τὴν ἀνάστασιν ἐμφυσήσας ὁ Κύριος τοῖς μαθηταῖς . . . οὐ δέδωκεν αὐτοῖς Πνεῦμα Ἅγιον ἀλλὰ σχήματι μόνον ἐνεφύσησε*[2]. But this was ground upon which the orthodox in West and East could meet without fear of collision; for both held the Homoousion and the Hypostatic Union, and the censure upon the Bishop of Mopsuestia was so expressed as to convey no more.

The Greek Church writers of the sixth century when they touch upon the Procession occupy themselves chiefly with distinguishing between the theological ideas conveyed by 'procession' and 'generation.' Thus Leontius of Byzantium writes: *ταῦτα τὰ Τρία οὐδὲν ἀλλήλων διαφέρουσιν εἰ μὴ μόνον κατὰ τὰ ἰδιώματα...τοῦτο μόνον διαφέρουσιν ὅτι ὁ μὲν Υἱὸς γεννᾶται ἐκ τοῦ Πατρός· τὸ δὲ Πνεῦμα ἐκπορεύεται ἐξ αὐτοῦ. πῶς δὲ γεννᾶται ὁ Υἱὸς ἐξ αὐτοῦ ἢ πῶς ἐκ-*

[1] *Supr.* p. 158. [2] Mansi, 9, p. 384.

πορεύεται τὸ Πνεῦμα τὸ Ἅγιον οὐ δεῖ περιεργάζεσθαι[1]. Similarly Anastasius of Mt. Sinai, Τρεῖς ὑποστατικαὶ ἰδιότητές εἰσιν ἐπὶ τῆς θεότητος· τὸ ἀγέννητον τοῦ Πατρὸς καὶ τὸ γεννητὸν τοῦ Υἱοῦ καὶ τὸ ἐκπορευτὸν τοῦ Ἁγίου Πνεύματος. οὐδὲ γεννητός ἐστιν ὁ Πατὴρ οὐδὲ ἐκπορευτὸς ὁ Υἱὸς οὐδὲ γεννητὸν τὸ Ἅγιον Πνεῦμα[2]. Another [?] Anastasius, the Patriarch of Antioch who died in the year 599 [?][3], sees a difference of use between the verbs *ἐξέρχεσθαι* and *ἐκπορεύεσθαι*: "Christ said of Himself 'I came forth from the Father;' but of the Spirit, 'Who proceedeth from the Father.' Although both the Son and the Holy Spirit are said to go forth from the Father, still *procession* is generally predicated of the Spirit, as *generation* of the Son...The Spirit proceeds from the Father, and receives from the Son all things which are the Father's...The Word is not without the Spirit, nor the Mind without the Word...The Spirit proceeds from the Father, but receives all that the Son hath, whose are all things that the Father hath : to shew that there is One Essence common to Him who receives, Him from whom He receives, and Him from whom He naturally proceeds...Such names as God Lord and Spirit are properly applied to each of the Persons, provided that we reserve to the Father the property of being Father, because He is the Sole Source of Godhead: to the Son the property of Sonship, seeing He alone is begotten: to the Paraclete the property of being Holy Ghost:

[1] Leont. Byzant. *de Sectis*, I. (Migne, LXXXVI. 1196) *ib.* IV. ὁ παρὰ τοῦ Πατρὸς ἐκπορεύεται is interpreted ὃ γέννημα ἐστὶ τῆς οὐσίας τοῦ Θεοῦ.

[2] Anastas. Sinaït. *Hodegus*, c. II. (Migne, LXXXIX. 60.) Cf. *supr.* τί πνεῦμα;...ἀσχημάτιστος ἐκπορευτὴ ὕπαρξις.

[3] Cf. Fabric. (ed. Harles) X. 595—6.

for He hath a procession from the Father which is peculiarly His own[1]." The above is from a Latin translation: the Greek original appears not to have been printed as a whole, but the following fragment presents substantially the same view: ὁμοούσιόν ἐστι Πατρὶ καὶ Υἱῷ καὶ συναΐδιον ὡς ἀεὶ συνυπάρχον· ὃ γὰρ ἐστὶ τὴν οὐσίαν ὁ γεννήσας Πατὴρ καὶ ὁ γεννηθεὶς Υἱὸς, τοῦτο καὶ τὸ Πνεῦμα τὸ Ἅγιόν ἐστι· καὶ ὥσπερ ὁ Υἱὸς ἐκ τοῦ Πατρὸς, οὕτω καὶ τὸ Πνεῦμα ἐξ αὐτοῦ, ὁ μὲν γεγεννημένος, διὸ καὶ Υἱός· τὸ δὲ ἐκπορευόμενον, καὶ ἐστὶ Πνεῦμα· μᾶλλον δὲ χρὴ λέγειν τὸν μὲν Υἱὸν ἀεὶ γεννώμενον, τὸ δὲ Πνεῦμα ἀεὶ ἐκπορευόμενον[2]. A second passage which is accessible in its Greek form comes nearer to the Western or at least to the Alexandrian view: ταύτῃ γὰρ καὶ Πνεῦμα στόματος αὐτοῦ (δηλονότι τοῦ Θεοῦ) τὸ Πνεῦμα τὸ Ἅγιον λέγεται, στόματος ὄντος τοῦ Μονογενοῦς· καὶ Πνεῦμα πάλιν ἐξ αὐτοῦ ἐκπορευόμενον καὶ ἀποστελλόμενον οὐ μόνον παρὰ τοῦ Πατρὸς ἀλλὰ καὶ παρὰ τοῦ Υἱοῦ...καὶ μὴν ὁ Κύριος δεικνὺς αὐτὸ ἐξ αὐτοῦ ὑπάρχειν ἐμφυσῶν τοῖς μαθηταῖς ἔλεγε, Λάβετε Πνεῦμα Ἅγιον[3].

The latent difference between East and West was at length brought to light by a fresh outbreak of Christological error at the beginning of the seventh century. Monothelitism, backed up by the Greek Emperor and the Patriarch of Constantinople, received a timid acquiescence if not a willing support from the Roman Pope Honorius. But on the death of Honorius in 638 the Roman See recovered its orthodoxy: John IV. and Theodore resisted the Eastern heresy, and the Lateran Council of 649 ana-

[1] Anastas. Antioch. *Or.* I. *de SS. Trin.* (Migne, LXXXIX. 1315 sq.)

[2] Cited by Theodorus Lascaris *de process. Sp. S.* l. 412—424.

[3] See Petavius *de Trin.* VII. § V. 10. Cf. Pusey, *Pref. to S. Cyril*, p. xxxv.

thematized its supporters[1]. At this Western Council the Constantinopolitan Creed was recited without the *Filioque;* the Greek and the Latin copies are equally free from the interpolation[2]. But the doctrine of the *Filioque* was known to be widely prevalent in the West, and to have received the sanction of Bishops, and even of certain of the Popes themselves. To the Monothelite East, smarting under the Roman anathema, this apparent departure of the West from the ancient faith offered a not unwelcome opportunity of revenge. Murmurs were heard at Constantinople that in his synodical letter Pope Martin had stated that the Holy Ghost proceeds from the Son as well as from the Father. The fact comes to our knowledge through a fragment of a letter written by S. Maximus to the Cyprian priest Marinus in the year 655[3]. This fragment is doubly valuable, as supplying the earliest direct evidence of opposition to the Latin view, and as offering a *concordat* at the very outset of the controversy. S. Maximus is defending the orthodoxy of Pope Martin; even the Constanti-

[1] Gieseler, II. 174—5.

[2] Mansi, 10, p. 1041. Τὸ ἐκ τοῦ Πατρὸς ἐκπορευόμενον, *ex Patre procedentem*, are the words.

[3] Migne XCI. 133 sq. and Mansi, 10, p. 695. A Latin version of the fragment is found among the works of Anastasius Bibliothecarius (Migne, P. L. CXXIX. 577 sq.) of which I subjoin the most important part. "Dixit [Papa], aiunt, procedere etiam ex Filio Spiritum Sanctum... Consonantia protulerunt testimonia Latinorum patrum necnon et Cyrilli Alexandrini...ex quibus non causam Spiritus Sancti Filium se facere monstraverunt. Unam enim norunt causam Filii ac Spiritus esse Patrem, alterius quidem secundum generationem, alterius vero secundum emissionem; sed ut hunc per eum prodire insinuarent et hinc substantiae communionem et indissimilitudinem demonstrarent......Nullam nunc usque fecerunt apologiam quia nec abjectionem eorum quae ab eis introducta sunt." For some interesting comments of Anastasius upon the letter of Maximus see the preface to his *Collectanea* addressed to John the Deacon (Migne, CXXIX. 560).

nopolitans (he says) found only two points to attack in his synodical letter, one touching the doctrine of the Incarnation, the other *περὶ θεολογίας, ὅτι (φασὶν) εἶπεν ἐκπορεύεσθαι κἀκ τοῦ Υἱοῦ τὸ Πνεῦμα τὸ Ἅγιον.* This latter statement had been confirmed by quotations from Latin fathers and from Cyril of Alexandria, and its consistency with the *μοναρχία* maintained: *συμφώνους παρήγαγον χρήσεις τῶν Ῥωμαίων πατέρων, ἔτι γε μὴν καὶ Κυρίλλου Ἀλεξανδρείας ἐκ τῆς πονηθείσης αὐτῷ εἰς τὸν εὐαγγελιστὴν ἅγιον Ἰωάννην ἱερᾶς πραγματείας· ἐξ ὧν οὐκ αἰτίαν τὸν Υἱὸν ποιοῦντας τοῦ Πνεύματος σφᾶς αὐτοὺς ἀπέδειξαν. μίαν γὰρ ἴσασιν Υἱοῦ καὶ Πνεύματος τὸν Πατέρα αἰτίαν...ἀλλ' ἵνα τὸ δι' αὐτοῦ προϊέναι δηλώσωσι, καὶ ταύτῃ τὸ συναφὲς τῆς οὐσίας καὶ ἀπαράλλακτον παραστήσωσι.* S. Maximus goes on to say that he had asked the Latins in vain for a more precise explanation of their dogma; it had become traditional in the West: perhaps the difference of language might in part account for their inability to satisfy the Greeks: *μεθερμηνεύειν δὲ τὰ οἰκεῖα, τοῦ τὰς ὑποκλοπὰς χάριν διαφυγεῖν τῶν ὑποπιπτόντων, κατὰ τὴν ὑμετέραν κέλευσιν παρεκάλεσα τοὺς Ῥωμαίους· πλὴν ἔθους κεκρατηκότος οὕτω ποιεῖν καὶ στέλλειν οὐκ οἶδα τυχὸν εἰ πεισθεῖεν*[1]. *ἄλλως τε καὶ τὸ μὴ οὕτως δύνασθαι διακριβοῦν ἐν ἄλλῃ λέξει τε καὶ φωνῇ τὸν ἑαυτῶν νοῦν ὥσπερ ἐν τῇ ἰδίᾳ καὶ θρεψαμένῃ καθάπερ οὖν καὶ ἡμεῖς ἐν τῇ καθ' ἡμᾶς τὸν ἡμέτερον.* For himself, Maximus evidently regretted the Latin terminology, and could have wished it withdrawn. His last words are almost a prophecy: γενήσεται δὲ πάντως αὐτοῖς πείρᾳ τὴν ἐπήρειαν μαθοῦσι καὶ ἡ περὶ τούτων φροντίς[2].

[1] *πιστεῖεν* (Combefis, Migne). The emendation in the text is due to a friend.

[2] The genuineness of this letter was disputed at Florence by some

So doubtful an apology is the more remarkable when we bear in mind the following facts. (1) It was to the interest of Maximus's party to support the Roman Bishop and Council against the Monothelites. (2) Maximus had travelled in the West; he had visited Africa and Rome; and the terms of his letter shew that he was acquainted with the interpretation which the Western Churches affixed to the Procession of the Spirit from the Son. (3) The *Filioque* had not yet, as we have seen, been added to the Roman version of the Constantinopolitan Creed, and there is no reason to suppose that S. Maximus was aware of the Spanish interpolation; his difficulty therefore has regard to the statement itself, and not to its irregular introduction into an Œcumenical symbol. (4) Lastly, there is evidence to shew that Maximus himself entertained the opinion which he represents as differing in form rather than in substance from the doctrine of the West, viz. the essential derivation through the Son. Thus in answer to the question, "Since we can say 'the Spirit of the Father and the Spirit of Christ,' why may we not speak conversely of 'the Father,' 'the Son, of the Spirit'?" he writes, Ὥσπερ ἐστὶν αἴτιος τοῦ Λόγου ὁ Νοῦς, οὕτως καὶ τοῦ Πνεύματος, διὰ μέσου δὲ τοῦ Λόγου. καὶ ὥσπερ οὐ δυνάμεθα εἰπεῖν τὸν λόγον εἶναι τῆς φωνῆς, οὕτως οὐδὲ τὸν Υἱὸν λέγειν τοῦ Πνεύματος[1]. Again in his discus-

of the Latins. Mr Ffoulkes states the arguments against it in *Christendom's Divisions*, II. p. 423 (note). On the other hand see Le Quien, *Diss. Damasc.* I. § xi. (Migne, *P. G.* XCIV. 204), who points out that besides the weighty testimony of Anastasius, the impartial tone of the letter speaks strongly in its favour. The writer is obviously not a partizan of either side, and no one but a partizan would have been likely to forge a letter on such a subject.

[1] *Quaest. et dubia* § XXIV. (Migne XC. 814).

sion of Zech. iv. 2, 3[1] the following very explicit avowal of the older Greek doctrine occurs: τὸ γὰρ Πνεῦμα τὸ Ἅγιον ὥσπερ φύσει κατ' οὐσίαν ὑπάρχει τοῦ Θεοῦ καὶ Πατρὸς, οὕτως καὶ τοῦ Υἱοῦ φύσει κατ' οὐσίαν ἐστὶν ὡς ἐκ τοῦ Πατρὸς οὐσιωδῶς δι' Υἱοῦ γεννηθέντος ἀφράστως ἐκπορευόμενον. We have had nothing so decisive from an Eastern since the age of S. Cyril, and we cannot but suspect that Maximus had felt the influence of the Western doctrine upon his own[2]. But into the formal statement 'the Holy Spirit proceeds also from the Son,' he as distinctly refuses to follow the Latins: their meaning may be orthodox, but he is at a loss to justify their phraseology. It was not the Monothelites alone who disliked the *Filioque:* Eastern Catholics had already begun to take exception to it. We hear indeed no more of the complaint: Monothelitism was vanquished, communion between Rome and Constantinople restored, and the lesser controversy forgotten for the time. But from this time forth there existed a nucleus of theological dissension between the two great Patriarchates which only awaited a fitting opportunity for developing itself into an open schism.

S. Maximus died in exile, A.D. 662, for his persistent confession of the Catholic Faith: eighteen years later the Faith triumphed at the Sixth Œcumenical Council. From the proceedings of this Council and of the provincial synods which preceded it we glean several interesting facts as to the state of the Procession-dogma both in East and West. We have records of three Western Synods

[1] *Quaest. ad Thalass.* § LXIII. (Migne, XC. 672).

[2] Pitzipios (*l'Église Orientale*, p. 29) calls attention to the fact that the Greek Church commemorates S. Maximus as a Confessor on Jan. 21).

which were held in 679—80 to ascertain the mind of Latin Christendom upon the Monothelite controversy. In each of these documents the Procession of the Holy Ghost is referred to, but with a singular difference of statement. The Archbishop of Milan and his suffragan Bishops drew up a profession of their faith in which the Procession from the Son is perhaps purposely ignored: the words are, "Cum nominamus Spiritum Sanctum, ab aeterni Patris persona eum procedere monstramus[1]." From Rome, where, on March 27, 680, some 125 Bishops met under the Presidency of Pope Agatho, there came a synodical letter, in which, after declaring their intention to keep inviolate the terms of the Catholic Apostolic Faith as hitherto preserved and delivered by the Apostolic See, the Council adopts the words of the Constantinopolitan Symbol, without the interpolation: "credentes... in Spiritum Sanctum dominum et vivificatorem ex Patre procedentem[2]." On the other hand, from England during this same year, and in a document addressed to Agatho, we receive a statement of the procession from the Son more distinct than any hitherto put forth, if we except the professions of the Spanish Councils.

The English Council was held at Bishop's Hatfield (Haethfelth) on Sept. 17, 680[3]. It was assembled by Archbishop Theodore, apparently in obedience to the desire of the Pope, who had sent over John, Precentor of the Church of S. Peter's,

[1] Mansi, 11, p. 206.

[2] *ib.* p. 289.

[3] See Mansi II. p. 176 sq.: Haddan and Stubbs, *Councils*, III. p. 141 sq.: Dr Smith's *Dict. of Chr. Antiqq.* I. pp. 760—1. The original authority is Bede, *eccl. hist.* IV. 17, 18 (Migne XCV. 108—200).

with a commission to report upon the state of religious belief in the Church of England[1]. Doubtless there was reason to fear that the Monothelite error might have crept in, under the rule of a Primate whose birth and education were Greek. It was not without misgivings on the part of Pope Vitalian that Theodore of Tarsus had been consecrated to the see of Canterbury. His friend Hadrian had procured the appointment only on the condition that he accompanied the new Archbishop to England and watched over his orthodoxy: "ut ei doctrinae cooperator existens (so Bede explains) diligenter attenderet ne quid illi contrarium veritati fidei Graecorum more in ecclesiam cui praeerat introduceret[2]." Now that the crisis of the struggle between the Faith and the Monothelite heresy had arrived, Agatho was naturally anxious to ascertain the result of Theodore's twelve years' episcopate. He would have been glad to have secured Theodore's presence at the Roman Council[3]; fail-

[1] Bede, *l. c.* "intererat huic synodo pariterque catholicae fidei decreta firmabat vir venerabilis Johannes, archicantator ecclesiae S. Apostoli Petri et abbas monasterii B. Martini, qui nuper venerat a Roma per jussionem papae Agathonis" partly to teach the English the Roman method of chanting, partly to report upon their spiritual condition: "aliud in mandatis ab apostolico papa acceperat, ut cujus esset fidei Anglorum ecclesia diligenter edisceret Romamque rediens referret."

[2] Bede, *hist. eccl.* IV. I. Theodore had received the Greek tonsure: "quatuor expectavit menses donec illi coma cresceret quo in coronam tonderi posset: habuerat enim tonsuram more Orientalium. See Dean Hook's *Lives of the Archbishops*, vol. I. ch. 4.

[3] Mansi, II, 286. *ἠλπίζομεν ἀπὸ Βρεταννίας Θεόδωρον τὸν σύνδουλον ἡμῶν καὶ συνεπίσκοπον, τῆς μεγάλης νήσου Βρεταννίας ἀρχιεπίσκοπον καὶ φιλόσοφον.* Dean Hook annotates (p. 149), "William of Malmesbury (G. Pontif. lib. I.) understood the invitation as relating to the general Council." But there is not a trace of this in Agatho's words, and when the Dean writes (p. 161) "Theodorus...was...regardless of the Pope's wish that he should attend as one of his representatives

ing that, he received with satisfaction the report of the Hatfield Council, which left no doubt as to the soundness of the faith professed by the Archbishop and the nation. This document is happily preserved in part by Bede. It accepts the first Five Councils, Nicaea, Constantinople, Ephesus, Chalcedon, Constantinople II, and the Lateran Synod of 649[1], at which the Roman Church had condemned the Monothelite doctrine. Then follows this additional profession, "Et glorificamus Dominum nostrum Jesum sicut isti glorificaverunt, nihil addentes vel subtrahentes . . . glorificantes Deum Patrem sine initio et Filium ejus unigenitum ex Patre generatum ante saecula et Spiritum Sanctum procedentem ex Patre et Filio inenarrabiliter, sicut praedicaverunt hi quos memoravimus supra, sancti apostoli et prophetae et doctores. Et nos omnes subscripsimus, qui cum Theodoro archiepiscopo fidem catholicam exposuimus."

From what source had the Bishops of England received the *Filioque* at this early period? It is not necessary to suppose that the Creed in its interpolated form had already made its way from Spain to Britain: or even that the influence of the Spanish Councils had been felt here at all. It has been suggested that the presence in England of the

at the Council of Constantinople (Mansi XI. 286)," he exceeds his authority and is probably in error. See Haddan and Stubbs, III. p. 141. Yet the statement that "the VIth general Council waited for" Theodore is endorsed by Dr Pusey (*pref. to S. Cyril*, p. xxxvi).

[1] In the proceedings of this Synod, of which a copy had been sent to England by the Pope, the Constantinopolitan Creed occurred without the *Filioque* (see p. 187 *supr.*). Yet in the face of this uninterpolated Creed, the Synod of Hatfield ventured to enunciate the procession from the Son: so little was the *ex Patre* thought to exclude the *ex Filio*.

Abbat Hadrian offers a more probable explanation[1]. Hadrian is thus described by Bede: "vir natione Afer, sacris literis diligenter imbutus, monasterialibus simul et ecclesiasticis disciplinis institutus, Graecae pariter et Latinae linguae peritissimus[2]." He was a well-read theologian, a master of Greek, an Italian monk, an African by extraction and probably by early education. Trained in the school of S. Augustine of Hippo and S. Fulgentius of Ruspe[3], he would regard the Procession from the Son as the legitimate and necessary consequence of the Procession from the Father, and as a doctrine essential to the full apprehension of Catholic truth. His relation to Theodore, and his ripe knowledge of both languages, would place his authority high in the estimation of the Greek scholar, whose previous residence in Rome, acquaintance with Latin Church literature and obligations to the Roman Pontiff and to Hadrian, would predispose him to receive what he had learned to regard as the orthodox Western belief. If the unanimity of Theodore's suffragans, to which Bede draws special attention[4], cannot be accounted for in the same way, may we not

[1] So Mr Ffoulkes, *The Athanasian Creed*, pp. 203—4: adding, "in that it [the profession at Hatfield] affects to have been drawn from the Creed we must infer also that the interpolated Creed had been received in England." The inference seems too hasty, and Mr Ffoulkes has modified it in his recent article on the Council in Dr Smith's *Dict. of Chr. Antiquities*, where he writes: "the assertion of procession from the Son as well as from the Father...may seem to indicate that the interpolated form of the Creed had got into Britain by then; but it may be explained in another way." The other way suggested is through the influence of Hadrian.

[2] *Hist. eccl.* IV. I. Theodore is less enthusiastically described: "vir et saeculari et divina literatura et Graece instructus et Latine."

[3] *Dict. of Chr. Antiqq.* I. p. 761.

[4] Bede, *l.c.* "nos omnes subscripsimus:" *infr.* "inventa est in omnibus fides inviolata Catholica."

hazard the conjecture that the doctrine had been brought into Saxon England with Christianity itself by S. Augustine of Canterbury, who had heard it from the lips of S. Gregory the Great [1]? Certainly on such a point it is more likely that Theodore would follow, than that he would lead, the national belief; and the tenacity with which the English Church has ever clung to the *Filioque* [2] seems to

[1] See above, p. 157. S. Augustine of Canterbury was dead only 75 years at the date of the Co. of Hatfield.

[2] After the Synod of Hatfield we have no further trace of the *Filioque* in England till the end of the next century, when the attention of the English Bishops was very possibly recalled to the subject by the Council of Frankfort (794) at which several of them were present (see below, ch. IX). The Cotton collection of MSS. contains a well-known volume (Cleopatra E. I), which opens with a series of English Episcopal professions ranging from the year 796 to the time of S. Thomas the martyr. Of these documents, a majority of those which are anterior to the end of the 9th century offer statements of the writer's faith in the Holy Trinity: and five, written between 798 and 857, embody the *Filioque*. (1) Denebert, Bishop of Worcester (798) cites the words of the *Quicunque*: "Spiritus S. a Patre et Filio, non factus nec creatus nec genitus, sed procedens." (2) A nameless Bishop of Lichfield (circ. 832) and (3) Diorlaf, Bishop of Hereford (857), agree in the use of a formula which sounds like a paraphrase of the interpolated Constantinopolitan Creed: "Credo et in Spiritum Sanctum, procedentem a Patre et Filio, vivificantem universa quae in caelis et quae in terris sunt." (4) Diorwulf, Bishop of London (839), writes, "ego confiteor...Spiritum Sanctum procedentem ex Patre et Filio." (5) Ethelwald, Bishop of Dunwich (845): "credo...Sanctum quoque Spiritum ex Patre et Filio procedentem." (Haddan and Stubbs, III. pp. 525–659). How intelligently as well as firmly the Augustinian view was held by the English Church before the Norman Conquest appears from such a passage as the following, taken from the Homilies of Ælfric (*ed.* Thorpe, vol. I. p. 280): "The Holy Ghost is the quickening God Who proceeds from the Father and the Son. How proceeds He from Him? The Son is the Wisdom of the Father, ever of the Father; and the Holy Ghost is the Will of them both...Ever was the Holy Ghost, Who is the Will and Love of them Both." The Cambridge MS. of these Homilies (circ. 1030) contains an A.S. version of the "Mass Creed" with the clause "Se gæth of tham Fæder and of tham Suna:" (Heurtley, *harm. symb.* p. 164). In mediæval England the *Filioque* was instilled with equal care into clergy and people.

suggest that in this island, as in Spain, the Western view of the Procession was received by the nation at its first conversion as an integral part of the Faith: that the Anglo-Saxons, like the Spanish Visigoths, had never known any other expression of the mystery.

The Œcumenical Council began to sit on Nov. 7, 680, and ended on Sept. 16 of the next year. It is remarkable that among the professions of faith and synodical letters read at its sessions the English profession finds no place. Did it reach Rome too late to be forwarded? or was it withheld by the Pope lest the *Filioque*, already known to be unpalatable to the East, might provoke discussion, and hinder the work of reunion? It is conceivable that Agatho, whilst heartily concurring[1] in the belief of the English

Every Bishop at his consecration was asked "Credis etiam Spiritum Sanctum...a Patre Filioque procedentem?" (Maskell, *ritualia eccl. Angl.* III. p. 249). The dying man was taught that one of the essentials of the Catholic Faith was to believe "Spiritum Sanctum...a Patre et Filio pariter procedentem": "si vis ergo salvus esse, frater (it was added), ita de mysterio Trinitatis sentias." (Maskell, I. p. 75.) One cannot open an English mediæval sermon-book and turn to the sermons provided for Whitsuntide, without encountering an attack upon the Greeks, and a defence of the Latin view of the Procession. Finally, the English Reformation was so far from abandoning in this particular the lead of the mediæval Church, that it laid fresh stress upon the *Filioque* (1) by importing it into the Litany, where the ancient "Spiritus Sancte Deus" was in 1544 rendered "O God the Holy Ghost proceeding from the Father and the Son": and (2) by giving it a place in the Elizabethan Articles of 1563 (Hardwick, *Hist. of the Articles*, p. 127). Of late it has been urged by one of the greatest of living English theologians that to concede anything to the Easterns would be regarded by the mass of the English people as nothing less than an abandonment of the entire doctrine of the Holy Trinity, of which the Procession from the Son has come to be viewed as an essential part.

[1] Of this there can be no doubt. The profession of Hatfield had been drawn up under the eye of Precentor John, the Pope's special envoy:

Bishops, may yet have been unwilling to put a stumblingblock in the way of his Eastern brethren.

The documents actually read at the Council[1] included the Milan letter and the letter of Agatho already noticed, the latter bearing the signature of Wilfrid, Theodore's opponent, who was at Rome when the Roman Synod was held, and subscribed for the Northern dioceses of England, for Scotland, and for Ireland[2]. Both of these Western expositions of doctrine were silent, as we have seen, upon the relation of the Holy Spirit to the Son, whilst both distinctly professed belief in His Procession from the Father. The former question was not so strictly excluded in the Eastern professions. Macarius of Antioch produced a paper, in which he reechoed the language of S. Gregory Thaumaturgus: *πιστεύω...εἰς τὸ Πνεῦμα τὸ Ἅγιον, τὸ ἐκ τοῦ Πατρὸς ἐκπορευόμενον καὶ δι' Υἱοῦ πεφηνός, δηλαδὴ τοῖς ἀνθρώποις*[3]. It will be noticed that by this time the last words stood in the text of Gregory's *ἔκθεσις*, unless they were now

and the document was received at Rome with universal approval: "exemplum catholicae fidei Anglorum (says Bede) Romam perlatum est atque ab apostolico papa omnibusque qui audiere vel legere gratantissime acceptum."

[1] For an account of the proceedings at the Council see Dr Swainson, *N. and A. Creeds*, 246—251, or the article on Councils of Constantinople in Dr Smith's *Dict. of Christ. Antiquities* (I. 444).

[2] In the *Concilia* Wilfrid is made to sign himself "legatus venerabilis synodi per Britanniam constitutae." "The form of this subscription shews it to be the invention of the notary who drew up the acts of the Council, for it is contradicted by Eddius and Bede." (Haddan and Stubbs, II. p. 141.) Eddius (*Vit. Wilfrid.* c. LI.) gives the true form: "Wilfridus...episcopus Eboracae civitatis...pro omni Aquilonali parte Britanniae et Hiberniae insulisque quae ab Anglorum et Britonum nec non Scotorum et Pictorum gentibus colebantur veram et catholicam fidem confessus est et cum subscriptione sua corroboravit." (*ib.* 140).

[3] Mansi 11, 351.

added as a gloss by Macarius[1]. At the 11th session a synodical letter was read from Sophronius of Jerusalem [*ob.* 636], who had been the earliest opponent of Monothelitism and the friend of Maximus the Confessor. It contained an original confession by the Patriarch. The following clauses relate to the Holy Ghost: *πιστεύω...εἰς ἓν Πνεῦμα Ἅγιον τὸ ἐκ Θεοῦ Πατρὸς [ἀϊδίως ?] ἐκπορευόμενον, τὸ φῶς καὶ Θεὸν καὶ αὐτὸ γνωριζόμενον καὶ ὃν ἀληθῶς Πατρὶ καὶ Υἱῷ συναΐδιον ὁμοούσιόν τε καὶ ὁμόφυλον καὶ τῆς αὐτῆς οὐσίας καὶ φύσεως, ὡσαύτως δὲ καὶ θεότητος......ἔστι μετὰ τοῦ εἶναι Θεὸς Πνεῦμα Ἅγιον τὸ Πνεῦμα τὸ Ἅγιον καὶ οὔτε Πατὴρ θεωρούμενον οὔτε Υἱὸς λαμβανόμενον, ἀλλ' ὅπερ ὁ Πατὴρ κατ' οὐσίαν πεπίστευται καὶ ὅπερ ὁ Υἱὸς κατὰ φύσιν ἀγγέλλεται*[2]. Further on a passage occurs which reminds us of S. Cyril of Alexandria: referring to the Insufflation, Sophronius says that Our Lord gave the Holy Ghost to the Apostles in virtue of the Homoousion: *Πνεῦμα τούτοις παρέχει πανάγιον ὡς συγγενὲς αὐτῷ καὶ ὁμόφυλον.*

However, whether through the forbearance of the Westerns or the importance of the primary subject of discussion, nothing passed upon the question of the Procession; the Constantinopolitan Creed was recited by the Council in Greek, and of course in its uninterpolated form: the special 'Definition' which followed, and the synodical letter to Pope Agatho, contain no allusion to the doctrine of the Holy Spirit. The murmurs which S. Maximus had overheard, and in which he was half disposed to

[1] "The Monothelite, Macarius of Antioch, glossed 'the Holy Spirit Who proceedeth from the Father and shone forth through the Son' with the words 'viz., to men.'" Dr Pusey (in the pref. to Mr P. Pusey's E. Tr. of *S. Cyril on S. John*, p. XLVII. note).

[2] Mansi 11, p. 466.

join, had died away before the Council, or were forgotten in the joyful prospect of reconciliation, and the *Filioque* controversy seemed to have been strangled at its birth. In point of fact it was but suspended till the next outbreak of hostilities between Eastern and Western Christendom. Crowded out by the pressure of the Monothelite disputes of the Seventh Century, it reasserted its right to a hearing in the Iconoclastic troubles of the Eighth[1].

[1] The *liber diurnus Romanorum Pontificum* (Migne CV. 44, sq.) contains certain professions of faith composed shortly after the sixth Œcumenical Council (at the end of the 7th century or beginning of the 8th), and intended for use at the consecration of a Pope. In one of these we read, "Dum de Patre Filius aeternaliter nascitur, Spiritus Sanctus de Patre procedere confirmatur; eundem Dei Filius de suo accipere perhibet, et in nomine suo mitti a Patre Spiritum Sanctum manifestat, et insufflando discipulis 'Accipite Spiritum Sanctum,' utpote de se procedentem adnuntiat." Another of these Papal Creeds declares "Credimus...Patrem quidem ingenitum, Filium autem ex Patre unigenitum, Spiritum vero Sanctum nec genitum nec ingenitum, sed de Patre Filioque procedentem." Thus the faith of the Roman See in reference to the Procession of the Holy Ghost was well-defined at this period and openly professed in the West, although a desire for peace may have led the Popes to suppress the *Filioque* in their intercourse with the Eastern Church. The Constantinopolitan Creed, however, retained its purity at Rome to a much later date.

CHAPTER IX.

THE FRANKS AND THE EASTERN CHURCH.

ἰδοὺ ἡλίκον πῦρ ἡλίκην ὕλην ἀνάπτει.

S. James III. 5.

ALMOST coincidentally with the invasion of Spain by the Visigoths, the Franks had obtained a permanent footing in North Gaul[1]; but it was not before the end of the fifth century that the rise of the Merovingians and the baptism of Clovis (A.D. 496) converted a roving and pagan population into a settled Christian community. Unlike the Visigoths, the Franks learnt their Christianity from the lips of a Catholic Bishop, and their King, before his baptism, made a solemn confession of his faith in the Holy Trinity[2]. It is not improbable that the *Filioque* found place in this confession, dictated as it was by S. Remigius, whose contemporaries in the South of Gaul certainly regarded the Procession from the Son as an integral part of the Faith[3]. Indications are not wanting that the dogma was already received in France during the following century. The Frank Church History of S. Gregory of Tours [*ob.* 595] opens with a Creed in which a very promi-

[1] Gibbon, *Decline* &c., c. XXXI.

[2] Greg. Turon. *hist. Franc.* II. 31 (Migne LXXI. 227): "rex omnipotentem Deum in Trinitate confessus, baptizatus est."

[3] *vid. supr.* pp. 154 sq.

nent place is given to it. About to write the story of the Church's conflicts with Pagans and heretics, this writer thinks it necessary first to evince his own soundness in the Faith by reciting the articles of his belief: "credo ergo," he proceeds, "in Deum Patrem Omnipotentem, credo in Jesum Christum Filium suum unicum...credo Sanctum Spiritum a Patre et Filio processisse[1]." A fragment of the Gallican liturgy, recently edited from a MS. written before the year 760, contains a *contestatio* which begins, "Omnipotens aeterne Deus, Pater, Unigenitus, Spiritus Sancte ex Patre et Filio mystica processione subsistens[2]." On the other hand it does not appear that the interpolated form of the Constantinopolitan Creed had found its way into Gaul at this time. A Paris MS. of the 8th century, known as the Gellone Sacramentary, presents a Latin version which gives simply *ex Patre procedentem;* and the Gelasian Sacramentary as used in France is said to have been equally free from the Spanish addition[3]. Nor (if we may believe Walafrid Strabo) had the Churches of Gaul and Germany

[1] *hist. Franc.* I. (prolog.) (Migne, 162). This profession is introduced with the words, "illud tantum studens ut quod in ecclesia credi praedicatur sine ullo fuco aut cordis haesitatione retineam." Hence it appears that the *Filioque* was already preached in the Churches of Gaul before the end of the 6th century.—The Benedictine editor annotates, "Hanc particulam *Filioque* [in Gregory's profession] habent omnes editi et MSS., cum codice Corbeiensi;" so that the reading may in this instance be regarded as tolerably certain.

[2] Mone, *lateinische und griechische Messen*, p. 19: cf. p. 10.

[3] See Dr Swainson's *N. and A. Creeds*, p. 146 note: and cf. Gerbert, *vet. liturg. Alemannica*, p. 313: "in veteri expositione symboli pro catechumenis in Sacramentario Gallicano Bobiensi nulla adhuc mentio fit de processione ex 'Filioque.'...Deest etiam in sacramentario Gelasiano vulgato, in quo Graece et Latine legitur ad traditionem symboli; itemque in psalterio Graeco MSco. San-Gallensi." Cf. also Dr Heurtley's *harm. symbolica*, pp. 158—160.

generally adopted the Spanish custom of singing the Creed at mass before the time of Charlemagne[1]: its liturgical use in this part of Europe is thought to have been confined at first to the administration of Baptism[2]. Thus even if the interpolated Creed was known in Gaul before the end of the 8th century, its influence upon the religious belief of the people was probably less than in Spain.

Under the Carlovingian Pepin the acceptance of the *Filioque* dogma by the Franks emerges into clearer light. France has the doubtful honour of being able to claim the first Council at which the question was formally raised as matter of controversy between East and West. Unfortunately the records of the Council held at Gentilly (Gentiliacum), near Paris, in the year 767, have perished, and our knowledge of its proceedings is derived from three chroniclers of the next century: Eginhard, the contemporary and biographer of Charlemagne, Ado, Archbishop of Vienne (*ob.* 874), and Regino, Abbot of Prüm (*ob. circ.* 908)[3]. The first and third of these writers tell us simply that the Council was held in consequence of dissensions having arisen between certain Greeks and Romans 'upon the subject of the Holy Trinity and the religious use of images[4].' Ado's

[1] Walafrid Strabo *de reb. eccl.* c. 22 (Migne CXIV. 947), "apud Gallos et Germanos post dejectionem Felicis haeretici sub gloriosissimo Carolo Francorum rectore damnati idem Symbolum latius et crebrius in missarum coepit officiis iterari." Cf. however Mabillon's remark (*de liturg. Gallicana*, p. 7): "quod ergo Galli etiam regnante Carolo M. symbolum lecto evangelio recitaverint, id ex veteri ordine Gallicano videtur manasse."

[2] So Dr Caspari (cited in *Dict. of Chr. Antiq.* art. 'Creeds').

[3] See Eginhard, *Annal.* (Migne CIV. 386); Ado Vienn. *Chronicon* (Migne CXXIII. 125); Regino Abbas, *Chronicon* (Migne CXXXII. 51).

[4] Eginhard says, "Orta quaestione de Sancta Trinitate et de sanctorum imaginibus inter Orientalem et Occidentalem ecclesiam

account is every way fuller: "facta est tunc temporis synodus anno incarnationis Domini DCCLXVII.; et quaestio ventilata inter Graecos et Romanos de Trinitate, et utrum Spiritus Sanctus sicut procedit a Patre, ita procedit a Filio; et de sanctorum imaginibus, utrumne fingendae aut pingendae erant in ecclesiis." Assuming the trustworthiness of an episcopal chronicler who writes from Gaul not more than a century after the facts[1], this brief statement is full of interest. We ask ourselves, who were these Greeks, and what brought them to the court of the Frank King? how, again, it happened that the question of the Procession was mixed up at Gentilly with a matter belonging to the Iconoclastic controversy? That controversy had broken out in the East some forty years before; but the crisis had been reached in 754, when the Emperor Constantine (Copronymus) held a Council at Constantinople which, claiming to possess Œcumenical authority, decreed the indiscriminate destruction of all images whether of Our Lord or of the Saints[2]. The answer

(id est, Romanos et Graecos) rex Pippinus conventu in Gentiliaco villa congregato synodum de ipsa quaestione habuit." Regino: "Rex in supra dicta villa synodum magnam habuit inter Romanos et Graecos de Sancta Trinitate vel [*i. q.*, et: *v.* Ducange, *s. v.*] de sacris imaginibus."

[1] There is really no valid reason for discrediting the statement of Ado (as Mr Ffoulkes has done, *Dict. of Ch. Antiq.*, art. 'Co. of Gentilly'). It is true, of course, that "there is no proof that the dispute between the two Churches on the Procession of the Holy Ghost had [elsewhere openly] commenced before 767:" but we have noticed indications of a latent difference sufficient to explain the occurrence of such a sudden outbreak whenever a favourable opportunity might present itself. Such an opportunity was probably afforded by the meeting at Gentilly: see below.

[2] See the records of the Council, preserved amongst the acts of the 2nd Co. of Nicaea, 6th session (Mansi 13, p. 203 sq.).

of Rome was delayed till the year 769[1], by which time Pepin had passed away, and the long reign of Charlemagne had begun. But in the interval the subject must have excited much attention in the West: and though under Charlemagne the Franks took an independent line with regard to the decisions of the Second Council of Nicaea, there is no reason to doubt that during the early stages of the controversy they would have been one with the Roman Church in condemning the rude iconoclasm of Copronymus and the Constantinopolitan synod[2]. Now we know that on more than one occasion during Pepin's reign communications passed between Constantinople and the Frank Court[3]: in 757 an embassy conveyed costly presents from Constantine to Pepin: at another time the Greek Emperor sought the hand of a Frank princess for his son Leo[4]. The negociation proved unsuccessful, partly, as it seems, through the exertions of the Pope. Nothing is more likely than that if the ambassador of Copronymus fell in with the Papal legates at the court of Pepin, they would be taunted by the Romans as εἰκονομάχοι:

[1] It was then given in no doubtful terms by a Lateran Council which pronounced, "Si quis sanctas imagines Domini nostri Jesu Christi et ejus genetricis atque omnium sanctorum secundum SS. patrum statuta venerari noluerit, anathema" (Mansi 12, p. 720).

[2] Neander, arguing against the supposition that the Frank Church under Charlemagne changed its front with regard to image-worship, admits that it would "have [had] to agree with the Roman [Church] in opposing the Greek destruction of images." (*Ch. Hist.* v. p. 323. *E. Tr.*).

[3] Pagi on Baronius, *anno* 766.

[4] See *Cod. Carol.* L. (Migne XCVIII. 258), where Pope Stephen III. writes to Charlemagne, "Hoc, peto, ad vestri referre studete memoriam, eo quod dum Constantinus imperator nitebatur persuadere... vestro genitori ad accipiendum conjugio filii sui germanam vestram nobilissimam Gisilam......nec contra voluntatem apostolicae sedis pontificum quoquo modo vos audere peragere."

nothing more likely than that if so attacked the Greeks would retort by resuscitating the charge of innovation in doctrine which had been cast in the teeth of the Roman Church as far back as the time of Maximus[1]. With regard to the line taken by the controversialists at Gentilly we are left to mere conjecture; unless it is safe to infer from the form of Ado's statement[2] that the Greeks were as yet prepared to condemn only such a construction of the *Filioque* as contradicted the Catholic doctrine of the *μοναρχία*; and that the Westerns in their defence fell back upon the distinction already drawn by S. Augustine between the procession of the Holy Spirit from the Father and His procession from the Son. The discussion seems to have turned simply upon the doctrine: there is no reason to suppose that the interpolation of the Creed was thought of by either side at Gentilly. The Greeks who were present, possibly even the Latins, were ignorant of the fact.

Among the most strenuous opponents of the *iconophobia* created by Leo the Isaurian was a monk of Damascus, who has won the honour of canonization both in East and West[3], and whose theology, accepted by the West, has long been regarded in the East as the standard of orthodoxy[4]. S. John of Damascus [*ob.* circ. 756] has happily left a full state-

[1] See above, p. 184.

[2] "Utrum sicut procedit a Patre, ita procedit a Filio." The question presented itself in the same form to Rusticus, more than two centuries before; and he interpreted the *sicut...sic* [=ita] as equivalent to "*eodem modo quo—*:" see above, p. 159.

[3] He is commemorated by the Latin Church on May 6, by the Greeks on Nov. 29 and Dec. 4. Cf. Cave, *h. l.* I. p. 482: Fabric. *bibl. Gr.* (ed. Harles), IX. p. 682 sq.

[4] "The S. Thomas of the Eastern Church:" Neale, *H. E. Ch.* Intr. I. p. 1159.

ment of his belief as to the Procession of the Holy Ghost: a statement the more valuable because it gathers into one the scattered teaching of the earlier Greek divines and presents the Eastern doctrine in a form which admits of easy comparison with the doctrine of the West, whilst it is beyond the suspicion of being animated by a hostile or controversial spirit. The following are the main points of his Pneumatology, gathered from the treatise *De fide orthodoxa:*

(1) The Holy Spirit is the Breath of God, which necessarily accompanies His Word[1]. Like the Word, He is a Person in the Divine Essence; a *δύναμις οὐσιώδης τοῦ Πατρὸς προερχομένη καὶ ἐν τῷ Λόγῳ ἀναπαυομένη καὶ αὐτοῦ οὖσα ἐκφαντική· οὔτε χωρισθῆναι τοῦ Θεοῦ ἐν ᾧ ἐστι καὶ τοῦ Λόγου ᾧ συμπαρομαρτεῖ δυναμένη*[2]. The Father alone is the *αἰτία ἀναίτιος Πατὴρ τοῦ Μονογενοῦς*, and the *προβολεὺς τοῦ Πνεύματος*[3]. The Father alone is ingenerate; the Son alone is generate: the Spirit alone, proceeding: the generation of the Son and the procession of the Spirit being alike *ἐκ τῆς τοῦ Πατρὸς οὐσίας: ἅμα δὲ καὶ ἡ τοῦ Υἱοῦ ἐκ τοῦ Πατρὸς γέννησις καὶ ἡ τοῦ Ἁγίου Πνεύματος ἐκπόρευσις*[4]. (2) But if the Spirit, like the Word, has His Source in the Essence of the Father, yet it is through the Word that He is communicated to the creature, even as the sun's light comes to us through the sunbeam: *ὥσπερ ἐκ τοῦ ἡλίου μὲν ἥ τε ἀκτὶς καὶ ἡ ἔλλαμψις (αὐτὸς γάρ ἐστιν ἡ πηγὴ τῆς ἀκτῖνος καὶ τῆς ἐλλάμψεως)· διά τε*

[1] *de f. o.* I. 7. (Migne XCIV. 804) δεῖ δὲ τὸν λόγον καὶ Πνεῦμα ἔχειν· καὶ γὰρ ὁ ἡμέτερος λόγος οὐκ ἄμοιρός ἐστι τοῦ πνεύματος.

[2] Migne, 805. Cf. *infra* (Migne, 856): Θεός καὶ τὸ Πνεῦμα τὸ Ἅγιόν ἐστι, δύναμις ἁγιαστικὴ, ἐνυπόστατος, ἐκ τοῦ Πατρὸς ἀδιαστάτως ἐκπορευομένη καὶ ἐν Υἱῷ ἀναπαυομένη ὁμοούσιος Πατρὶ καὶ Υἱῷ.

[3] Migne, 809.

[4] Migne, 817, 824.

[διὰ δὲ?] τῆς ἀκτῖνος ἡ ἔλλαμψις ἡμῖν μεταδίδοται. Thus, whilst we do not speak of the Spirit as being from (out of) the Son, we call Him, nevertheless, the 'Spirit of the Son'; we confess that through the Son He is manifested and conveyed to us; although the converse statement is not admissible: ἐκ τοῦ Υἱοῦ τὸ Πνεῦμα οὐ λέγομεν, Πνεῦμα δὲ Υἱοῦ ὀνομάζομεν.....τὸν δὲ Υἱὸν οὔτε τοῦ Πνεύματος λέγομεν οὔτε μὴν ἐκ τοῦ Πνεύματος[1]. (3) Further, though the Son is excluded from being in any sense the Cause or Principle of the Holy Ghost (μόνος γὰρ αἴτιος ὁ Πατήρ)[2], yet the ἔλλαμψις δι' Υἱοῦ, which has been admitted, is inseparably connected with the ἐκπόρευσις: made apparent to us by the temporal Mission of the Spirit, it depends, nevertheless, upon the eternal order of the Life of God: the Father is λόγου γεννήτωρ καὶ διὰ λόγου προβολεὺς ἐκφαντορικοῦ Πνεύματος: the Holy Spirit is ἐκφαντορικὴ τοῦ κρυφίου τῆς θεότητος δύναμις τοῦ Πατρὸς, ἐκ Πατρὸς μὲν δι' Υἱοῦ ἐκπορευομένη[3]. Thus the Holy Ghost is the Spirit of the Father as proceeding

[1] Migne, 833. Cf. *de hymno Trisagio* (Migne XCV. 60): τὸ Πνεῦμα, ἐνυπόστατον ἐκπόρευμα καὶ πρόβλημα· ἐκ Πατρὸς μὲν, Υἱοῦ δὲ, καὶ μὴ ἐξ Υἱοῦ, ὡς Πνεῦμα στόματος Θεοῦ, Λόγου ἐξαγγελτικόν.

[2] Migne, 850.

[3] Migne, 848. Cf. *dial. c. Manich.* 5 (Migne, 1512), ὁ Πατὴρ ἀεὶ ἦν, ἔχων ἐξ ἑαυτοῦ τὸν αὐτοῦ Λόγον καὶ διὰ τοῦ Λόγου αὐτοῦ ἐξ αὐτοῦ τὸ Πνεῦμα αὐτοῦ ἐκπορευόμενον. According to Basil (not writing however with a view to this subject) the difference between ἐξ οὗ and δι' οὗ is chiefly verbal: *de Sp. S.* v. ἐφ' ὧν διωρίσθη τὸ δι' οὗ κυρίως λέγεσθαι, ἐπὶ τῶν αὐτῶν τούτων τὸ ἐξ οὗ μετελήφθη. Pitzipios (*L'Eglise Orientale*, I. p. 61) remarks that the Procession δι' Υἱοῦ is repeatedly affirmed by the Greek service-books. He cites the following examples: Σὺ γὰρ ποταμὸς θεότητος ἐκ Πατρὸς δι' Υἱοῦ προερχόμενον. Τὸ Πνεῦμα τὸ Ἅγιον Θεὸς συμφυὲς καὶ σύνθρονον Πατρὶ καὶ Λόγῳ γνωρίζεται, φῶς ὑπερτέλειον ἐκ φωτὸς ἐκλάμψαν, ἐξ ἀνάρχου Πατρὸς καὶ δι' Υἱοῦ προερχόμενον. Pitzipios adds (*infr.* p. 115), "Ce qui donna motif aux pères de l'Eglise Orientale de faire usage...de l'expression διὰ τοῦ Υἱοῦ...est le sens principal de la préposition ἐκ."

from, i.e., out of (ἐκ) the Father: and the Spirit of the Son as proceeding through, not out of, the Son, the Father being the common Source of Both: ὁ Πατὴρ πηγὴ καὶ αἰτία Υἱοῦ καὶ Ἁγίου Πνεύματος... τὸ Πνεῦμα τὸ Ἅγιον, Πνεῦμα τοῦ Πατρὸς ὡς ἐκ τοῦ Πατρὸς ἐκπορευόμενον... καὶ Υἱοῦ δὲ Πνεῦμα, οὐχ ὡς ἐξ αὐτοῦ, ἀλλ' ὡς δι' αὐτοῦ ἐκ τοῦ Πατρὸς ἐκπορευόμενον[1]. (4) Lastly, the meaning of procession 'through the Son' is illustrated by two familiar figures. (*a*) The Spirit is the Image of the Son, as the Son is the Image of the Father: εἰκὼν τοῦ Πατρὸς ὁ Υἱὸς, καὶ τοῦ Υἱοῦ τὸ Πνεῦμα, δι' οὗ ὁ Χριστὸς ἐνοικῶν ἀνθρώπῳ δίδωσιν αὐτῷ τὸ κατ' εἰκόνα[2]. (*b*) As the Spirit is the middle term between Generate and Ingenerate, so on the other hand it is through the Son that the Spirit is knit to the Father—i.e., the life of the Father may be regarded as flowing through the Son into the Spirit: Θεὸς τὸ Πνεῦμα τὸ Ἅγιον μέσον τοῦ ἀγεννήτου καὶ τοῦ γεννητοῦ, καὶ δι' Υἱοῦ τῷ Πατρὶ συναπτόμενον[3].

It might have been hoped that an exposition of the Eastern Pneumatology, so careful and yet

[1] Migne, 849. This chapter (*de f. o.* I, 12) is missing in the most ancient MSS., but was received as genuine by Johannes Veccus and Georgius Scholarius: Migne, 845: cf. Neander, *Hist. of Dogma*, II. 435. With the last clause of the quotation cf. *hom. in Sabb.* 4 (Migne XCVI. 605) τοῦ Υἱοῦ λέγεται ὡς δι' αὐτοῦ φανερούμενον καὶ τῇ κτίσει μεταδιδόμενον, ἀλλ' οὐκ ἐξ αὐτοῦ ἔχον τὴν ὕπαρξιν.

[2] Migne, 855. On the theological import of εἰκών, cf. Dr Lightfoot's exhaustive note on Coloss. i. 15.

[3] *ibid.* Cf. Dr Pusey's remark (in the pref. to S. Cyril on S. John (E. Tr. p. xxxix.): "Although those among whom he [S. John Damascene] lived had dropped the expression 'from,' it is clear that he himself held the 'through' in no other sense than the old Greek fathers, of the mode of existence of the Holy Trinity, and that he rejected the 'from' as involving in his conception, the denial of the monarchia."

so temperate, set forth in the 8th century by a theologian whom East and West united to honour, would go far to prevent a serious conflict of opinion upon this point between the Latin and Greek Churches. Neander has pointed out that the doctrine of S. John of Damascus presents the "point of mediation by which the two Churches may come together[1]," and a living Catholic theologian has sagaciously adopted the writings of Damascene as the basis of a practical scheme which still excites the liveliest hopes among the friends of reunion[2]. But the age which followed the death of their author was an era of controversy, not of conciliation, and at the time the voice of the peacemaker was lost in the noisy strife of combatants.

A year after the Council of Gentilly the death of Pepin made way for the accession of Charles the Great, whose long reign [768—814], momentous in its influence upon the politics, the social condition, and the literature of Europe, was equally fruitful in the field of theology. Himself no mean theologian, Charles was surrounded by a circle of divines drawn from the principal schools of Western Christendom; Alcuin, Theodulf, Paul Warnefrid, Paulinus, met at the Frank Court—a band of scholars, who, under

[1] *Ch. Hist.* VI. pp. 294—5. Cf. *supr.* "The great dogmatist of the Greek Church, John of Damascus, laid down this doctrine in his doctrinal system according to its peculiar form in the Greek Church, yet *he did it in such a way as to leave room for a middle course.*" A full and careful summary of Damascene's doctrine on this point will be found in *die trinitarische Lehrdifferenz*, pp. 109—120.

[2] See above, p. 3, note 2. The saving clause in the Bonn statement—"in Sinne der Lehre der alten ungetrennten Kirche," will, it may be hoped, prevent the Easterns from regarding the scheme as a concession to the modern Greek view which confuses the 'Procession through the Son' with the 'Temporal Mission.'

Charles's patronage, could afford to be independent at times even of Papal decisions. Three questions of theological controversy engaged the attention of this powerful Western faction: the religious use of Images; the Adoptionist heresy: and (in connection sometimes with the former, sometimes with the latter of these two points) the doctrine of the Procession of the Holy Ghost.

In the East a strong reaction in favour of Image-worship had set in under the auspices of the Empress Irene, and Tarasius, the new Patriarch of Constantinople. A correspondence was opened between the Patriarch and the Pope, which led to the assembling of a great Council at Nicaea in the year 787. Into the wisdom of the conclusion arrived at by this Council or into its claim to Œcumenicity, it is unnecessary to enter here: we have simply to note the position which it took up with reference to the doctrine of the Procession. Speaking roughly, it seems to have sanctioned alike the old Constantinopolitan statement of the Procession, in which no reference was made to the Person of the Son, and the phrase which had so commonly obtained amongst orthodox Greek theologians, and of which S. John of Damascus had been the latest exponent, "from the Father through the Son." At the 3rd Session a letter was produced which had been addressed by Tarasius, when entering upon office, to the other Patriarchs of Christendom. It contained the words, *Πιστεύω...εἰς τὸ Πνεῦμα τὸ Ἅγιον, τὸ κύριον καὶ ζωοποιοῦν, τὸ ἐκ τοῦ Πατρὸς δι' Υἱοῦ ἐκπορευόμενον*[1]. Both the Pope and the Eastern Patriarchs had expressed their approval of this profession; and the

[1] Mansi 12, 1122.

Council added its formal acceptance[1]. On the other hand, no exception was taken to the synodical profession of Theodore of Jerusalem and the Bishops of Palestine, although they were content to say, Πιστεύομεν εἰς ἓν Πνεῦμα Ἅγιον τὸ ἀϊδίως ἐκ τοῦ Πατρὸς ἐκπορευόμενον καὶ ὃν ἀληθῶς Πατρὶ καὶ Υἱῷ συναΐδιον ὁμοούσιόν τε καὶ ὁμόφυλον, καὶ τῆς αὐτῆς οὐσίας καὶ φύσεως, ὡσαύτως δὲ θεότητος[2]. And at its closing Session the Council itself recited the uninterpolated Creed[3], prefacing the recital with the emphatic declaration, Οὐδὲν ἀφαιροῦμεν, οὐδὲν προστίθεμεν· ἀλλὰ πάντα τὰ τῆς καθολικῆς ἐκκλησίας ἀμείωτα διαφυλάττομεν[4]. There is no reason, however, to suppose that these words were directed against the

[1] Mansi, 1154: πᾶσα ἡ...ἁγία σύνοδος...τὸν νυνὶ ἀναγνωσθέντα χάρτην, ὅρον ὀρθοδοξίας...Ταρασίου ὄντα, ἀποδεχόμενοι στοιχοῦμεν.

[2] Mansi 12, 1136. In another Creed recited at Nicaea the Procession was omitted altogether. Basil, Bishop of Ancyra, upon submitting to the prevalent doctrine of image-worship, professed his faith in the Holy Trinity as follows: πιστεύω καὶ ὁμολογῶ εἰς ἕνα Θεὸν Πατέρα παντοκράτορα, καὶ εἰς ἕνα Κύριον Ἰησοῦν Χριστὸν τὸν Υἱὸν αὐτοῦ τὸν μονογενῆ, καὶ εἰς τὸ Ἅγιον Πνεῦμα τὸ Κύριον καὶ ζωοποιόν· Τριάδα ὁμοούσιον καὶ ὁμόθρονον. No exception was taken to this confession by Tarasius or by any other member of the Council: see Mansi 12, 1010.

[3] At Florence it was stated that an old MS. copy of the Latin acts exhibited *Filioque* (Mansi 31, 550). The addition may very possibly have been due to the zeal of some Western copyist in or after the Photian age. Photius makes much of the fact that six Œcumenical Councils in succession had been content with ἐκ τοῦ Πατρός: *Mystagog.* § 5 (Migne CII. 285): τίς εἶπε τῶν ἱερῶν καὶ περιωνύμων πατέρων ἡμῶν τὸ Πνεῦμα τοῦ Υἱοῦ ἐκπορεύεσθαι; ποία σύνοδος;...ἐδογμάτισεν εὐθὺς τῶν οἰκουμενικῶν καὶ ἁγίων ἑπτὰ συνόδων ἡ δευτέρα τὸ Πν. τὸ Ἅ. ἐκ τοῦ Πατρὸς ἐκπορευεσθαι· διεδέξατο ἡ τρίτη· ἐβεβαίωσεν ἡ τετάρτη· σύμψηφος ἡ πέμπτη κατέστη· συνεκήρυξεν ἡ ἕκτη· ἐπεσφραγίσεν λαμπρῶς ἀγωνίσμασιν ἡ ἑβδόμη.

[4] Mansi 13, 376. The recitation was followed by an anathema against Arianism and Macedonianism: βδελυττόμεθα δὲ καὶ ἀναθεματίζομεν Ἄρειον...Μακεδόνιόν τε καὶ τοὺς περὶ αὐτὸν καλῶς ὀνομασθέντας Πνευματομάχους. Were these points of agreement purposely put forward with the view of shutting out minor differences?

Filioque. No Eastern at Nicaea breathed a word upon the subject of the *προσθήκη*; the Westerns who were present discreetly forbore to mention it. All were content to have succeeded in reversing the iconoclastic decrees of the Constantinopolitan Synod of 754: to the Patriarch Tarasius it seemed as if East and West were now lastingly united in the bonds of a true faith: *ἡ φιλονεικία πέπαυται* (he exclaimed), *καὶ τὸ μεσότοιχον ἤρθη τῆς ἔχθρας· ἀνατολὴ γὰρ, δύσις, ἄρκτος, καὶ μεσημβρία, ὑπὸ ζυγὸν ἕνα καὶ μίαν συμφωνίαν γεγόναμεν*[1].

The joy of the good Patriarch proved to be premature. Though the proceedings of the Nicene Synod had received the consent of Rome, they failed to commend themselves to the Frank theologians. Whether their rejection by Charles was owing in part at least to political circumstances, is uncertain; that under Charles's influence they were rejected by the West, with the solitary exception of the Roman Church, seems tolerably clear. A letter is extant in which Pope Hadrian I. sets himself to answer a *capitulare* which had been sent to Rome by Charles upon the receipt of the Nicene decrees[2]. It contained a string of objections to various statements made or allowed by the Council. First among these, strangely enough, there comes a

[1] Mansi 12, 1153. The Council responded: *Δόξα σοι ὁ Θεὸς ὁ ἑνώσας ἡμᾶς.*

[2] Migne XCVIII. 1257. (Mansi 13, 760). Charles had entrusted this document to a confidential and experienced servant of the court: "praeterea directum a vestra...potentia suscepimus fidelem familiarem vestrum, videlicet Engelbertum abbatem et ministrum capellae, qui paene ab ipsis infantiae rudimentis in palatio vestro enutritus est et in omnibus consiliis vestris receptus...Edidit nobis capitulare adversus synodum quae pro sacrarum imaginum erectione in Nicaea acta est."

demurrer to Tarasius's doctrine of the Procession: "quod Tarasius non recte sentiat qui Spiritum Sanctum non *ex Patre et Filio* secundum Nicaenum symbolum, sed *ex Patre per Filium* procedentem in suae credulitatis lectione profiteatur." The Pope's reply took no notice of the fact which Charles had unconsciously disclosed, that the Franks were now in the habit of using the interpolated Creed; yet without condemning the interpolation, still less the Western doctrine, Hadrian reasserted against Charles the orthodoxy of the Patriarch's phraseology, and its consistency with Catholic belief: "hoc dogma Tarasius non per se explanavit, sed per doctrinam sanctorum patrum confessus est." The *per Filium* was certainly permissible, for it had been taught not only by S. Athanasius and S. Basil in the East, but by the greatest of Western fathers, by S. Hilary, S. Ambrose, S. Augustine himself: it was part of the traditional belief of the Roman see: "responsum reddidimus, non quemlibet (absit) hominem defendentes, sed olitanam traditionem sanctae catholicae et apostolicae Romanae ecclesiae priscam praedecessorum nostrorum sanctorum pontificum sequimur doctrinam."

The *capitulare* conveyed to Hadrian by Engelbert seems to have formed the nucleus of the famous *Libri Carolini*[1], which appeared under

[1] Cf. Hefele, *Conciliengeschichte*, b. III. p. 671: "dass aber die nach Rom gesandten Capitula ein auf der Synode zu Frankfurt gefertigter Auszug der *libri Carolini* seien, wie Petavius vermuthete, möchte ich weniger annehmen, und halte für wahrscheinlicher, dass unsere Carolinen eine etwas spätere von Carl befohlene Ueberarbeitung und weitere Begründung der ursprünglich viel kürzeren, nur in einzelnen Sätzen bestehenden *capitula* seien, und dass Form und Text dieser gerade so waren, wie sie uns noch jetzt in dem Antwortschreiben Hadrians entgegentreten."

Charles's name[1] about the year 790[2]. The third of these books enters at considerable length upon the Procession-doctrine of Tarasius. It is curious to see how completely the great defender of the Western interpolation anticipates the East in throwing upon his opponent the charge of having added to the Catholic Faith. 'Had Tarasius merely omitted the *Filioque*, he would not have complained: many had done so who nevertheless believed the fuller doctrine of the Universal Church. The point of the Patriarch's offence lay in appending the *per Filium*, which presented quite another view of the Spirit's relation to the Son[3]: "alteram namque vim habet *ex* praepositio, et alteram *per*." The *per Filium* was dangerous, inasmuch as (1) it was ambiguous; whereas ambiguity is never more to be deprecated

[1] From Simeon of Durham (an annalist of the 12th century, but probably deriving his account from an 8th century record) we learn that in 792 a copy of the Nicene acts was sent to England by Charlemagne, and that the English Bishops entrusted their reply to Alcuin: "contra quod scripsit Albinus epistolam ex authoritate Divinarum scripturarum mirabiliter affirmatam; illamque cum eodem libro et persona Episcoporum ac Principum nostrorum regi Francorum attulit." Cf. Hardwick, *Ch. Hist. of the Middle Ages*, p. 78: Haddan and Stubbs, III. pp. 468—9. Haddan and Stubbs say, "It is probable that Alcuin as being the most learned man at the Frank Court...had a share in the composition of the *Libri Carolini*, and possible that that work was based upon Alcuin's letter mentioned in the text." The latter supposition, however, must be abandoned, if the *Libri Carolini* are held to have been written in 790. See next note.

[2] So at least we gather from the preface, which says of the Nicene Council, "Gesta praeterea est *ferme ante triennium* et altera synodus illis in partibus." (Migne XCVIII. 1003.) Cf. Hefele, III. p. 653.

[3] *Libr. Carol.* III. 3 (Migne XCVIII. 1117): "quod Tarasius non 'ex Patre' tantum (sicut quidam qui quamquam eum ex Filio quodammodo tacuerint tamen ex Patre et Filio procedentem omnino crediderint); neque 'ex Patre et Filio' (sicut omnis universaliter confitetur et credit ecclesia eum procedere); sed 'ex Patre per Filium' in suae fidei professione confessus est."

than when it occurs in definitions of the Faith[1]: (2) it had an Arian tendency, since the Arians used the same phrase to express their doctrine of the Spirit being the creature of a created Son: (3) it was unauthorized: "dum...ex Patre et Filio ab omni catholica ecclesia procedere credatur, quaerendum est utrum necesse sit eum per Filium a Patre et non potius ex Patre et Filio procedere profiteri, cum hujuscemodi professio neque in Nicaeno neque in Chalcedonensi symbolo a sanctis patribus facta inveniatur"...... "per Filium eum a Patre procedere profiteri synodicae confessioni inusitatum est." In any case (the Caroline writer concludes) the language adopted by Tarasius ought not to be forced upon the Church: "sufficiat hoc credere, hoc firmiter tenere, hoc toto corde fateri, Patrem ingenitum, Filium genitum, Spiritum vero Sanctum nec creatum nec genitum, sed ex Patre et Filio procedentem; ita duntaxat ut in confessione fidei omnes operationes, omnes verborum novitates caveantur et his verbis hisque sententiis fidelium confessio roboretur quae sanctae et universales synodi in Symbolo taxaverunt."

But neither the *capitulare* nor the fuller refutation of the Nicene decision offered by the Caroline Books satisfied the zeal of Charles. In the year 794 he succeeded in bringing together at Frankfort an assembly at which Bishops were present from Italy, Gaul, Aquitaine, and Britain[2], as well as from every

[1] "Multo magis fidei definitio dilucida et perspicua et omni ambiguitate sive tortuositate carens esse debet"—a characteristic sentiment.

[2] So Charles himself affirms in the letter to Elipandus: "necnon et de Britanniae partibus aliquos ecclesiasticae disciplinae viros convocavimus:" *infra:* "tenet et tertius libellus orthodoxam sanctorum patrum episcoporum et virorum venerabilium fidem, qui in Germaniae Galliae Aquitaniae et Britanniae partibus dignis Deo deserviunt officiis." Alcuin certainly took part in the proceedings,

part of Germany. Two episcopal legates, whose names are recorded, but of whose sees no mention is made, appeared on behalf of the Pope, and are represented as having subscribed the acts of the Council[1]. The accounts of this great Western Council are meagre and perplexing: but it seems that two controversies occupied the special attention of the Bishops—Adoptianism, and the question of Icon-worship. On both points the Council was unanimous. All agreed to reject the heresy of Elipandus and Felix: all refused submission to the Nicene decree; "omnimodis adorationem et servitutem renuentes contempserunt atque consentientes condemnaverunt[2]." Attached to the Frankfort Canons in the *Concilia* is a collection of four important documents bearing upon the former of these questions: a letter

but as an expert; cf. *capitulare Francoford.* c. LIV.: "Commonuit etiam ut Alcuinum ipsa sancta Synodus in suo consortio sive in orationibus recipere dignaretur, eo quod esset vir in ecclesiasticis doctrinis eruditus." Haddan and Stubbs (III. pp. 481—2), after quoting the above, say, "It is quite possible that he may have participated......as a representative of the English Church." The words of the *capitulare* seem to me to exclude this view.

[1] So Eginhard (*Annal.* a. 794. Migne CIV. 445—5): "adfuerunt etiam in eadem synodo et legati S. R. E., Theophylactus ac Stephanus episcopi, vicem tenentes ejus a quo missi sunt Hadriani papae." Mr Ffoulkes (*Dict. of Chr. Antiq.* I. p. 690) suggests that the legates of the Pope may have left before the discussion on Icon-worship began. Both the Annalists and Charles (*Ep. ad Elipand.*) claim the consent of the Papal legates only for the condemnation of Adoptianism: but, on the other hand, not a word is said of their withdrawal from the Council.

[2] This account is confirmed by Eginhard, *Annal.* a. 794 (Migne, *l. c.*): "Synodus etiam quae ante paucos annos in Constantinopoli (*sic*) sub Herena [*v.l.* Irene] et Constantino filio ejus congregata et ab ipsis non solum septima verum etiam universalis est appellata ut nec septima nec universalis haberetur diceretur ve, quasi supervacua in totum ab omnibus abdicata est." Similarly the *Annales Laurissenses* (Migne, *ibid.*): "pseudosinodus Graecorum quam falso septimam vocabant et pro adorandis imaginibus fecerunt, rejecta est a pontificibus."

from Pope Hadrian to the Bishops of Spain: a *libellus episcoporum Italiae contra Elipandum*, which was sent in the name of the Archbishop of Milan and the Bishops of Liguria, Istria, &c., but had been composed by Paulinus, Patriarch of Aquileia[1]; a Synodical Epistle to the Spanish Church from the Bishops of Gaul and Germany; and lastly, an Epistle to Elipandus from Charlemagne himself. Three of these compositions distinctly assert the *Filioque*. The Pope's testimony is express: "Spiritus.... Sanctus cum.... ex Patre Filioque essentialiter procedat, quo pacto credi potest super Deum [sc. Filium] descendisse....a quo ineffabiliter semper procedit?" Paulinus writes that the Catholic doctrine of the Holy Trinity provides for the distinction of the Persons "ita sane ut alius credatur Pater, quia Pater est.... et alius credatur Filius, quia Filius est.... et alius credatur Spiritus Sanctus, quia Spiritus Sanctus est et a Patre Filioque procedit[2]." In Charlemagne's letter the Procession from the Son is twice affirmed in the course of a profession which ends with the words, "Haec est fides catholica et ideo nostra[3]."

At Frankfort the *Filioque* was referred to incidentally; at Friuli, two years later[4], the interpolation of the Creed was for the first time openly defended before a Synod of the Church. The Council of Friuli (the Venetian *Forum Julii*) seems to have been a provincial gathering of the suffragans of Aquileia.

[1] This is implied in the wording: "Ego Paulinus licet indignus peccator...una cum reverendissimo et omni honore digno Petro Mediolanensis sedis archiepiscopo."

[2] Mansi 13, 878.

[3] Mansi, 905—6.

[4] A.D. 796: cf. Hefele, *Conciliengeschichte*, III. 674, note: "nicht 791 wie nach Baronius die Meisten annahmen. Das 23. Jahr Carls, das in Protokoll dieser Synode genannt ist, muss vom Anfange seiner Herrschaft in Italien gerechnet werden, da diese Synode eine italische ist. *Pagi*, ad ann. 791, 6 sqq."

Paulinus presided, and opened the proceedings with a long address upon dogma which bears the mark of careful preparation. Its tone is apologetic; its apparent aim is to secure the acceptance by the Patriarchate of the interpolation which the less remote provinces of the Frank Empire had already embraced. The Patriarch begins by remarking that the first duty of the Council was to lay the foundations of a sound faith. In attempting this, their work must be tested at every step by the Creed—the plumb-line of the spiritual builder[1]. By the Creed he meant that inviolable form of belief which had been composed with the aid of the Holy Ghost by the fathers of Nicaea and Constantinople. Later Councils had forbidden the drawing up of any other symbol; nor was he about to commit or suffer a breach of this rule: "non alteram componere vel docere fidem consentio, sed eam quae a sanctis patribus traditam omnia sinceriter saecula susceperunt." But for the sake of the unlearned, it was allowable to expound the necessarily brief and terse language of the ancient formula. The original Nicene Creed had stopped short with the words, "And in the Holy Ghost": all that followed was added by the fathers of Constantinople; yet the identity of the Creed had not been lost through an addition which was simply an expository gloss: "suppleverunt quasi exponendo eorum sensum, et in Spiritum Sanctum confitentes

[1] Mansi 13, 835: "primum ergo visum est mihi in primi ordinis fronte ipsum textum symboli...quasi lineam in directum normulatim aequo moderamine in fundamenta hujus spiritalis aedificii mole intrinsecus ac forinsecus tendere, ut coaequata juxta illius rectitudinis normulam tota nostri operis fabrica hinc inde Catholicae fidei libratim submissa perpendiculo, rectius ad altiora excrescens, convenienter in utroque pariete aequis disputationum metita funiculis, in summa scientiae arte perfectionis culmen veridicis assertionibus fulciatur," &c., &c.

se credere dominum ac vivificatorem ex Patre procedentem." In the same way, when at a later time heresy began to whisper that the Spirit proceeds from the Father alone, to the exclusion of the co-essential Son, the meaning of the Creed had been further expounded by the addition of *Filioque*[1]. We do not blame the Constantinopolitan fathers for introducing into the Creed the doctrine of the procession from the Father which they drew from the Gospel of S. John. Nor should censure fall upon those who upon similar authority filled up the outline more completely. The *Filioque* is involved in the *Homoousion* which was taught in the original Creed: "si ergo inseparabiliter et substantialiter est Pater in Filio et Filius in Patre, quo pacto credi potest ut consubstantialis Patri Filioque Spiritus Sanctus non a Patre Filioque essentialiter et inseparabiliter semper procedat?" It follows that the shorter and the fuller forms of the Creed are equally sound, equally defensible: "quam catholice et sancti patres .... a Patre Sanctum Spiritum procedere sunt professi! quam gloriose et illi qui eum ex Patre Filioque procedere confitentur[2]." At the end of this elaborate defence we have the "textus symboli"—the interpolated Latin, of course, followed by the Patriarch's own exposition of its contents. In the latter we read, "Spiritus Sanctus verus Deus, vere et proprie Spiritus Sanctus est, non geni-

[1] "Sed et postmodum propter eos videlicet haereticos qui susurrant Spiritum Sanctum solius esse Patris et a solo procedere Patre, additum est: 'qui ex Patre Filioque procedit.' One is curious to know to whom Paulinus refers, and whether he had any distinct theory as to the date of the interpolation. His address gives no information on these points. Walch (*Hist. Contr.*, p. 23) understands him to be defending the *Filioque* against the Greeks.

[2] The same view had been taken in the Caroline Books: *supr.* p. 210.

tus nec creatus, sed ex Patre Filioque intemporaliter et inseparabiliter procedens.... non est personaliter Pater vel Filius, sed de utroque procedit."

The Patriarchate of Aquileia appears to have accepted the interpolation without a murmur. But before long it began to provoke angry controversy in the East, to which the Latin Creed had now been carried by Frank settlers.

In the month of November, 809, the Emperor[1] held a great council at Aix-la-Chapelle (*Aquisgrani*) for the express purpose of coming to a decision upon the *Filioque* question. "Imperator, de Arduenna Aquas reversus (writes Eginhard), mense Novembrio consilium habuit de processione Spiritus Sancti[2]." "In qua synodo (adds Ado of Vienne) quaestio agitatur utrum sicut procedit a Patre, ita procedat a Filio[3]." From these accounts Pagi inferred that at Aix, as at Gentilly, the discussion turned upon the point of doctrine only, not upon the interpolation[4]. But that the latter was the real, if not the acknowledged subject of the Aix debate, is

[1] It is significant that the beginning of the *Filioque* troubles almost synchronizes with the rise of the Western Empire. Cf. Ffoulkes, *Chr. Div.* II. p. 398: "A new era had dawned with the division of the Empire, with the Christmas-day A.D. 800 that witnessed the coronation of Charlemagne as Emperor of the West. The Empire which had long been disintegrating was rent asunder at last, and united Christendom, was it destined to weather the political earthquake......and remain one? This was in reality the problem which those simple monks of Mt. Olivet...were the first to agitate, and Charlemagne to consider."

[2] Migne CIV. 472.

[3] Migne CXXIII. 132. Ado adds, "Cum regula et fides ecclesiastica firmet Spiritum S. a Patre et Filio procedere non creatum non genitum sed Patre et Filio coaeternum et consubstantialem. Nomen autem processionis a Patre et Filio in Apocalypsi ita aperte est positum [quoting Rev. xxii. 1]." Cf. *supr.* p. 8, note 2.

[4] *In annales Baronii* a. 802. Baronius had taken the opposite view.

placed beyond doubt by a series of most interesting documents[1] which have survived to supplement the meagre annals of the chroniclers.

The discussion at the Council of 809 originated in a monkish fray at Jerusalem: thus much the chroniclers tell us[2], but we are left to glean the particulars from a letter addressed to Pope Leo III. by one of the parties engaged in the controversy. On the mount of Olives a party of Frank monks had founded a convent under the direct patronage, as it seems, of the Western Emperor[3]. A Greek monk named John, belonging to the monastery of S. Sabas[4], chose (we know not why) to open war upon the Latin community. "You Franks (he cried) are all heretics: a worse heresy than yours does not exist." On Christmas-day [808?] John publicly repeated his charge, adding "Your books are heretical:" and an attempt was made to eject the Franks from the Church of the Nativity where they were keeping

[1] See Appendix A.

[2] So Eginhard: "quam quaestionem Joannes quidam monachus Hierosolimis primum commovit." Similarly Ado of Vienne. "It was at Jerusalem—the city of peace—that the first sparks of controversy seem to have been elicited" (Ffoulkes, *Christendom's Divisions*, II. 71).

[3] From the letter it appears that Charles had presented them with several of their MSS.: and the writer at least had formerly been in attendance on the Emperor ("dum essem ego Leo servus vester...ad pia vestigia domni Caroli...audivimus in capella ejus dici in symbolo fidei," &c.). In 807 the Abbat Egilbald and one of the brethren, Felix by name, had been sent over to the French court by the Patriarch of Jerusalem: cf. Eginhard. *Annal.* a. 807 (Migne CIV. 468).—Mr Ffoulkes (*Chr. Div.* II. 71) suggests that the Frank Convent on Mt Olivet may have been "possibly the one frequented or founded there by Rufinus of Aquileia." Cf. Le Quien, *diss. Damasc.* I. § xiv.

[4] Montfaucon (*palaeogr. Graec.* p. 89) describes a MS. (*saec.* XVI.) with the inscription, ἐγράφη ἐν τῇ μόνῃ τοῦ ἁγίου Σάβα εἰς τὸ σπήλαιον καὶ ἐν τῇ ἁγίᾳ πόλει Ἱερουσαλήμ. Cf. *bibl. Coist.* p. 273, &c. For an account of the present monastery of Mar Sâba, see Porter, *Handbook for Syria*, p. 196 sq.

the festival. Shortly afterwards, on a Sunday during divine service in the Church of the Holy Sepulchre, they were examined by the Archdeacon and clergy of Jerusalem upon their faith and, in particular, as to their recension of the Creed. They admitted that they differed from the Greeks in the wording of four formularies[1], the *Gloria Patri*, the *Gloria in excelsis*, the *Pater noster*, and the *Creed:* in the last-named, they said "Qui ex Patre Filioque procedit." For this they had been called heretics: although their use was none other than that of the Holy Roman Church. This explanation seems to have satisfied or checked the scruples of the Jerusalem clergy: but the irrepressible John was not silenced so easily: he went round the monasteries preaching opposition to the *Filioque* and a crusade against the Franks. Under these circumstances the persecuted monks of Mt Olivet appealed to the Pope; and their letter is full of the interest which belongs to a simple and unadorned narrative of facts which has floated down to us from a distant age. In support of their own view they plead (1) that they had heard the *Filioque* chanted as part of the Creed in the Emperor's own chapel: (2) that it was professed in "the Faith of S. Athanasius"[2]: (3) that the doctrine was taught in two books which they had received from the hands of Charles himself, copies of one of Pope Gregory's homilies[3] and of the Rule

[1] To the first the Latins added *sicut erat in principio* (Conc. Vasens. A.D. 529: cf. Walafrid. Strab. *de reb. Eccl.* c. 25): to the second, *tu solus altissimus* (cf. *Constit. Apost.* vii. 47). In the third they omitted the doxology: see Freeman, I. p. 108.

[2] Cf. Swainson, *N. and A. Creeds*, p. 445. As to the influence of the *Quicunque vult* on the *Filioque* controversy, see above, p. 176.

[3] See above, p. 157, and cf. Le Quien *diss. Damascen.* I. § XVIII. (Migne, *P. G.* XCIV. 214): "nullus dubito quin significent sibi traditam

of S. Benedict[1]. With an honest desire to know the truth, they beg the Pope to institute an enquiry into the facts of the case, and especially to satisfy himself as to the genuineness of the *Filioque* in the Constantinopolitan Creed, and its use in the Emperor's chapel.

If the Pope vouchsafed any direct reply to the monks of Mt Olivet, his letter is lost, or lies buried in the recesses of some monastic library. A like fate seems to have befallen a letter addressed to Leo by Thomas, Patriarch of Jerusalem, which may have referred to this recent controversy. We possess, however, a profession of faith which was very possibly enclosed in the Papal answer to the Frank monks, but bears the title "Leo, to all the Churches of the East"; and a letter sent by the Pope to Charlemagne together with a copy of the Mt Olivet appeal. The letter to the Emperor is purely formal and seems purposely to abstain from entering into the merits of the question. The Symbol, on the other hand, is lengthy and elaborate. It lays down the doctrine of the Roman Church with a view to its acceptance by the Catholic East: and in the heart of this authoritative exposition of what Rome now regarded as *de fide* we find an unflinching statement of the Procession from the Son.

It was on the receipt of this communication from the Pope that Charles summoned his Bishops to meet him at Aix. On the doctrinal question

a Carolo fuisse collectionem homiliarum...quam Paulus diaconus ipsiusmet imperatoris jussu congesserat. Nam in hac collectione homilia illa Gregorii quam citant reperitur pro die octava Paschae".

[1] Le Quien, *l. c.*: "nihil ejusmodi habetur hodie in regula S. Benedicti. Arbitror professionem hanc fidei appendicis cujusdam instar fuisse quae postmodum regulae subnexa sit a monachis recitanda."

no real hesitation could have been felt: the Franks were as one man in believing the *Filioque:* the creed which the Pope had sent to the East testified his assent in the strongest terms. Perhaps it was by way of declaring his independence that the Emperor allowed the subject to be discussed, and returned to the Pope a string of scriptural and patristic testimonies, 'sufficient, as he trusted, to overwhelm the enemy and compel his return to the bosom of the Catholic Church'—from which (it appears) he had been separated by his rejection of the Western doctrine. The other controverted point, as Charles was doubtless sagacious enough to perceive, required more delicate handling. Upon the interpolation the Pope had preserved a discreet silence: the Roman Church was known to be still holding aloof from the practice of the Court. The Council therefore could decide nothing; but it sent a mission to Rome to confer with the Pope, and, if possible, to gain his adhesion. According to Eginhard[1], the members of this mission were Bernhar, Bishop of Worms, and Adalhard, Abbat of Corbie: the latter seems to have been accompanied by his neighbour and diocesan, Jesse, Bishop of Amiens, whose interest in the question had possibly been awakened by a previous visit to the East[2].

Nothing in the literature of this controversy surpasses in interest or importance the account which has reached us of the meeting between Charles's

1 "Cujus definiendae causa Bernharius (*v. ll.*, Bernhardus, Bernarius) episcopus Wormacensis et Adalhardus abbas monasterii Corbeiae Romam ad Leonem papam missi sunt" (Migne CIV. 472).

2 Cf. Petav. *de Trin.* VII. 1, "quibus addendus est Jesse Ambianensis episcopus, ut ex actis collationis cum Leone papa liquet." He had been sent by Charlemagne to Constantinople in 802 on a political mission: Cave, *Hist. lit.* a. 799.

legates and the Pope[1]. To the dogmatic statement of the Council, Leo III. gave his ready assent: he was also at one with the Franks in denouncing as a heresy the wilful rejection of the *Filioque* doctrine. But in the next stage of their negociations the *missi* were less successful: the Pope refused to declare the acceptance of the doctrine to be in all cases necessary to salvation; whilst to the insertion of *Filioque* in the Creed he was inexorably opposed. It was pleaded that thousands of the unlearned gained their knowledge of this truth simply from hearing it sung at Mass: and that the singing of the Creed at Mass had been permitted by the Pope himself. Leo replied that other points of doctrine equally true and important found no expression in the Creed: that as for his permission, it had reference to the original symbol, not to an interpolated form: even the Roman Church had not presumed to add to the ancient Creed, much as it might seem to need expansion[2]. As a last resource, the legates pointed out the danger to simple souls in the excision of words which they had been taught to regard as a part of the Faith: the doctrine would be lost, they argued, with the words. The Pope admitted the danger and suggested a way to meet it. Let the singing of the Creed at Mass be gradually given up: the excision might then be made without attracting popular remark: the true doctrine would continue to be held, whilst the unauthorized addition (which seems to have been confined to the

[1] It was held in the *secretarium* of S. Peter's, A.D. 810. (Hefele, III. p. 702.)

[2] Neander (*Ch. Hist.* VI. 296) remarks, "The Pope proceeded at this time on the same principle with that followed in the Greek Church, which would allow no alteration to be made in the decisions of a General Council illuminated by the Holy Ghost."

Creed as inserted in the missals) would eventually disappear[1].

Charles did not attempt to renew the negociation. He could not have hoped for any concession during the lifetime of a Pope whose answer shewed him at once so fearless and so wise; and Leo outlived the Emperor[2]. The latter seems to have judged it best to submit in silence to the Papal rebuke, whilst he neglected the advice by which it was accompanied. There is no reason to suppose that the chanting of the interpolated Creed ceased or was even suspended in consequence of the conference at Rome. Sixty years after the Council of Aix, Aeneas Parisiensis argues against the Greek rejection of the *Filioque* on the ground that the whole Gallican Church chanted the words at Mass on every Lord's Day[3]. And whilst the use of the interpolated Creed at Mass continued, the doctrine of the *Filioque* was now propagated with all the zeal which is excited by the consciousness of being pledged to the defence of a disputed and doubtful opinion. Probably it is to the years which followed the Council of Aix that we owe the two earliest specimens of the controversial literature which afterwards sprang up in such rank abundance on the field of the *Filioque* dispute. (1) The treatise of Theodulf, Bishop of Orleans, *de Spiritu Sancto*

[1] This report is given at length in App. A.: an English translation will be found in Neale, *H. E. Ch.*, Intr. ii. pp. 1163—6. The original is due to the Abbat Smaragdus, who was present at the Conference: Fabric. *Bibl. Lat.* VI. 493.

[2] Leo III. died in 816: Charles in 814.

[3] *Lib. adv. Graec.* c. XCIII. (Migne CXXI. 721), "item in fide catholica quam die dominica decantat ad missam universalis Galliarum ecclesia sic canitur inter cetera: 'Credo et in Spiritum S. Dominum et vivificatorem, qui ex Patre Filioque procedit.'"

opens with a dedication to the Emperor in elegiac verse, which connects the work with the first years of the controversy. The writer took up his pen at the command of Charles:

"imperii vestri rex inclyte jussa secutus
 defero Theodulfus haec documenta libens.
perge, libelle, celer Caroli ad vestigia celsi
 regis et 'o pie' dic 'induperator ave:
inclyta sanctorum mecum est sententia vatum
 quos bene spiramen Flaminis hujus agit.
tuque manum injicies, vegetat quem Spiritus ille
 causa tuo cujus tempore coepit agi[1].'"

The book itself is better than the prefatory verses, and presents a formidable list of authorities, more or less trustworthy, in support of the Latin doctrine. (2) The treatise on the Procession which bears the name of Alcuin[2], if genuine, must have been written some years before the Aix Council, since Alcuin died in 804. But the authorship is uncertain: the style is said to be unlike that of the great English scholar[3]; and as the work was executed at the express desire of Charlemagne ("secundum vestrae sublimitatis jussionem") we are led to connect it with a period of his reign, when the Emperor's mind is known to have been occupied with the *Filioque* controversy[4].

The Pope on the other hand, if he felt himself unable to dictate to Charles, was resolved, as far as in him lay, to guard the Roman Church against the

[1] Migne CV. 241.

[2] Alcuin, *de processione Sp. S.* (Migne CI. 64, sq.). [3] Migne, 63.

[4] In 813, by desire of Charles, a Council was held at Arles, to deal with certain matters of discipline. Its canons open with a profession of faith in which the *Filioque* is prominent, and which ends as follows: "Haec est catholicae ecclesiae fides, hanc confessionem servamus atque tenemus: quam quisque firmissime custodierit perpetuam salutem habebit." (Mansi 14, 58).

insertion in its Creed of the interpolated words. Anastasius Bibliothecarius, who flourished in the next generation, relates that Leo 'for the love he bore to the orthodox Faith and out of his care for its preservation' caused two silver shields on which the Creed had been engraved in Greek and Latin to be set up on either side of the *confessio* in S. Peter's[1]. Writers of the 11th and 12th centuries—S. Peter Damian, Abelard, and Peter Lombard—omitting the mention of the two languages and the second shield, volunteer a statement which they would have been little likely to invent, that in the Creed which Leo set up the *Filioque* was omitted: the Father alone was mentioned in reference to the procession of the Holy Ghost[2]. Photius twice alludes to the same circumstance[3], although with some minor differ-

[1] *Hist. de vitis Rom. Pontif.* (Migne CXXVIII. 1238): "hic vero [Leo III.] pro amore et cautela orthodoxae fidei fecit ubi supra [*sc.* in basilica ipsius Apostoli (beati Petri)] scuta argentea duo scripta utraque symbolo, unum quidem literis Graecis et aliud Latinis, sedentia dextra laevaque super ingressum corporis." S. Peter Damian (*de process. Sp. S.* c. II.: Migne CXLV. 635), Peter Lombard (*sentent.* I. *dist.* XI. § 2, Migne CXCII. 552) and Peter Abelard (*intr. ad theol.* II. Migne CLXXVIII. 1073) speak of a single "tabula argentea," which was set up by Leo "ante sacratissimum corpus beati Pauli Apostoli" [P. Damian] or "post altare beati Pauli" [P. Lombard]. Peter Lombard represents the words "pro amore &c." as Leo's own ("ut ipse ait"). Possibly they formed part of the heading.

[2] S. Peter Damian says, "Beatus Leo... inter ceteras suae fidei symbolas ait, 'Et in Spiritum S...ex Patre procedentem.'" Peter Lombard expressly, "In quo quidem symbolo in processione Spiritus solus commemoratur Pater."

[3] *Mystagog.* (Migne CII. 395), *οὗτος δὲ ὁ Λέων τὸ θησαυροφυλάκιον τῆς ἀποστολικῆς ἐκκλησίας Ῥωμαίων διανοίξας ἀσπίδας δύο τοῖς ἱεροῖς κειμηλίοις συναποτεθησαυρισμένας ἐξήνεγκεν Ἑλληνικοῖς* [*καὶ*] *γράμμασι καὶ ῥήμασιν ἐχούσας τὴν εὐσεβῆ τῆς πίστεως ἔκθεσιν, καὶ ταύτας ἐνώπιον ὑπαναγνωσθῆναι τοῦ Ῥωμαϊκοῦ πλήθους ἐδικαίωσεν.* *Epist.* I. 24 (Migne, 799), *θυρεοῖς τισιν...ἀναγραψάμενος...κατὰ τὰς πύλας τῆς ἐκκλησίας προσέπηξεν.* In both passages Photius also states that Leo [III. ?] required the Creed to be recited at mass in Greek, *ὡς ἂν κατὰ μηδένα τροπον μηδαμῶς*

ences of detail: the shields, he says, had been discovered by Leo in the treasury of S. Peter's, and were of ancient workmanship: they were affixed to the doors of the Church, not to the *confessio.* But whenever the inscription was made, or wherever it was set up, all agree that Leo adopted this method of preserving the Creed inviolate. It was a practical answer to the temerity of the Franks: as Charles had popularized the interpolation among his subjects by ordering it to be chanted at Mass: so the Pope sought to root the old Creed in the affections of the Roman people by exhibiting it constantly before their eyes in connection with the most sacred of their local shrines[1]. The plan appears to have succeeded for a time; and it has been thought that the interpolated symbol obtained no recognized footing at Rome until, exactly two hundred years after the death of Charlemagne, the Emperor Henry II. prevailed upon Benedict VIII. (1014) to adopt the German use of chanting the symbol at the Holy Mysteries[2]. But the tact and

παραχαράττοιτο βαρβάρῳ γλώσσῃ τὸ ἄχραντον ἡμῶν τῆς εὐσεβείας μάθημα. But he appears to have confused Leo III. with Leo IV. the predecessor of Benedict III. (cf. Migne, 395), and the use of the Greek Creed at Baptism with its introduction into the Mass. See Art. on 'Creeds' in *Dict. of Chr. Antiq.* (I. p. 492).

[1] Hefele (III. p. 703) connects the setting up of the shields with the Roman conference of 810.

[2] Cf. Bernonis abbatis Augiensis *de officio missae* c. II. (Migne CXLII. pp. 1061—2.) ["Symbolum] Romani usque ad haec tempora divae memoriae Henrici imperatoris nullo modo cecinerunt. Sed ab eodem interrogati cur ita agerent, me coram assistente, audivi eos hujusmodi responsum reddere, videlicet, quod Romana Ecclesia non fuisset aliquando ulla haereseos faece infecta, sed secundum S. Petri doctrinam in soliditate catholicae fidei permaneret inconcussa; et ideo magis his necessarium esse illud Symbolum saepius cantando frequentare, qui aliquando ulla haeresi potuerunt maculari. At dominus imperator non antea desiit quam omnium consensu id

moderation of Leo did not save the peace of Christendom even for the next two centuries. Scarcely more than fifty years had elapsed, when Photius Patriarch of Constantinople gave vent to the hidden spark of discord, and it burst forth into a flame[1].

domino Benedicto apostolico persuasit ut ad publicam missam id decantarent." Dr Neale (*H. E. Ch.* Intr. ii. p. 1167), says "Nicolas I. has to answer for the final insertion." See, however, Voss. *de tribus Symbolis*, p. 77, and cf. Walch. *hist. contr. de process. Sp. S.*, pp. 18, 19.

[1] The encyclical letter of Photius to the Patriarchs was written in A. D. 867.

APPENDIX.

(A). DOCUMENTS RELATING TO THE COUNCIL OF AIX, A. D. 809.

1. *Epistola peregrinorum Monachorum, &c.*

Sanctissimo ac reverentissimo domino in Christo patri LEONI summo pontifici et universali papae sedis sanctae apostolicae urbis Romae congregatio montis Oliveti.

Domine pater, te dignatus est Dominus exaltare super omnes sacerdotes, et exaltata est sedes tua sancta super omnes sedes Christianorum, quia suo ore dignatus est Christus dicere: *Tu es Petrus*, etc. Benignissime pater, nos, qui sumus hic in sancta civitate Jerusalem peregrini, ullum hominem super terra non amamus plusquam vos, et in quantum valemus in istis sanctis locis pro vobis die noctuque Domino fundimus preces prostrati omnes servi tui super terram cum lacrymis. Itaque notam tibi facimus tribulationem nostram, quam hic patimur. Johannes, qui fuit de monasterio S. Sabae, quem Theodulus iguminus servus vester scit, ipse levatus est super nos dicendo quod 'Franci qui sunt in monte Oliveti haeretici sunt,' et dixit nobis quia 'omnes Franci haeretici estis,' et reprobat fidem nostram dicendo quia 'non est major haeresis.' Et nos ei dicimus: 'Frater, sile. Quod si nos dicis haereticos, de sede sancta apostolica dicis haeresim.' Et usque in tantum nos conturbavit ut in die natalis Domini in sanctam Bethleem in sancto praesepio, ubi noster Dominus redemptor humani generis pro mundi salute nasci dignatus est, submitteret laicos homines qui nos foras proicere vellent, dicendo quod 'haeretici estis, et libri quos habetis haeretici sunt.' Sed per vestram sanctam orationem et fidem confortavit nos Dominus. Non enim potuerunt nos foras eicere. Diximus omnes: 'Hic volumus mori. Nam foras nos non eicietis.' Unde et fecimus vocem nostram omnes nos servi vestri pariter dicendo ad sacerdotes qui sunt in sancta civitate: 'Videte, patres et fratres, de isto homine qui contra nos tanta et talia loquitur et contra fidem sanctam Romanam, quia talia verba nunquam audivimus de gente nostra.' Et post haec die sancto dominico congregati sunt sacerdotes cum clero et populo contra sanctum sepulcrum Domini et inter sanctum Calvariae locum, et interrogaverunt nos de fide nostra ipsi sacerdotes, qualiter crederemus symbolum. Nos autem dicendo quod 'sic credimus sicut sancta Ecclesia Romana,' diximus 'et dicimus in nostra lingua quae vos non dicitis in Graeca; et in *Gloria Patri* non dicitis *sicut erat in principio*, et in *Gloria in excelsis* non dicitis *tu solus altissimus*, et *Pater noster* alio modo dicitis, et in symbolo nos dicimus plus quam vos, *qui ex Patre Filioque procedit*, unde dicit iste Johannes inimicus animae suae propter hunc sermonem eo quod haeretici simus.' Quos Hierosolymitas rogavimus dicentes: 'Nolite audire hunc hominem, nec dicatis de nobis haereses.' Quod si nos dicitis haereticos, de throno beati Petri dicitis haeresim. Et si hoc dicitis, peccatum inducitis super vos. Et sacerdotes scripserunt nobis cartam de fide nostra quam licet crederemus, dicendo nobis: 'Creditisne sicut sancta resurrectio Domini?' Nos autem diximus quod 'sic credimus quomodo sancta resurrectio Domini et sedes sancta apostolica Romana.' Post haec ipse archidiaconus in sancto Constantino una nobiscum ascendit in pergo et legit ipsam cartam in populo. Et nos servi vestri anathematizavimus omnem haeresim et omnes qui de sancta sede apostolica Romana dixerint haeresim. Et nunc, domine pater benignissime, cogitare digneris de nobis servis tuis, qui etsi de longinquo simus, oves tuae sumus, et tibi commissus est omnis mundus, sicut vestra sanctitas scit, sicut ait Dominus Petro: *Si diligis me, Petre, pasce oves meas*. Benignissime pater, dum essem ego Leo servus vester ad sancta vestigia vestra et ad pia vestigia domni Karoli piissimi imperatoris filiique vestri, audivimus in capella eius dici in symbolo fidei *qui ex Patre Filioque procedit*, et in homilia sancti Gregorii, quam nobis filius vester domnus Karolus imperator dedit, in parabola octavarum Paschae, ubi dixit: *Sed ejus missio ipsa processio est, qui de Patre procedit et Filio*. Et in regula sancti Benedicti, quam nobis dedit filius vester domnus Karolus, quae habet fidem scriptam de sancta et inseparabili Trinitate, dicit: *Credo Spiritum sanctum Deum verum ex Patre procedentem et Filio*. Et in dialogo quem nobis vestra sanctitas dare dignata est similiter dicit. Et in fide sancti Athanasii eodem modo dicit. Itaque per ipsum Johannem facta est nobis grandis confusio in sancta civitate, quoniam dicit quod Spiritus Sanctus non procedit de Patre et Filio, et de hoc misit grandem errorem per omnia monasteria, et requirebat fidem nostram et libros nostros, et de domino Gregorio dicit quod non sint recipiendi ejus libri. Unde iterum atque iterum, sancte pater, in terram prostrati cum lacrymis postulamus et rogamus te per Patrem et Filium et Spiritum sanctum, qui Trinitas inseparabilis unus dicitur, ut digneris inquirere tam in Graeco quam in Latino de sanctis patribus qui symbolum composuerunt istum sermonem ubi dicitur *ex Patre Filioque procedit.* Et in Graeco non dicunt sicut nos, sed dicunt *qui ex Patre procedit*, et vident istum sermonem gravem quem nos dicimus in Latino. Et mandare digneris domno Karolo imperatori filio vestro quod nos istum sermonem in ejus capella audivimus, *qui ex Patre Filioque procedit.* Et nos hic servos vestros certos facere digneris, quia nulla species hujus sacramenti tam nobis amabilis videatur quam sanctus vester vultus et sancta oratio et deprecatio seu memoria vestra. Unde et poscimus, benignissime Pater, vestram sanctissimam pietatem ut hos servos vestros [et] Johannem presbyterum, quando Deo gubernante ad sacrosanctam vestram gravitatem pervenerint, benigne suscipere dignemini et nobis servis vestris certum mandatum dirigere. Commendamus nos Dominicus, Theodorus, Arimundus, Gregorius, Johannes, Leo, et omnis congregatio de monte sancto Oliveti humilis servi vestri vestris sacris ac Deo dignis orationibus. Deus et Dominus noster te, sanctissime pater, cum omnibus tuis ad exaltationem sanctae suae Ecclesiae et ad salutem animae tuae et ad gaudium nostrum regere, protegere, et pia miseratione in omnibus et per omnia custodire dignetur: qui dicitur benedictus in saecula[1].

2. *Leo Papa III. Karolo Augusto.*

Domino piissimo et serenissimo victori ac triumphatori filio amatori Dei et Domini nostri Jesu Christi KAROLO Augusto LEO episcopus servus servorum Dei. Omnia quae de singulis partibus nobis accidunt necesse est ut vestrae intimemus imperiali potestati. Praesenti siquidem anno direxerunt nobis epistolam monachi qui in sancto monte Oliveti morantur fidei contentionem continentem quam inter se habebant. Nos vero symbolum orthodoxae fidei illis misimus, quatenus omnes secundum hanc nostram sanctam catholicam et apostolicam Ecclesiam rectam et inviolatam teneant fidem. Quam vero epistolam vestrae imperiali

[1] Baluz. *Misc.* VII. 14 sq. (Migne CXXIX. 1257 sq.)

potentiae misimus relegendam. Interea revertentes praesentes fideles servientes vestri, Agamus videlicet et Roculphus, a Hierosolymis detulerunt nobis epistolam Thomae Hierosolymorum patriarchae. Quam relegentes reperimus ut per nostram precatoriam epistolam vestrae pietati eos commendaremus. Qua de re precamur vestram imperialem potentiam ut, sicut soliti estis super omnes fideles vestros impertire suffragium, ita cum eis misericordiam facere jubeatis. Ipsam vero epistolam quam nobis praedicti fideles vestri detulerunt vestrae serenitati misimus. His praelibatis, omnipotens Deus sua vos protectione custodiat, atque a perfidis omnibus regnum vestrum sui extensione brachii defendat, vosque post longa annorum curricula ad gaudia aeterna perducat. Piissimum domini Karoli imperium gratia superna custodiat, eique omnium gentium colla substernat[1].

3. *Symbolum orthodoxae fidei Leonis Papae.*

LEO episcopus servus servorum Dei omnibus orientalibus Ecclesiis. Hoc symbolum orthodoxae fidei vobis mittimus ut tam vos quam omnis mundus secundum Romanam sanctam catholicam et apostolicam Ecclesiam rectam et inviolatam teneatis fidem. Credimus sanctam Trinitatem, id est, Patrem, Filium, et Spiritum Sanctum, unum Deum omnipotentem, unius substantiae, unius essentiae, unius potestatis, Creatorem omnium creaturarum, a quo omnia, per quem omnia, in quo omnia: Patrem a se ipso, non ab alio; Filium a Patre genitum, Deum verum de Deo vero, lumen verum de lumine vero, non tamen duo lumina, sed unum lumen; Spiritum Sanctum a Patre et a Filio aequaliter procedentem, consubstantialem, coaeternum Patri et Filio. Pater plenus Deus in se, Filius plenus Deus a Patre genitus, Spiritus Sanctus plenus Deus a Patre et Filio procedens. Non tamen tres deos dicimus, sed unum Deum omnipotentem, aeternum, invisibilem, incommutabilem, qui totus est ubique praesens, non per partes divisus, sed totus in omnibus, non localiter, sed personaliter, qui sine commutatione sui mutabilia creavit et creata gubernat, semper manens id quod est, cui nihil accidens esse poterit, quia simplici divinitatis naturae nihil addi vel minui potest, quia semper quod est, cui semper primum est, cui sempiternum est, cui idem est esse, vivere, et intelligere. Et haec tria unus Deus. Haec tria idem Deus et Dominus,

[1] Baluz. *Misc.* VII. 17. (Migne CXXIX. 1259 sq.)

vera et sempiterna Trinitas in personis, vera et sempiterna Unitas in substantia, quia una est substantia Pater et Filius et Spiritus Sanctus. Haec vero sancta Trinitas [nihil amplius?] est in tribus personis simul nominatis quam in una qualibet persona semel dicta, quoniam unaquaeque persona plena est substantia in se, non tamen tres substantiae, sed unus Deus, una substantia, una essentia, una aeternitas, una magnitudo, una bonitas, Pater et Filius et Spiritus Sanctus. Nec aliud est Pater in natura quam Filius vel Spiritus Sanctus, nec aliud Filius et Spiritus Sanctus quam Pater in natura, quibus est una natura. Sed alius est Pater in persona, alius Filius in persona, alius Spiritus Sanctus in persona. In Patre aeternitas, in Filio aequalitas, in Spiritu Sancto aeternitatis aequalitatisque connexio. Unum omnes in substantia et essentia, omnipotentia, et divinitate. Sicut enim eadem sancta Trinitas inseparabilis est in substantia, ita inseparabilis est in operibus, quamvis opera Dei quibusdam personis specialiter conveniant, sicut Patri vox illa quae de caelo sonuit super Christum baptizatum, et ad Filii personam humanitatis tantummodo pertinet susceptio, et Spiritus Sancti personae proprie congruit illa columba in cujus specie idem Spiritus Sanctus descendit super eumdem Filium secundum hominem baptizatum. Tamen absque omni dubitatione illam vocem et illam columbam in Christi humanitatem tota sancta Trinitas operata est, cujus opera inseparabilia sunt. Credimus eumdem Filium Dei Verbum aeternaliter natum de Patre, consubstantialem Patri per omnia, temporaliter natum de Spiritu Sancto et Maria virgine, duas habentem nativitates, unam ex Patre aeternam, alteram ex matre temporalem, qui etiam Filius Dei suae carnis conceptione conceptus est et suae carnis nativitate natus. Deum verum confitemur conceptum et Deum verum natum, eumdem verum Deum verum hominem, unum Christum Filium Dei unigenitum, perprimum et perfectum in duabus naturis in unius personae singularitate, impassibilem et passibilem, mortalem atque immortalem, crucifixum in infirmitate nostra, eundemque semper viventem in virtute sua, qui mortuus est carnis suae morte et sepultus, atque ab inferis, damnato et spoliato principe totius iniquitatis, rediens tertia die resurrexit, atque cum triumpho gloriae videntibus discipulis caelum ascendit, sedens in dextera Patris, id est, majestate divinitatis, inde jam venturus judicare vivos et mortuos, quem impii judicantem videbunt in ea forma qua crucifixus est, non in ea humilitate qua injuste judicatus est, sed in ea claritate qua juste judicaturus est mundum; cujus majestatis visio aeterna est omnium sanctorum beatitudo. Qui secundum hanc fidem rectam non crediderit, hunc damnat sancta catholica et apostolica Ecclesia, quae fundata est ab ipso Jesu Christo Domino nostro, cui est gloria in saecula. Amen[1].

4. *Karoli M. Ep. ad Leonem III. Papam.*

Quaestio quae de Spiritus Sancti processione est nuper exorta, jamdudum est diligentissime a sanctis Patribus ventilata. Sed quia jam diu a quaerentibus neglecta jacebat, non quievit quasi antiquitus ventilata, sed quasi quaedam his temporibus nobis subito emersit occulta, quod divinitus spiratum fideliter credens non dubito. Crebris etenim quaestionum ictibus praesens ecclesia tunditur, ut doctrinis catholicis erudita, sanaeque fidei confessionibus elimata, in aeternum quandoque haereditate filiorum percepta vivere cum Domino valeat feliciter regnatura. Sed quia, ut praefatus sum, haec quaestio diu a quaerentibus indiscussa jacebat, voluit omnipotens Deus in eamdem suscitare corda pastorum, ut negligentiae torpore sublato, exercitationis sanctae brachio caelestem valeant perfodere thesaurum. Sermonis etenim Dominici sarculo saepius divinarum Scripturarum pastores debent proscindere campum, ne zizania satoris iniqui semenque malignum formosi tritici valeat opprimere fructum, aut volans passim volucris haeretica semen catholicum a cordibus rapiat parvulorum, horridaque spinarum emersio Domini nitidam possit suffocare segetem. Lectionis etenim sacrae cognitio imbecillis baculum, nervosis arma ministrat, hostium subdolas fortiter premit insidias, et victoribus aeternas feliciter promittit coronas. Ergo procul a pastoribus negligentiae torpor abscedat; procul a mentis acumine inertia damnosa recedat, mollisque lascivia corporis membra relinquat, et altus sopor mollisque somnus in rigidas lucrosasque lectionis emergat excubias, ut Ecclesiae ager opimus doctorumque semine satus, valeat centenos Omnipotenti reddere fructus. Jam nunc aggrediar de Spiritus Sancti processione.

[Testimonies from Scripture and the Fathers follow. The letter concludes thus:]

Haec a nobis summo opitulante Opifice de Spiritus Sancti processione multiplicia sanctarum Scripturarum aggregata sunt testimonia, ut divinorum librorum sententiis victus, multorumque

[1] Baluz. *Misc.* VII. 18. (Migne CII. 1030. CXXIX. 1260.)

orthodoxorum nube testium pressus veritati non valeat resistere inimicus; sed potius sententiis catholicis veridicisque suasus testimoniis, revertatur ad tutissimum Ecclesiae sinum, ut pariter catholico educatus in gremio, quandoque aeternum cum filiis mereatur accipere regnum[1].

5. *Acta collationis Romanae.*

Lectis a praedictis missis per ordinem testimoniis, atque a domno apostolico diligentissime auditis, ait: Ita sentio, ita teneo, cum his auctoribus, et sacrae Scripturae auctoritatibus. Si quis aliter de hac re sentire vel docere voluerit, defendo; et nisi conversus fuerit, et secundum hunc sensum tenere voluerit, contraria sentientem funditus abjicio. His dictis, novi quod nonnulla colloquendo potius quam disputando praecesserunt: quorum series sensuum seu verborum, nisi tantum quod inde fuit, non satis memoriae occurrit. Cumque eadem collatio ad hoc usque procederet, ut jam magis certa disputatio, quam ut supra collocutio habenda esset; et si non eadem fuit proprietas sermonum, in quantum recordari valeo, iste tamen fuit cursus sensuum, et summa conclusio novissimarum definitionum.—MISSI. Quia vero, ut dicitis, ita certissimum credendum est, credendo immutabiliter tenendum, tenendo vero, sicubi necesse fuerit, constantissime defendendum est, numquid non id nescientes docendum, scientibus autem, ut id attentius teneamus, confirmandum est?—PAPA. Ita est.—MISSI. Si ita est, si quis hoc nescierit, vel ita non crediderit, num salvus esse poterit?—PAPA. Quisquis ad hoc sensu subtiliore pertingere potest, et id scire, aut ita sciens credere noluerit, salvus esse non poterit. Sunt enim multa, e quibus istud unum est, sacrae fidei altiora mysteria subtilioraque sacramenta, ad quorum indagationem pertingere multi valent; multi vero, aut aetatis quantitate, aut intelligentiae qualitate praepediti, non valent. Et ideo, ut praediximus, qui potuerit et noluerit, salvus esse non poterit.—MISSI. Si ergo ita est, imo quia ita est, quod non credere non licet, et non tacendo docere licet, cur non licet cantare, vel cantando docere?—PAPA. Licet, inquam, licet docendo cantare, et cantando docere. Sed illicite in prohibitis nec scribendo nec cantando licet inserere.—MISSI. Quia ergo utrisque notum est, quod ideo a vobis ut id symbolum cantando vel scribendo inseratur illicitum ducatur vel dicatur,

[1] Migne XCVIII. 923 sq.

quia illi qui idem symbolum condiderunt non indiderunt, ut cetera, et sequentes principales synodi, Chalcedonensis scilicet quarta, Constantinopolitana quoque quinta et sexta, ut novum ultra symbolum a quoquam qualibet necessitate seu salvandi homines devotione condere, et in veteribus tollendo, addendo, mutandove quicquam inserere prohibuerunt, non est ibi diutius immorandum. Sed hoc quaero, hoc ut dicatur rogo: quia id credere bonum est, bonum hodie sicut ad credendum ita ad cantandum tunc esse, si ab eis insertum fuisset.—PAPA. Bonum certe, et valde bonum, utpote tam fidei sacramentum magnum, quod non licet non credere, quisquis ad hoc valet pertingere.—MISSI. Numquid non bene idem tunc auctores fecissent, si quatuor tantum addendo syllabas, tam pernecessarium fidei sacramentum cunctis deinceps saeculis perspicuum redderetur?—PAPA. Sicut non audeo dicere non bene fecisse si fecissent, quia procul dubio sicut cetera quae vel omiserunt, scientes utique, et non tam humana quam divina illuminati sapientia fecerunt, ita quoque non audeo dicere istud eos nobis minus intellexisse [seu] perpendisse cur dimiserunt, vel cur dimissum, ne ultra mitteretur, sicut et cetera prohibuere. Tu et tui videte quid sentiatis de vobis. Nam et ego me illis non dico praeferam, sed etiam illud absit mihi ut coaequare praesumam.—MISSI. Absit etiam, pater, Deo nostro protegente, illud a nobis, ut nos quicquam horum cogitemus vel dicamus, vel superbia inflati, vel in divinis rebus humanae laudis cupidine provocati, ac si nosmet illis non tantum praeferre, verum etiam coaequare praesumamus: sed tantum secundum hujus temporis qualitatem, imbecillitatem fratrum nostrorum caritate compatientes, illud quaerimus, in eo laboramus, ut, quia finis mundi appropinquat, in quo sicut praedicta sunt tempora periculosa, etiam ideo inter cetera maxime fratribus nostris prodesse valeamus. Quo ergo fideles in Domino in sacramento fidei reddere studeamus: et idcirco quia praefatum symbolum a quibusdam ita cantari reperimus, et quod id ecclesiasticae congruere fidei, sicut sentimus, utique cognovimus: atque per hoc et nunc jam plurimos doctos, et sine fine usque in finem saeculi de tanto mysterio, si ita teneatur, instruendos esse cognovimus, qui nequaquam instrueretur, nisi cantaretur: melius nobis visum fuit cantando tantos instruere, quam tacendo indoctos relinquere. Si enim sciret paternitas tua, quanta sunt hodie millia id scientium quia cantatur, qui numquam scituri essent nisi cantaretur, fortasse nobiscum teneres, et id tuo etiam consensu ut cantaretur acquiesceres. — PAPA. Interim assentio. Verumtamen, quaeso, responde mihi: Num universa hujusmodi fidei mystica sacramenta, quae symbolo non continentur, sine quibus quisque, qui ad hoc pertingere potest, catholicus esse non potest, symbolis inserenda, et propter compendium minus intelligentium, ut cuique libuerit, addenda sunt?—MISSI. Nequaquam: quia non aeque omnia necessaria sunt.—PAPA. Etsi non omnia, certe plurima sunt his similia, quae nisi a capientibus credantur, catholici esse non possunt.—MISSI. Dabisne aliquid, non dico sublimius, sed saltem huic simile symbolo deesse?—PAPA. Nempe dabo, et abundanter dabo.—MISSI. Da primo unum, et si necesse fuerit, adde alterum.—PAPA. Quia amica agitur contentione quod agitur, et pro utrarumque partium quaeritur salute quod quaeritur (atque utinam quoties aliquid hujusmodi in majoribus seu in minoribus ecclesiasticis vel catholicis utilitatibus quaeritur, ita per omnia pacifice sine perversa intentione quaereretur!), ne quid forte de tam reverendis mysteriis temere loquamur, detur considerandi locus, et dabimus quicquid de his dederit Dominus.—*Et nocturna dilatione congrua data, ait* PAPA: Numquid magis salutare est credere, periculosumve non credere, Spiritum Sanctum a Filio sicut a Patre procedere, quam Filium sapientiam Deum a sapientia Deo, veritatem Deum a veritate Deo genitum esse, et tamen utrumque unam sapientiam, unam veritatem essentialiter Deum esse, cum tamen constet id a sanctis Patribus eidem symbolo inditum non esse? Si ergo haec duo, sicuti sapientes decet in tam familiari disputatione, ad hoc valent, ut nobiscum sentiatis et cognoscatis tot priores catholicos Patres, qui hoc unde agitur vel symbolis non inseruerunt, vel inserere quemadmodum cetera, ut supra dictum est, prohibuere, non praesenti ignorantia, non futuri negligenti providentia praetermisisse, et praetermissum ne mitteretur prohibuisse, a coacervandis testimoniis libentissime quiescimus. Sciendum vero, non solum secundum essentiam divinitatis, verum etiam secundum mysterium Dominicae incarnationis, tanta Deo auctore, et ex eorumdem patrum auctoritate damus et talia quanta non solum sapientibus satisfacere, sed etiam stultos valent opprimere.—MISSI. Non, inquam, necesse est in eo laborare, an nesciamus quod scimus: quia quicquid exinde ceteri sciunt, nos Deo auctore scimus, aut scire possumus, si non scimus.—PAPA. Hoc est, inquit, quod miramur, qui sine profectuoso labore potestis quiescere, laboratis ne quiescatis.—MISSI. Non ideo laboramus ne quiescamus, sed ne propter inertiam pii laboris praemium amittamus; et salva diligentiore inquisitione, declinataque pertinaci contentione, adhuc majus aestimamus lucrum, quod per hoc in corde quaerentium acquiritur, quam detrimentum in eo fieri illorum qui addiderunt, ac si per contumaciam contemptores paternarum constitutionum existerent. Aliud est enim per arrogantiam transiliendo bona contemnere, aliud bona per benevolentiam meliora efficere.—PAPA. Istud quoque etsi in quibusdam ut agatur bonum est, non tamen ideo ubique agendum est. Qua de re multa id ita esse probantia addi poterant testimonia: sed res per se admodum patet, quanto melius sit, ut quisque quodlibet bonum ita ut est utile reddere studeat: aut, si forte id ipsum bonum melius efficere nititur, hoc primo caveat, hoc magnopere perpendat, ne et se ultra quam debuit temerarium praesumendo, et illud quod per se salubre erat reddat noxium corrumpendo. Nisi quis forte asserere velit de praesenti unde agitur, vel similibus capitulis, quae sine periculo suo docere licet et discere, ut ordo docendi licitus dimittatur, et ibi deserantur, ubi numquam deinceps docens aut discens innocens, sed semper sane in transgressionis crimine merito culpabilis uterque judicetur. Quod te fortasse, si non dedigneris audire, non immerito tangit: qui [quia?] hic quod hactenus in Ecclesia Dei, et sibi quisque sapiens scire, et sine cogitatione delicti insipienter potuit docere, jam deinceps non dico stultus discere, sed nec ipse sapiens sine praevaricatione possit cantare, cantandove ut vultis quemquam docere, et dum multis alio quam debetis tramite prodesse eligitis, nullum in hac duntaxat parte dimittitis, cui si vos secutus fuerit non noceatis. Nam de eo quod supra docuistis, non aeque judicandus vel habendus sit ille qui tale aliquid devote fructum quaerendo ageret, illo qui hoc contumaci jussione praesumeret. Haec defensio, vel, si dici liceat, tergiversatio, non huc respicit, non istud intendit: quia non idem patres discernendo vel decreverunt nec sanxerunt, ut ipsum benevolus praesumeret, non malevolus, sed tantummodo nullus.—MISSI. Numquid non a te id ipsum symbolum est data in ecclesia cantandi licentia? Numquid a nobis huc usus ille cantandi processit? Hinc etenim illuc mos idem cantandi, non a nobis huc advenit: et quomodo illum usque hodie cantamus?—PAPA. Ego licentiam dedi cantandi; non autem cantando quippiam addendi, minuendi, seu mutandi: et ut expressius aliquid, quia vos cogitis, loquar, quamdiu vobis in hoc satis fuit, quomodo in hujusmodi cantando vel celebrando sacrosanctis mysteriis sancta Romana tenet Ecclesia, nequaquam aut nobis in talibus laborare, aut aliis laborandi occasionem neccesse fuit ingerere. Quod vero asseritis ideo vos ita cantare, quoniam alios in istis partibus vobis priores audistis cantasse, quid ad nos? Nos enim id ipsum non cantamus, sed legimus, et legendo docere, nec tamen legendo aut docendo addere quippiam eidem symbolo inserendo praesumimus. Quae vero praedictis symbolis fidei tantum non congruentia deesse cognoscimus, non, ut saepe dictum est, inserere praesumimus, sed locis temporibusve opportunis quibus competit ministrare curamus.—MISSI. Ergo, ut video, illud a vestra paternitate decernitur, ut primo illud, de quo quaestio agitur, de saepe fato symbolo tollatur, et tunc demum a quolibet licite ac libere, sive cantando, sive tradendo, discatur et doceatur.—PAPA. Ita procul dubio a nostra parte decernitur: ita quoque ut a vestra assentiatur, a nobis omnimodis suadetur.—MISSI. Quamquam ergo, ut supra ipse dixisti, pro ambarum partium quaeritur salute quod quaeritur, sublatis his quae vultis, bonum est ut idem symbolum cantetur.—PAPA. Bonum sane. Quod tamen non imperando, sed ut prius permittendo dicimus: quia illud sicuti tunc ita et nunc, si sincere agatur, utile indigentibus esse posse non ignoramus.—MISSI. Quia vero, ut dicitis, et verum dicitis, bonum est cantare id ipsum symbolum, numquid enim si sermo plenus recta fide e medio tollatur, idem sermo ab omnibus ac si contra fidem sit condemnabitur? Quale ergo dabis consilium, ne id ipsum ad aliquod transeat exitium?—PAPA. Si priusquam ita cantaretur interrogatus essem, ne insereretur utique respondissem. At nunc, quod tamen non affirmando, sed vobiscum pariter tractando dico, quantum menti occurrit, ita mihi videtur posse utrumque fieri: ut paulatim in palatio, quia in nostra sancta ecclesia non cantatur, cantandi consuetudo ejusdem symboli intermittatur: sicque fiat, ut quod id ipsum ut cantaretur non quaelibet imperantis auctoritas, sed potius audiendi id fecerat novitas; si dimittatur a vobis, dimittetur ab omnibus: et ita fortasse quantum esse potest, non incongrue utrumque fieri possit: ut quod jam nunc a quibusque prius nescientibus recte creditur credatur, et tamen illicita cantandi consuetudo sine cujusque fidei laesione tollatur[1].

[1] Sirmondi, *Conc. antiq. Galliae*, t. II. p. 256—260. (Migne CII. 971 sq.)

(B). RESOLUTIONS ADOPTED BY THE BONN CONFERENCE, AUG. 13—15, 1875.

[This Conference, over which Dr von Döllinger presided, was attended by more than twenty Easterns, including three members of the Episcopate, and by nearly fifty Anglicans, among whom was the Bishop of Gibraltar. The Anglicans were not in any way authorized to represent the English Church: but since the conference the resolutions to which they assented have engaged the attention of a Committee of the Southern Convocation. An English translation of part of these resolutions has been given above, p. 3, note: the following is the complete German text[1].]

1. Wir stimmen überein in der Annahme der ökumenischen Symbole und der Glaubensentscheidungen der alten ungetheilten Kirche.

2. Wir stimmen überein in der Anerkennung, dass der Zusatz des Filioque zum Symbolum nicht in kirchlich rechtmässiger Weise erfolgt sei.

3. Wir bekennen uns allerseits zu der Darstellung der Lehre vom h. Geiste, wie sie von den Vätern der ungetheilten Kirche vorgetragen wird.

4. Wir verwerfen jede Vorstellung und jede Ausdrucksweise, in welcher etwa die Annahme zweier Principien oder ἀρχαί oder αἰτίαι in der Dreieinigkeit enthalten wäre.

Wir nehmen die Lehre des heiligen Johannes von Damaskus über den heiligen Geist, wie dieselbe in nachfolgenden Paragraphen ausgedrückt ist, im Sinne der Lehre der alten ungetrennten Kirche an.

1. Der h. Geist geht aus aus dem Vater (ἐκ τοῦ Πατρός) als dem Anfang (ἀρχή), der Ursache (αἰτία), der Quelle (πηγή) der Gottheit. (*De Rectâ Sententiâ*, n. 1: *Contra Manich.*, n. 4.)

2. Der h. Geist geht nicht aus aus dem Sohn (ἐκ τοῦ Υἱοῦ), weil es in der Gottheit nur Einen Anfang (ἀρχή), Eine Ursache (αἰτία) gibt, durch welche alles, was in der Gottheit ist, hervorgebracht wird. (*De Fide Orthod.* I. 8: ἐκ τοῦ Υἱοῦ δὲ τὸ Πνεῦμα οὐ λέγομεν, Πνεῦμα δὲ Υἱοῦ ὀνομάζομεν.)

[1] I owe my copy to the kindness of the Rev. Prebendary Meyrick.

3. Der h. Geist geht aus aus dem Vater durch den Sohn (*De Fide Orthod.* I. 12: τὸ δὲ Πνεῦμα τὸ Ἅγιον ἐκφαντορικὴ τοῦ κρυφίου τῆς θεότητος δύναμις τοῦ Πατρὸς, ἐκ Πατρὸς μὲν δι' Υἱοῦ ἐκπορευομένη. *Ibidem:* Υἱοῦ δὲ Πνεῦμα, οὐχ ὡς ἐξ αὐτοῦ, ἀλλ' ὡς δι' αὐτοῦ ἐκ τοῦ Πατρὸς ἐκπορευόμενον. *C. Manich.* n. 5: διὰ τοῦ λόγου αὐτοῦ ἐξ αὐτοῦ τὸ Πνεῦμα αὐτοῦ ἐκπορευόμενον. *De Hymno Trisag.* n. 28: Πνεῦμα τὸ Ἅγιον ἐκ τοῦ Πατρὸς διὰ τοῦ Υἱοῦ καὶ λόγου προϊόν. *Hom. in Sabb.* s. n. 4: τοῦτ' ἡμῖν ἐστι τὸ λατρευόμενον...Πνεῦμα Ἅγιον τοῦ Θεοῦ καὶ Πατρός, ὡς ἐξ αὐτοῦ ἐκπορευόμενον, ὅπερ καὶ τοῦ Υἱοῦ λέγεται, ὡς δι' αὐτοῦ φανερούμενον καὶ τῇ κτίσει μεταδιδόμενον, ἀλλ' οὐκ ἐξ αὐτοῦ ἔχον τὴν ὕπαρξιν).

4. Der h. Geist ist das Bild des Sohnes, des Bildes des Vaters (*De Fide Orthod.* I. 13: εἰκὼν τοῦ Πατρὸς ὁ Υἱὸς, καὶ τοῦ Υἱοῦ τὸ Πνεῦμα,) aus dem Vater ausgehend und im Sohne ruhend als dessen ausstrahlende Kraft (*De Fide Orthod.* I. 7: τοῦ Πατρὸς προερχομένην καὶ ἐν τῷ λόγῳ ἀναπαυομένην καὶ αὐτοῦ οὖσαν ἐκφαντικὴν δύναμιν. *Ibidem* I. 12: Πατήρ...διὰ λόγου προβολεὺς ἐκφαντορικοῦ Πνεύματος).

5. Der h. Geist ist die persönliche Hervorbringung aus dem Vater, dem Sohne angehörig, aber nicht aus dem Sohn, weil er der Geist des Mundes der Gottheit ist, welcher das Wort ausspricht. (*De Hymno Trisag.* n. 28: τὸ Πνεῦμα ἐνυπόστατον ἐκπόρευμα καὶ πρόβλημα ἐκ Πατρὸς μὲν, Υἱοῦ δὲ, καὶ μὴ ἐξ Υἱοῦ, ὡς Πνεῦμα στόματος Θεοῦ, λόγου ἐξαγγελτικόν.)

6. Der h. Geist bildet die Vermittlung zwischen dem Vater und dem Sohn und ist durch den Sohn mit dem Vater verbunden (*De Fide Orthod.* I. 13: μέσον τοῦ ἀγεννήτου καὶ γεννητοῦ καὶ δι' Υἱοῦ τῷ Πατρὶ συναπτόμενον).

[The Report of the Committee of Convocation has now been presented to both Houses of Convocation, although not yet discussed. Through the courtesy of the Chairman, I have received a copy in time to print here the decision at which the Committee have arrived. After examining each of the six resolutions in detail, they conclude:

"The Committee having thus, in accordance with the instructions of the Upper and Lower Houses of this Convocation, reviewed these Resolutions, report:—that they do not find in them anything contradictory to the Formularies of the Church of England, or contrariant to sound doctrine, or that may not be held with a safe conscience."]

INDEX I.

INDEX II.

16

INDEX III.

INDEX IV.

(Councils, &c.)

INDEX V.

(Creeds and Confessions of Faith.)